INFORMAL ECONOMY
CENTRESTAGE

INFORMAL ECONOMY CENTRESTAGE

New Structures of Employment

EDITED BY

RENANA JHABVALA
RATNA M. SUDARSHAN
JEEMOL UNNI

SAGE Publications

New Delhi • Thousand Oaks • London

First published in 2003 by

Sage Publications India Pvt Ltd
B-42, Panchsheel Enclave
New Delhi 110 017

Sage Publications Inc
2455 Teller Road
Thousand Oaks, California 91320

Sage Publications Ltd
6 Bonhill Street
London EC2A 4PU

Published by Tejeshwar Singh for Sage Publications India Pvt Ltd, Typeset in 9.5/11.5 Century 751BT by C&M Digitals (P) Ltd, Chennai and printed at Chaman Enterprises, New Delhi.

Library of Congress Cataloging-in-Publication Data

Informal economy centrestage : new structures of employment / edited by Renana Jhabvala, Ratna M. Sudarshan, Jeemol Unni.
   p.   cm.
   1. Informal sector (Economics)—India. 2. Labor supply—India. 3. Income distribution—India. I. Renana Jhabvala. II. Sudarshan, Ratna M. III. Unni, Jeemol.

HD2346.I5I4685   330—dc21   2003   2003007029

ISBN: 0–7619–9710–5 (US–Hb)   81–7829–187–8 (India–Hb)

Sage Production Team: K.E. Priyamvada, Sunaina Dalaya, Rajib Chatterjee and Santosh Rawat

Contents

List of Tables

List of figures

List of Abbreviations

ASI	Annual Survey of Industries
BPL	Below Poverty Line
CFC	Consumption of Fixed Capital
CIF	Chief Inspector of Factories
CSO	Central Statistical Organisation
DES	Directorate of Economics and Statistics
DI	Directorate of Industries
DIC	District Industry Centre
DME	Directory Manufacturing Establishment
ESIS	Employees' State Insurance Scheme
FSU	First Stage Unit
GDP	Gross Domestic Product
GIC	General Insurance Corporation
GIDR	Gujarat Institute of Development Research
GVA	Gross Value Added
HDI	Human Development Indicators
HH	Household
ICLS	International Conference of Labour Statisticians
ICSE	International Classification of Status in Employment
ICT	Information and Communication Technologies
IIP	Index of Industrial Production
ILO	International Labour Organisation
ITGLWF	International Textile, Garment and Leather Workers Federation
LIC	Life Insurance Corporation of India
MCH	Maternal and Child Health
MIMAP	Micro Impact of Macro Adjustment Policies
NAS	National Accounts Statistics
NCAER	National Council of Applied Economic Research
NCO	National Classification of Occupations

NDME	Non-Directory Manufacturing Establishment
NDP	Net Domestic Product
NGO	Non-Governmental Organisation
NIC	National Industrial Classification
NICL	National Insurance Corporation Limited
NSS	National Sample Survey
NSSO	National Sample Survey Organisation
OAE	Own-Account Enterprise
OAME	Own-Account Manufacturing Enterprise
OPD	Out Patients Department
PF	Provident Fund
PPS	Probability Proportioned to Size
RBI	Reserve Bank of India
SAM	Social Accounting Matrix
SDP	State Domestic Product
SEF	Self-Employment in Farming
SENF	Self-Employment in Non-Farming
SEWA	Self-Employed Women's Association
SIDO	Small Industry Development Organisation
SNA	System of National Accounts
SSI	Small Scale Industry
SSU	Second Stage Unit
UN	United Nations
VAW	Value Added per Worker
WIEGO	Women in Informal Employment Globalising and Organising
WPI	Wholesale Price Index
WPR	Workforce Participation Rate

Preface

This book is the result of a creative collaboration between research and action, which began as a response to a question asked by members of the Self-Employed Women's Association (SEWA)—'Can we quantify the contribution of the informal workers to the economy?' SEWA, a trade union of women in the informal economy, has been trying, for the last 30 years, to organise for women and bring them into the mainstream of the economy. One of the main obstacles that we faced is the perception of most people towards informal workers, and especially towards women. Although, in the course of our work, we saw that these women workers were working hard and contributing to the livelihoods of their families, as well as to their economics, policy-makers saw them as marginal and unproductive.

We needed to convince policy-makers that these women were indeed productive workers, and so they should receive from the economy what they gave to it. One way was through numbers and statistics—people always seemed to find numbers convincing. One statistic we had been using was the number of the informal (or unorganised) workers, who formed around 90 per cent of the workforce. This figure did convince people of the size of the problem. However, it left the impression that these hundreds of millions of workers were a 'problem' for which a solution had to be found. In an era where economic growth was the 'mantra' a huge workforce of 'unproductive' workers was looked on with dismay. So we needed to show that not only was the size of the informal workforce large, but so was their contribution to the economy.

We started with a meeting of researchers and SEWA activists in Gujarat, and were surprised to find that in fact the Central Statistical Organisation (CSO) did collect extensive information on this sector for purposes of the National Accounts, and that the share of the unorganised sector in National Income was 63 per cent.* The questions

---

*For the year 1993–94.

we posed, interested some researchers first in Gujarat and later in New Delhi, and eventually we were fortunate to have a joint collaboration with the Gujarat Institute of Development Research (GIDR) and the National Council of Applied Economic Research (NCAER), in particular Jeemol Unni and Ratna Sudarshan.

This collaboration has succeeded beyond our expectations. For example, the research on Ahmedabad city by Jeemol Unni, brought out how the workforce has shifted from being mostly formal to being mostly informal, which has convinced the Government of Gujarat and the Ahmedabad Municipality to focus policies and budgets on them. The research used a methodology for measuring the informal sector, which caught the attention of the CSO, and laid the basis for the National Sample Survey (NSS) labour force survey and especially of the informal sector. The figures from the NSS are being used by the Second National Commission on Labour and also by the Government to frame schemes and policies for various categories of workers such as home-based workers and salt workers.

Based on the model developed here, an international collaboration of researchers, activists and policy-makers was developed called WIEGO— Women in Informal Employment Globalising and Organising. WIEGO works closely with international agencies, such as the International Labour Organisation (ILO) and the World Bank, to develop an understanding of workers in the informal sector and formulate policies, especially social protection policies, for bringing them into the mainstream.

We see this collaboration as a start of a longer and deeper association between researchers and activists in the cause of social justice for informal workers. We are grateful to the Ford Foundation, New Delhi, for providing financial support to this programme.

I would especially like to thank Jeemol Unni and Ratna Sudarshan for the patience and the creativity with which they approached the problem and the intelligence and rigour with which they carried out and coordinated the studies. I would especially like to acknowledge Elaben Bhatt as the inspiration behind it all.

Renana Jhabvala

Measuring the Informal Economy

RATNA M. SUDARSHAN AND JEEMOL UNNI

INTRODUCTION

The existence of the informal economy complicates analysis of economic and social systems. Informal activity in the developing world consists primarily of unregulated but productive activity, generally seen as a survival activity of the very poor. In the developed world, this kind of activity is relatively small. An element of illegality is usually present in the informal activity in developed countries, most often tax evasion in production/distribution. A third type of informal activity is unpaid household work, which again has engaged greater attention in the developed world. In this book, we focus on the first category of informal activity, the dimensions of which are large: for employment, between 35–85 per cent of non-agricultural employment in Asia, 40–97 per cent in Africa and 30–75 per cent in the Latin America–Caribbean region. In India, 86 per cent of women in the non-agricultural labour force are engaged in informal activity, as are 83 per cent of men (ILO 2002: 19).

These empirical facts are now fairly well-documented, thanks to a worldwide resurgence of interest in informality. The reasons behind the contemporary concern with informality in developed countries are to be found in the changing economic structure. This concern is visible in many ways, and more so in the priorities and policy statements of the United Nations (UN) bodies. The reasons for this renewed interest, discussed ahead, stem from specific concerns of the developed countries, and are rather different from the concerns of developing countries. From the point of view of policy design, conventional categories for collecting data on income and employment now appear inadequate; for example, new technology has changed the manner of interaction between organisations, and between employer and employee. Over the last two decades, there has been a trend towards informal contracts and weaker employer–employee contracts in the developed world, made possible both by developments in technology and by emerging new structures of governance and contract. On the one hand, it is technically feasible to work from home, and to work for multiple employers, largely as a result of the new Information and Communication Technologies (ICT) structures. There is also probably a benefit to employers in reducing their fixed costs by contracting out wherever possible. The result is a much more complex structure of employment, and greater difficulty in defining the one-to-one relations on the basis of which tax regimes, for example, have been constructed in the past. As a result, Statistics Divisions all over the world are engaged in efforts to count and systematise the informal sector. It is recognised that a large and rapidly growing unrecorded economy can bias key indicators such as unemployment rates, savings rates, productivity and price levels. Macroeconomic policies based on systematically biased information can produce counterproductive outcomes (see for example, Feige 1990).

The new thinking and new data collection methodologies that have been generated have been welcomed by those concerned with informal employment in developing countries. This is because the official language and statistical techniques can be usefully modified to examine informal workers in very different situations. Understanding informality, thus, is one of the sources of an emerging convergence, not just between empiricism and theory, but also in a concern mutual to the developed and developing world.

The emergence of networks and international funding support has enabled these issues to be raised in different forums, to maintain a certain level of advocacy, and has certainly played a part in stimulating research in the area. Networks have succeeded in converting the activist's concern to the level of policy debate.[1]

This book is primarily, although not exclusively, about measurement. The informal economy in India has a place in official statistics;

we argue here that the methodology of data collection as it exists is inadequate to capture its actual size and contribution to macro-economic aggregates. Capturing informality more accurately leads us also to question some standard assumptions about the economic behaviour of workers and producers in the informal economy. In many ways the research presented here is of a preliminary nature. We hope to establish the need for a closer look at the assumptions that lie behind both measurement and theory.

As explained in the preface, the research process through which this book has been developed, was one of engagement between researchers and activists. One of the outcomes of this engagement has been a constant need to formulate assumptions and test our findings against ground level experience. In this chapter, we start by examining the tension between theory and empiricism, especially in relation to informality, and how this may have influenced thinking on the informal economy. The section titled Defining Informality reviews the definition of informality in national accounting and as used in this book. The section discussing the book presents a preview of the remaining chapters in the book.

INFORMAL SECTOR AND ECONOMICS

First used in the early 1970s, the informal sector concept has generated a fairly large stream of empirical work in India and elsewhere, despite the fuzzy nature of the concept itself. Although dualism has been largely discredited, the persistence of different modes of employment and work and the resulting insecurities are reasonably well-captured by an informal-formal dichotomy. Empirical work has tried to establish the key features of informality, including establishing the large size of the sector, the different types of linkages between formal and informal employment and enterprises, and the special relevance of the concept to understanding female labour force participation. One of the greatest contributions has been, simply making visible the large number of small, scattered and low productivity occupations, in which people engage, or 'lifting the shroud'.

However, all of this empirical work has not made any clear dent in mainstream economic analysis and macro policy-making. The informal sector is still largely seen as 'residual', 'peripheral', often 'invisible'. The driving force of the economy is not to be located here. Hence, while measuring the size and contribution of the sector may be able to influence policy, to some extent, the significance of informality as a determinant of economic behaviour has not been widely recognised.

One area of economics that has been an exception to this general indifference is labour market studies, which have attempted to incorporate informality into their analysis. Economic models of labour force participation have recognised informal sector work (i.e., 'self employed or family workers') as conceptually distinct from working as an employee. While early models were dualistic in structure, others have allowed for a wider range of choices, and have generally concluded that the decision to engage in family or informal work is not identical to the decision to work as an employee (see for example, Mazumdar 1976).

For the larger world of economics, informality has remained a feature important for policy, and hence for empirical work, but has not warranted any modification of theory. Studies of the informal sector conducted in the 1970s were not too worried by the limited analytical usefulness of the concept as articulated by the ILO Kenya Mission. This concept was 'somewhat vague', but it was felt at the time that once more data became available, 'a definition of the target group having greater analytical significance is expected to emerge' (Sethuraman 1976: 77). The usefulness of the concept to the ILO's World Employment Programme, perhaps largely explains its quick diffusion and popularity at the time (see Bromley 1978). The large volume of empirical work that followed shows that informal employment is not being replaced by formal employment in developing countries, and that informal employment is increasing in developed countries. But the concept itself has not lost its nebulous quality. The result has been an increasing dissatisfaction with the use of the term, because the heterogeneity of the 'informal sector' means that 'different definitions lead to quite different inclusions and exclusions', and it may be best 'to avoid using the term entirely' (Mead and Morrisson 1996: 1617).

THEORY AND EMPIRICISM

Tensions between the pure theorist and the empiricist exist in all disciplines, and economics is no exception. Unlike sociology, which offers greater scope for theorising on the basis of small samples, economic theorists are not as compelled to take note of each empirical work. Although no less a science of human behaviour, the economic method offers greater scope for distancing theory from empiricism, by emphasising the need to eliminate 'noise'. The result is that very often, empirical analysis and theory have followed distinct routes. However, ultimately economic theory requires numbers to validate its propositions, and the collection of data requires an underlying conceptual framework. It is questionable whether any social science theory can remain alive for long without empirical backing; or whether empirical work can remain liberating and exciting forever without any conceptual apparatus. If that is so, an increasing divergence between the two may be an indication that convergence can be expected.

The fact that reality is difficult to incorporate into neat models, poses few problems to the practitioner: 'more than good economic analysis goes to the making of good decisions in economic policy' (Roll 1961: 526). Likewise students of development are encouraged to use 'holistic' and 'multi disciplinary' approaches, neither of which is necessarily conducive to neat theorising. This may be one of the reasons why a large amount of 'development studies' literature is regarded as distinct from 'economics', a perception that is generally much sharper in the developed world. The policy-maker and the development activist draw upon empirical findings explicitly, but on theoretical assumptions more often implicitly, rather than explicitly. Tensions between conceptual apparatus and statistical methodology begin to be of concern in periods of divergence, because the validity of analysis and prescription may be weakened during such phases.

Relevance to reality is at the root of convergence between theory and empiricism; the less this is valued, the more likely is divergence to be sustained. The forces in favour of convergence usually stem from policy-makers/activists, and not from theorists per se. Empirical findings are an essential input for the formulation of appropriate policies and institutional frameworks, and deviations from theoretical propositions are both permissable and frequent for policy-makers. Nonetheless, a supportive theoretical framework is needed, both to ensure a steady supply of data, and to be able to counter those who argue in favour of a different set of policies.

The period of the Second World War and immediately after, is a well-recognised period of convergence. Writing in 1953, on the history of economic thought, Eric Roll spoke of 'a powerful trend towards synthesis in economics' (Roll 1961: 518). The war had played an important part in bringing together the theoretical structure of economics and statistical concepts and techniques: without better statistics of national income and product, 'a war in which all the nation's resources were engaged could not be successfully prosecuted' (Roll 1961: 514). Post-World War II, economic and statistical analysis were probably well-blended in Britain and the USA. The development of conceptual frameworks for statistical measurement, specially in relation to national accounting, did a great deal to strengthen economic analysis (Maddison 1982: 21; Hoover 1995: 726). As Diebold puts it, 'The intellectual marriage of statistics and economic theory was reflected in the growth of the Econometric Society and its journal *Econometrica*.' (Diebold 1998: 177), with the result that in the post-war period 'The literature on the advanced countries has been largely technocratic, concerned with models and production functions' (Maddison 1982: 22). The volume of data generated in the post-World War II period has also stimulated the 'pure' empiricists, who seek patterns from the data without necessarily starting out with any conceptual framework of analysis. This divergence between those using theoretical frameworks and the empiricists can be observed in any branch of study. For example, an increasing divergence between theory-based statistical work, or 'structural' forecasting, and 'nonstructural economic forecasting' has been noted in this period (Diebold 1998). The limitations of econometric analysis are more evident in the context of developing countries (see Stiglitz 2000), but even in the context of developed countries, it is true that 'economic performance ... is influenced by institutions and policy' (Maddison 1982: 25).

The 1990s has brought together several forces favouring a stronger synthesis between empirical and theoretical work in relation to national accounting, for the second time in this century. It is increasingly recognised that systems of data collection need to use new or modified concepts to accurately capture the reality of the situation, and that theoreticians could/should contribute to the development of new concepts and corresponding methodologies. The post-war period has seen challenges to the perceived rigidity of economic concepts, and these have come most sharply from environmental and feminist thought, and more recently from the worldwide resurgence of interest in informal employment. All three of these movements have questioned the conventional categories of analysis, specially in relation to national income accounting. Thus, the System of National Accounts (SNA) 1993 is not just a framework for national accounting to be primarily used by statisticians; it is also an indication of the extent to which critiques of the basic concepts can be accommodated within the existing framework of analysis.

To introduce their concerns into mainstream debate, both feminist economists and environmentalists have made use of techniques of valuation. For example, counting in women's unpaid work can double the estimates of the GDP (see Ironmonger 1996). However, while such use of existing concepts is useful in starting a debate, it cannot substitute for the shift in perspective that underlies the debate. Real concern, for example, for ecological sustainability can hardly be satisfied by a valuation of the losses entailed by some particular production activity.

National income accounting has been at the forefront of debate, and the SNA (1993) is central to current discussions on the informal economy. The contemporary concern with the informal economy can be seen as a movement towards greater convergence between concerns of empiricism and theory, as well as of some concerns of the developed and developing world.

INFORMALITY AND ECONOMIC GROWTH

Empirical evidence of the existence of the informal sector in developing countries and its refusing to wither away in spite of the predictions is a challenge to theory. The theories of the informal sector so far have viewed this sector as a residual. Marx propounded the concept of a 'reserve army' consisting of unemployed persons and 'petty commodity producers' waiting in the ranks to fit into the grand scheme of capitalist production. The capitalists squeezed the labourers with the threat of unemployment looming large, to extract surplus. The concept of 'petty commodity producers' persisted and in current terminology they are the 'self employed workers' constituting the low productivity informal sector. Lewis (1954), Fei and Ranis (1964), Hariss and Todaro (1970) continued to use the concept of 'surplus labour' and how this 'residual' would facilitate the transition of the economies from agriculture to industry and rural to urban locales in different ways. All these theories continued with the expectation that the informal sector would wither away.

In recent years, there has been some rethinking of the concept with a view to focus on the positive aspects of this sector. This emerged at first in the 1980s with the literature on 'flexible specialisaton' based on the experience of small-scale production in industrial clusters in the developed countries (Holmstrom 1993; Piore and Sabel 1984). Whether these production units can really be considered part of the informal sector is debatable. However, the idea that small-scale can be part of a flexibilisation strategy was highlighted. In the 1990s, the impact, of the structural adjustment programmes, was beginning to be felt in many countries that had embarked on this programme in the previous decade. The positive features of micro-enterprises were lauded and the search for micro-entrepreneurs began, fueled by World Bank funding. Micro-enterprises and the informal sector were seen as the immediate solution for retrenched workers affected by 'downsizing' and other processes of the adjustment programmes.

In the advanced countries, the debate concerning how to explain the existence of informal employment, revolved around whether such work is a leftover of classical capitalism or a new form of advanced capitalism (Williams and Windebank 1998). The former was the formalisation thesis that suggested the formal sector was growing and would eventually absorb all marginal workers. The latter or informalisation thesis, explained the growth of the informal sector as a new form of advanced exploitation (Amin 1996; Castells and Portes 1989; De Soto 1989).

LABOUR MARKETS AND INFORMAL EMPLOYMENT

The labour market in developing countries is markedly different from that in the developed countries. In fact, the notion of the labour market has been questioned on the ground that it is not clear what is sold in this market and that it is in fact different from a commodity market (Standing 1999). Conventional analysis considers a labour market as the place where prospective employees offer themselves for work and enter into an explicit or implicit contract with an employer for a wage. The determination of the wage rate is the major topic of analysis in the literature on the labour market. This depends on the relative 'bargaining' power of the employer and employee. However, this notion of a labour market calls into question the position of the self-employed workers.

In the classic conflict between capital and labour, or employers and employees, the self-employed workers do not figure. In most theories of the labour market, or frameworks of enquiry, the self-employed workers are assumed to be a transient category, which will disappear with development. When their existence is recognised, these workers are dismissed as engaged in 'petty commodity production' or 'petty trade'. Or else they are subsumed in the capitalist production process, being linked to it through subcontracting arrangements. Self-employed workers are a nebulous category because they neither have sufficient capital nor are they purely labour. Self-employed workers combine the use of, primarily, their own capital and own or family labour to generate employment and incomes for themselves. The distinguishing feature of self-employment is a lack of a clear-cut employer–employee relationship, even of a temporary nature.

The self-employed workers in developing countries, however, engage in multiple activities and also often offer themselves for wage employment. They in fact make a choice between self-employment and wage employment (Unni 1996). Self-employed workers affect the supply side of the wage equation. If a large proportion of the self-employed offer themselves for wage employment, they would in fact drive down the wage rate. Therefore, any notion of the labour market has to consider the self-employed workers as part of it. This is particularly true of the developing world where the self-employed constitute a large proportion of the labour force.

This large component of the self-employed, constitutes a major portion of the informal sector in developing countries. While the proportion of self-employed workers may have declined over the last two decades, they still constitute a major segment of the labour market. In short, they refuse to disappear. The character of the informal sector in the developed and developing worlds are, therefore, different.

DEFINING INFORMALITY

Conceptually, a primary attribute of informal employment is the absence of regular or written contracts. The consequence is that direct measurement becomes difficult. Most informal employment may be similar to formal employment in terms of the work done, with the difference that it is performed without regular contracts, generally for small and unregistered enterprises and within a different system of incentives and controls. But, there are categories of informal employment that do not have a counterpart within the formal system. These include self-employed workers, such as home-based workers, street vendors and workers engaged in productive household activity such as dairying/livestock. At the upper end of the spectrum, consultants and tele-workers also fall outside the conventional categories. There are other aspects to informality that make counting difficult, such as workers engaging in multiple activities adding up to a long day's work, but not in any single activity. These problems are compounded by the difficulty in distinguishing 'housework' from 'productive activity' in developing countries.

The importance of getting an accurate count is explained by the fact that work and production are two sides of the same coin. At the heart of the debate on work is the concept of what constitutes productive work and how to measure production. This problem is discussed here in the context of international recommendations by various organisations concerned with these issues. There have been many recent efforts—to include more of household production, informal sector activities and women's work in the production boundary—and attempts to provide some estimates for the same.

Employment is viewed as an indicator of the level of economic activity in a country. The work of individuals when combined with other factors of production yields an output valued by society. At the macro level the notion of 'work' and 'production' is theoretically interconnected. 'Production' is the result of the economic activities of producers and 'work' is input supplied in the process of production. The two concepts are complementary. Hence, there has to be a correspondence between the measurement of 'persons producing' and 'production'.

International standards for the measurement of 'economically active population' and 'production' as suggested by international bodies like the ILO and the UN aim at establishing this correspondence. While the concepts regarding the 'economically active population' are proposed in the various International Conferences of Labour Statisticians (ICLS), the concept of the production boundary is suggested by the United Nations' System of National Accounts (SNA). International recommendations on the measurement of national product, employment and related statistics, serve to provide guidelines for the development of national statistics on the subject and improve international comparability of the statistics gathered.

PRODUCTION BOUNDARY IN NATIONAL ACCOUNTS

The origins of the SNA can be traced back to the Sub-Committee Report on National Income Statistics of the League of Nations Committee of Statistical Experts published in 1947. The first explicit reference to the drawing of a production boundary for national accounts purposes, can be found in the SNA (1953). Unlike the 1947 system, the 1953 system explicitly took the needs of developing countries into consideration. The problem of separation of households from enterprises and the inclusion of production for home consumption in the total product were recognised. 'Accordingly the report attempted to provide clearly defined rules for drawing the production boundary' (SNA 1993: xxxix).

The production boundary in the 1993 SNA is only slightly different from the one in the 1968 SNA.

In defining the production boundary, the 1993 SNA draws on the distinction between goods and services. It includes the production of all goods within the production boundary, and the production of all services except personal and domestic services produced for own final consumption within households (other than the services of owner occupiers and those produced by employing paid domestic staff) (SNA 1993: 527).

The 1993 SNA removed the 1968 SNA limitation with regard to own-account production. This

excluded the production of goods not made from primary products, the processing of primary products by those who do not produce them and the production of other goods by households who do not sell any part of them in the market (ibid.).

These seemingly small changes in the production boundary actually extends the production boundary to include a number of activities undertaken in the household, mainly by women, particularly in developing countries, such as processing of agricultural produce. It also includes the gathering of wild fruit or berries and firewood and carrying water from one location to another.

The informal sector consists of a diverse set of economic activities and does not lend itself easily to statistical measurement. The informal sector resolution adopted by the Fifteenth ICLS represents the first internationally approved guidelines for the development of statistics on the informal sector. The relevance of the resolution goes beyond employment statistics, since it forms part of the SNA (1993).

One of the new features of the SNA 1993 is the recommendation to introduce, where relevant, sub classifications of the household sector, including a distinction between the formal and informal sectors. Such a distinction makes it possible for the accounts to quantify the contribution of the informal sector to the national economy (Hussmanns 1996).

The main cause of the underestimation of the informal sector is the difficulty of identifying and estimating the work of women in this sector. The cause of this underestimation stems from various reasons: Women are engaged in those activities, which are most difficult to capture and measure, e.g., home-based work and street vending. The non-response rate is also higher for women. They are engaged, more than men are, in second or multiple jobs and the non-measurement of this phenomenon is a source of underestimation. Their production activities are hidden behind their status of so-called housewives, or family worker (Charmes 1999).

An increasing concern in national and international fora has been that the usual labour force surveys carried out at country levels do not capture the activity pattern of certain groups of workers, particularly women. They obviously belong to the informal sector and their activities are mostly invisible. Information on such invisible groups of workers belonging to the informal sector would be available only if the required probes or questions are introduced in the survey questionnaire to obtain clear-cut answers to identify and categorise them. Any failure in a survey to fully capture the activity pattern of such persons will underestimate the volume of employment in the informal sector. Most such workers are engaged in some entrepreneurial activities without fixed premises of operation and are not easily detected in a survey. Obviously, an enterprise survey, which does not fully capture such persons and their activities, will underestimate the output generated in the informal sector. It may therefore be necessary that any survey to estimate the size and output of the informal sector should be linked and detailed probes undertaken, to identify such persons and account for their output. That is, the correspondence between persons engaged in producing goods and services (work) and the value of production (value added) has to be maintained in the informal sector as well.

DEFINITION AND METHODOLOGY: EFFORTS THROUGH NATIONAL AND INTERNATIONAL NETWORKING

The data on labour force that are currently collected through the official statistical systems in India, and at the international level, are not able to capture the new processes of informalisation adequately. The contention of the methodological studies included here is that improved concepts and definitions are required to estimate this new dimension of informalisation of the labour force.

International organisations, such as the ILO, are currently concerned with these changes in the labour force. The new System of National Accounts (1993), has reflected this concern. An International Expert Group on Informal Sector Statistics has also been constituted, called the 'Delhi Group'. In its meetings so far it has deliberated on the definition of the informal sector and reviewed the data collection procedures in various countries. The Delhi Group has been meeting every year since 1997. This group is one of the City groups of the United Nations Statistical Commission. The work of this group is to prepare an inventory of country practices of data collection, evaluate the data collecting systems, discuss and implement the international definition of the informal sector (ICLS 1993), prepare guidelines for collection of data on the informal sector, suggest a minimum data set to be collected by countries, etc. The Delhi Group has been successful in getting many countries to better understand and conduct country surveys of the informal sector using the ICLS 1993 definition. At the Fifth Meeting of the group, held in September 2001, the ILO argued the need to distinguish between informal employment and the informal sector; the proposed format to be tested by India and Mexico.

We have participated at the Delhi Group meetings every year as data users, representing Women in Informal Employment, Globalising and Organising (WIEGO), an international coalition of academics, activists, NGOs and trade unionists. We felt that, while the current international definition is useful to identify the size of the informal sector and for national accounts, the size and contribution of some of the vulnerable groups of workers need to be estimated separately. These workers were home-based workers and homeworkers, street-based workers and street vendors, domestic and other informal wage workers, and informal employment in the formal sector. It was also pointed out that a variable like the 'place of work' will help to identify some of these workers.

In India, the Expert Group on Defining the Informal Sector (November 1998), constituted by the Government of India, felt that the definition of the informal sector adopted by the 15th International Conference of Labour Statisticians (ICLS–1993) was conceptually close to that defined by the Indian Statistical System. SEWA, which was represented in the Expert Group, pointed out that when the ICLS–1993 definition, which is enterprise-based, is implemented through an enterprise survey (such as the Unorganised Sector Surveys of the National Sample Survey Organisation [NSSO]), it tends to miss out certain categories of single person own-account enterprises. This is because it is difficult to identify such workers as enterprises. For example, certain persons providing services, or undertaking manufacturing or processing of goods on contract, often at home and persons working on the streets without fixed premises, even though such enterprises are included in the international definition of the informal sector. Certain service providers who work for households such as domestic servants, chowkidars, gardeners, etc., are in any case excluded from the informal sector by the international definition. Such workers are more easily captured through a household survey.

While it is an important goal to net all categories of workers, it is also necessary to assess their contribution in terms of output, that is, to maintain the correspondence between 'work' and 'production'. There is a need to link the worker approach with the enterprise approach in order to estimate both the size in terms of employment, and contribution, in terms of value added, of the informal sector (see next chapter for details on these approaches). It is necessary to canvass a minimum set of questions to assess the output or income of these workers, immediately after the household survey, to a sample of enterprises identified in the survey. In order to do this, GIDR–SEWA conducted a Linked Household-Cum-Enterprise Survey of the informal sector in Ahmedabad city in 1998–99 (Unni 2000). The purpose of the survey was similar to that outlined above. Some of the results of the household survey, used to estimate the size of the informal sector, were circulated to the Expert Group. The CSO requested GIDR–SEWA to conduct a methodological study in rural areas as a precursor to the NSS Pilot Survey on the Informal Sector to be conducted along with the Employment Unemployment Survey of the NSSO, 1999–2000. The purpose was to test a questionnaire and suggest a survey design to link the worker and enterprise approach to arrive at estimates of the size and contribution of the informal sector.

The NSSO conducted its first ever nationwide survey on informal non-agricultural enterprises, incorporating a module on the informal sector, along with its Employment and Unemployment Survey during July 1999 to June 2000, the 55th Round. Following the ICLS definition, all unincorporated proprietary and partnership enterprises have been defined as informal sector enterprises. This definition differs from the concept of unorganised sector widely used in Indian data collection, and may be considered a sub-set of the unorganised sector (CSO 2000).

DEFINITION OF INFORMALITY USED IN THIS BOOK

In this book, more than one definition of informality has been used. Each paper included here has chosen a definition to suit the primary objective of the study. The chapters based on secondary and official data—Chapters Five, Six and Seven—have started with the definition as used in the Indian statistical system, i.e., of the 'unorganised' sector. According to Kulshreshtha and Singh (1999), in the Indian NAS, the unorganised sector refers to a collection of those operating units whose activity is not regulated under any legal provision and/or which do not maintain any regular accounts. The unorganised segment broadly covers all of the agricultural sector except plantation crops, operations of the government irrigation system, minor minerals, unregistered manufacturing units and all units of non-manufacturing activities except those in the public, private corporate and cooperative sector. Two of the chapters—Five and Seven—go on to develop the concept of 'informal households'. While the term informality is widely used in relation to workers and enterprises, consumption and savings decisions are generally taken at the level of the household and data on such variables is presented at the household level. In trying to understand the impact of informality on consumption/savings behaviour, it becomes necessary to classify households into 'formal' and 'informal'. The criterion used to do this in Chapters Five and Seven is 'the primary source of income of the household'.

In contrast, the methodological chapters—Two and Three have been able to experiment with the concept and to collect data accordingly. Essentially, these chapters have tried to develop the distinction between 'informal employment' and 'informal sector'.

THIS BOOK

The understanding that informal employment is an integral and growing part of the present day economic system, then, has motivated this book. Several of the papers in this book have taken as their starting point the contribution made by the informal economy to the nation. This contribution could take different forms: it creates productive work, self and wage employment; creates value added through production of goods and services; creates savings and investment which is eventually converted to capital formation; and provides revenues to the government through taxes. Further, the self-employed workers create their own jobs and incomes and perform a useful role of reducing poverty and income disparities.

Chapter Two by Jeemol Unni and Uma Rani uses a new approach, a two-stage methodology, comprising of a Linked Household-cum-Enterprise Survey. Besides estimating the total size of informal employment, the study was able to effectively enumerate specific vulnerable groups of workers, such as home-based workers, home-workers and street vendors on whom there is an international focus (Chen et al. 1999). The study was also able to bring out the need to focus on the growing component of informal employment or precarious employment in the formal sector. The two-stage approach was able to separately estimate the contribution of these groups to the value addition in the economy.

India's urban population has been growing twice as fast as the rural population in the last decade. Providing the urban population with productive activities is proving a daunting task. This paper also analyses the role and contribution of the informal economy in a city in Gujarat. About three-quarters of the employment and nearly half of the income was generated in the informal economy in the city. It is often assumed that the informal economy does not pay taxes to the city authorities. In order to get a rough idea of resources generated by the informal economy we tried to estimate the amount of legal and illegal fees paid by this sector to the city economy. About 60 per cent of the fees paid by the informal economy was illegal.

Chapter Three by Keshab Das employs a sub-sector approach to study the ceramic ware industry in Gujarat. This approach starts with the selection of a product group in which small enterprises are important and identifies and analyses the principal functions, participants and channels in the sector. A sub-sector map highlights the vertical relationships and competitive positions of sub-sector participants. The strengths and weaknesses of different actors in the value chain, and the 'nodes' or points where action should be taken to derive maximum benefit for the sector can be identified through this methodology. The classic sub-sector method of identifying value chains, drawing maps of vertical and horizontal linkages and identifying nodes, was not strictly followed. However, an important focus of the study was on the underestimation of the industry group, at the three-digit industrial classification, in the official data sources on unorganised manufacturing sector. The study also addressed important aspects of production organisation, labour process, terms of employment and mode of payment which could highlight the varying dimensions of informal production arrangements in one sub-sector of the unorganised manufacturing sector. Besides the generation of jobs, the study argued for the need to emphasise vital issues such as terms of employment, mode of payment and earnings, relating to the quality of employment generated in the informal economy. As an issue of production organisation, the case study found that there is a fairly high degree of informality in labour arrangements within the formal enterprises. These issues are not addressed in the official statistics on this sector. Further the study also demonstrated that the conventional notion of small firms being essentially dependent on their large counterparts could be quite misleading.

Chapter Four by Anushree Sinha, N. Sangeeta and K.A. Siddiqui presents a disaggregation of the economy using a social accounting matrix framework in which factors of production and households are divided into formal and informal. The study looks at informality from three axes—goods market informality, factor market informality and households. The special focus of this paper is to show the strong overlap between gender, informality and poverty.

Chapter Five by N. Lalitha uses the official secondary data sources, the Unorganised Manufacturing Sector Survey of the NSSO, to analyse the growth of this sector at the national level. The method of estimation of the income contribution of the unorganised sector in the National Accounts is critically examined in this chapter with suggestions for improvement.

Chapter Six by Basanta Pradhan, P.K. Roy and M.R. Saluja uses data from a survey of 5,000 households to estimate the contribution of informal households to total household savings. Households surveyed have been grouped into six occupational categories, on the basis of principal source of income. Except for those households whose major source of income originates from salary received from the organised sector, all other households have been defined as working in the informal sector. It is seen that almost 60 per cent of total household savings are found to originate in informal households. Although the average level of savings of formal households is three times that of informal households, the savings rate of informal households averaged 17.9 per cent and compares well with that of formal households—25.4 per cent. Sixty-two per cent of informal savings took the form of physical investment, if consumer durables are excluded from the definition; and 55 per cent if both consumer durables and gold and jewelry are excluded. The corresponding numbers for formal households are 26 per cent and 7 per cent. The distribution of physical investment is also different by type of household. These findings have important implications for growth: institutional mechanisms to collect and channel savings from informal households may have a good chance of success.

Chapter Seven moves on to discussing a different aspect of the informal economy, that is the need for social security. This chapter by Anil Gumber and Veena Kulkarni presents a study of health needs and perceptions, and a comparative study of existing forms of health insurance in and around Ahmedabad. It confirms both the need for insurance for unorganised workers and their willingness to pay. Mirai Chatterjee contributes some insights from the SEWA experience to this chapter.

The last chapter by Renana Jhabvala looks at the process of bringing informal workers 'centrestage' in India, through the experiences and insights gained by the Self-Employed Women's Association.

NOTE

1. Special mention could be made of WIEGO and HomeNet, networks that have been active and vocal in issues of concern to informal workers.

REFERENCES

Amin, S. (1996), 'On Development: For Gunder Frank', in S.C. Chew and R.A. Denmark (eds), *The Underdevelopment of Development*, London: Sage.

Bromley, Ray (1978), 'Introduction—The Urban Informal Sector: Is it Worth Discussing?', *World Development*, vol. 6, no. 9/10: 1033–39.

Castells, M. and A. Portes (1989), 'World Underneath: The Origins, Dynamics and Effects of the Informal Economy', in A. Portes, M. Castells and L.A. Benton (eds), *The Informal Economy: Studies in Advanced and Less Developing Countries*, Baltimore: John Hopkins University Press.

Charmes, J. (1999), 'The Quality of Women's Employment: A Review of Statistical and Empirical Evidence Towards an Improvement of Their Situation at Work', Paper prepared for the International Labour Office, Department of Development Policies (POLDEV), Programme 'Improving the Quality of Women's Employment'.

Chen, M., J. Sebtad and L. O'Connell (1999), 'Counting the Invisible Workforce: The Case of Homebased workers', *World Development*, vol. 27, no. 3.

CSO (2000), *Report of the Time Use Survey*, Central Statistical Organisation, Ministry of Statistics and Programme Implementation, Government of India, New Delhi.

Diebold, Francis X. (1998), 'The Past, Present and Future of Macroeconomic Forecasting', *Journal of Economic Perspectives*, vol. 12, no. 2: 175–92.

Fei, J.C.H. and G. Ranis (1964), *Development of the Labour Surplus Economy: Theory and Policy*, Irwin: Illinois.

Feige, Edgar L. (1990), 'Defining and Estimating Underground and Informal Economies: The New Institutional Economics Approach', *World Development*, vol. 18, no. 7: 989–1002.

Hariss, J.R. and M.P. Todaro (1970), 'Migration, Unemployment and Development: A Two Sector Analysis', *American Economic Review*, vol. 60, no. 1.

Holmstrom, M. (1993), 'Flexible Specialisation in India', *Economic and Political Weekly*, vol. 28, no. 35.

Hoover, Kevin D. (1995), 'Why Does Methodology Matter for Economics?', *The Economic Journal*, 105: 715–34.

Hussmanns, R. (1996), 'ILO's Recommendations on Methodologies Concerning Informal Sector Data Collection', in Bohuslav Herman and Wim Stoffers (eds), *Unveiling the Informal Sector: More than Counting Heads*, Aldershot: Avebury.

ICLS (1993), 'Report of the Fifteenth International Conference of Labour Statisticians', International Labour Organisation, Geneva.

ILO (2002), Women and Men in the Informal Economy: A Statistical Picture, Geneva: International Labour Office.

Ironmonger, D. (1996), 'Counting Outputs, Capital Inputs and Caring Labour: Estimating Gross Household Product', *Feminist Economics*, vol. 2, no. 3: 37–64.

Kulshreshtha, A.C. and Gulab Singh (1999), 'Gross Domestic Product and Employment in the Informal Sector of the Indian Economy', *The Indian Journal of Labour Economics*, vol. 42, no. 2: 217–30.

Lewis, W.A. (1954), 'Economic Development with Unlimited Supplies of Labour,' *The Manchester School*, vol. 22: 139–91.

Maddison, Angus (1982), *Phases of Capitalist Development*, New York: Oxford University Press: 21–25.

Mazumdar, Dipak (1976), 'The Urban Informal Sector', *World Development*, vol. 4, no. 8: 655–79.

Mead, Donald C. and Christian Morrisson (1996), 'The Informal Sector Elephant', *World Development*, vol. 24, no. 10: 1611–19.

Piore, M.J. and C.F. Sabel (1984), *The Second Industrial Divide: Possibilities for Prosperity*, New York: Basic Books.

Roll, Eric (1961), *A History of Economic Thought*, London: Faber and Faber.

Sethuraman, S.V. (1976), 'The Urban Informal Sector: Concept, Measurement and Policy', *International Labour Review*, vol. 114, no. 1 (July–August): 69–81.

SNA (1993), *System of National Accounts, 1993*, Commission of the European Communities, World Bank, Washington, D.C.

Soto, Hernando de (1989), *The Other Path: The Invisible Revolution of the Third World*, London: I.B. Tauris.

Standing, Guy (1999), *Global Labour Flexibility: Seeking Distributive Justice*, London: Macmillan.

Stiglitz, Joseph (2000), 'Scan Globally, Reinvent Locally: Knowledge Infrastructure and the Localisation of Knowledge', in Diane Stone (ed.), *Banking on knowledge: The genesis of the global Development Network*, London and New York: Routledge: 24–43.

Unni, Jeemol (1996), 'Occupational Choice and Multiple Job Holding in Rural Gujarat', *The Indian Economic Review*, vol. 31 no. 2.

——— (2000), Urban Informal Sector: Size and Income Generation Processes in Gujarat, Part I, SEWA–GIDR–ISST–NCAER, Report No. 2, National Council of Applied Economic Research, New Delhi.

Williams, Colin C. and Jan Windebank (1998), *Informal Employment in the Advanced Economies: Implications for Work and Welfare*, London and New York: Routledge.

❷

Employment and Income
in the Informal Economy:
A Micro-Perspective

JEEMOL UNNI AND UMA RANI

INTRODUCTION

The labour market in developing countries is markedly different from
that in the developed countries. The most striking feature of labour
markets in the developing countries is their non-homogeneous
character. The labour markets in these two worlds differ in their
sectoral composition with the vast majority of employment being in
the non-agricultural sectors in the developed world, whereas the
developing world is still predominantly agricultural. The status of the
vast majority of workers in the developed countries is of wage and
salary earners. Whereas in the developing countries there is a
predominance of self-employment.

This non-homogeneous character of the labour markets in developing countries also implies that the nature of employment and the
manner in which it is created is different in the two worlds. 'Almost
all the employment in developed economies is created within the
recognised institutional framework as the economic agents which
create these jobs operate within the existing laws and regulation'
(Sethuraman 1998). These economic agents are the government,

and private enterprises, including non-corporate entities, and the employment thus created is governed by the prevailing labour laws and regulations. In contrast, in the developing countries the vast majority of the population is left to fend for itself and create employment out of its own ingenuity, skills and capital. This leads to vast differences in the nature of employment and the creation of a dualistic structure of 'formal' and 'informal' components of the labour market.

The term 'informal sector' has come into wide usage during the last two decades, although its precise meaning has remained a subject of controversy. It is an umbrella concept, used to describe a variety of activities producing goods and services through which individuals gain employment and incomes (Hussmanns 1996). The development strategies pursued were heavily biased in favour of modern, large-scale enterprises. The informal sector was considered a transitory phenomenon that would fade away as the formal sector created more and more jobs. However, economic recession, structural adjustment policies and continued high rates of urbanisation and population growth, forced the modern sector enterprises, especially those owned by the government, to retrench workers or reduce wages drastically. This led to an unprecedented expansion of the informal sector in many countries. In fact, in some countries it was the informal sector alone, which absorbed the labour force. This has increasingly led to the belief that a large and growing segment of the labour force in most developing countries will be engaged in the informal sector for many years to come, and that the informal sector will remain an important, and probably expanding, part of national economies. Researchers and policy makers are beginning to acknowledge that the informal sector can no longer be ignored and that it needs to be integrated into the overall development process (ibid.).

The theoretical basis of the concept of the 'informal sector' grew out of labour market studies that emphasised the dualistic tendencies in the urban economies of the developing countries in the 1950s and 1960s (Lewis 1954; Fei and Ranis 1964). However, it was Hart (1973), who first used the term to suggest such a dichotomy in his dual model for urban workers in Ghana which was based on one simple characteristic, namely the distinction between income opportunities in wage employment and self-employment. The concept however, started gaining attention after its wide usage in a number of country and city studies in Asia, Latin America and West Africa, carried out by the ILO in the 1970s. Since then, the concept of the 'informal sector' has dominated the debate regarding urban employment policies in the developing countries, where a large part of the urban labour force is engaged in low productivity, low income, activities outside the organised modern sector.

The major achievement of the ILO's country missions was to shift the emphasis from a development strategy based mainly on economic growth, whereby employment was obtained as a residual, to a strategy which focused on employment as the prime objective. The ILO's definition of the informal sector in the early 1970s was descriptive. It specified a set of characteristics to distinguish informal enterprises: small-scale of operation, family ownership, reliance on indigenous resources, labour intensive and adaptive technology, skills acquired outside the formal system and operation in unregulated and competitive markets. The problem with applying such multiple criteria is that all of them could be found in units pursuing different objectives. They are also difficult to apply. In practice, most of the early ILO studies ended up using a single index of the employment size.

In the 1990s, the idea that the informal sector is a feature unique to the developing countries came to be questioned. It was noted that there was increasing evidence of informal sector activities existing and proliferating in advanced industrialised countries as well. This was due in part to increasing 'flexibilisation' of large enterprises and in part to economic recession. The literature on 'flexible specialisation' based on case-studies in industrial economies, highlighted the comparative advantages of small-scale production and forced a substantial re-evaluation of its role in the development process (Holmstrom 1993). Piore and Sabel (1984), describe the growth of small-scale production units combining flexible technology and specialised production in developed countries such as Italy, Germany and Japan. The growth of the informal sector was thus attributed to the rapidly changing market demand and technological advances. This view also finds its echo in the developing country studies on subcontracting, ancillarisation and industrial clustering.

In this chapter we analyse the contribution of the informal economy in generating employment and income, from a micro-perspective of a district in the industrially developed state of Gujarat. In the next section we juxtapose the enterprise-based definition of the informal sector with a new definition of informal employment focussing on the degree of informality of the status of the worker. An empirical estimate of informal employment, disaggregated by the 'invisible' groups of workers constituting it, is presented in the third section. This is contrasted with the estimate of employment in the informal sector. Informal enterprises by their place of work and the gender dimensions of proprietorship are discussed in the next two sections. The value addition generated by these enterprises and homeworkers is highlighted in section six. The contribution of the informal economy to the city in terms of employment, incomes and legal and illegal fees paid to the authorities, is discussed in section seven.

DEFINITION OF THE INFORMAL SECTOR: ICLS/SNA 1993

At the international level, after several years of negotiations, an agreement was reached on the definition of the informal sector, in the Fifteenth International Conference of Labour Statisticians (ICLS) 1993 and which was adopted in the new System of National Accounts (SNA) (1993). Due to the complexity and looseness of the concept, the labour statisticians decided to distinguish one single statistical definition for the purpose of data collection from the several definitions that varied according to the needs of the users and could be differentiated at the tabulation stage.

The SNA (1993), characterises the informal sector as consisting of units engaged in the production of goods or services with the primary objective of generating employment and incomes to the persons concerned. They form part of the household sector as unincorporated enterprises owned by households. They are distinguished from corporations and quasi-corporations on the basis of their legal status and the type of accounts they hold. These household enterprises do not have a legal status independent of the households or household members owning them.

The Fifteenth ICLS 1993, adopted an operational definition of the informal sector that is irrespective of the kind of workplace, the extent of fixed assets, the duration of the activity of the enterprises and its operation as a main or secondary activity. Within the household sector, the informal sector comprises: (i) Informal own-account enterprises that are single member or partnership household units that do not hire workers on a continuous basis; (ii) enterprises of informal employers are household units owned and operated by employers, singly or in partnership, which employ one or more employees on a more or less continuous basis. For operational purposes the latter may be defined in terms of either, the size of unit below a specified level of employment or, non-registration of the enterprise or its employees.

CRITIQUE OF THE ICLS/SNA DEFINITION

The ICLS/SNA definition of the informal sector is based on the legal status of the enterprise. To distinguish employment in the informal sector one will have to assume that all persons working in such units are workers in this sector. That is, informal employers, and employees in the enterprises of informal employers, own-account workers and unpaid family helpers in informal enterprises. This definition of the informal sector, focussing on the enterprise, hides the heterogeneity in the status and working conditions of the workers in them. It will not be correct to assume that all workers in the formal sector are better off than all workers in the informal sector, or that all workers in the informal sector are equally badly off.

In recent years many writings have expressed the view that such a dichotomised classification of the 'formal' and 'informal' sector is unrealistic and tends to hide more than it reveals. It also fails to capture three things which are important from the point of view of social protection for workers, particularly women: 'the continuing process of informalisation of the formal economy; the great diversity within the informal economy itself; and the linkages between the formal and informal parts of the economy' (Lund and Srinivas 2000).

The term 'informal sector' is giving way to the term 'informal economy'. For example in an important paper called 'Decent work', the Director General of the ILO used the term informal economy (ILO 1999). Sethuraman (1998) argued that 'it is now widely accepted that such a dichotomy into the formal and informal is but a caricature of the real economy because both the formal and informal parts exhibit considerable diversity'. Employment in the informal economy is not only inferior to that in the formal economy, in terms of wages and benefits received, but also varies in terms of quality. 'Some jobs tend to be more informal than others in the sense that the extent of deviation from the established quality norms is greater.'

The ICLS definition of the informal sector actually distinguishes the status of the enterprise. This is useful for National Accounts and in estimating the gross value added accruing from the two sectors. The concept of the 'informal economy' in fact tries to characterise the workers depending on the degree of informality of their work status. This is more useful for persons concerned with wages, working conditions and access to social protection to workers.

A second problem with the enterprise-based definition arises, when it is used in an establishment survey to distinguish the unit. This definition tends to leave out more invisible groups of own-account enterprises, such as those operating on the streets or in their homes. A labour force survey with clear questions on the place of work and nature of contract may be better able to net all such workers.

We argue that the enterprise-based dichotomous definition (SNA) is important from the point of view of estimating the contribution of this sector in the gross national product. However, an additional worker-based approach is required to identify the status of workers within the two sectors and invisible groups of workers often missed out through an enterprise approach (Unni 2000a).

DEFINITION OF INFORMAL EMPLOYMENT

Within a wider concept of the informal economy we define informal employment as employment created outside the recognised institutional framework, that is, by unincorporated enterprises and households. The concept of informal employment characterises the workers depending on the degree of informality of their work status. Informal employment can be distinguished into wage and non-wage employment.

The international definition of the informal sector distinguishes two kinds of enterprises, namely, own-account enterprises and enterprises of informal employers. The activity status of employment is the closest that this enterprise-based definition can get to distinguishing the informal employment. The present activity status classification of the International Classification of Status in Employment (ICSE) 1993, ILO consists of the following categories: employees, employers, own-account workers, members of producer's cooperatives, contributing family members, workers not classifiable by status.

COMPONENTS OF THE INFORMAL EMPLOYMENT

Following the worker approach, workers in the informal economy can be broadly distinguished into wage employment and non-wage employment, each consisting of the following components:

FIRST COMPONENT: NON-WAGE EMPLOYMENT

- Own-account workers.
- Employers/owners of informal enterprises with at least one hired worker.
- Unpaid family helpers in both types of informal enterprises.

SECOND COMPONENT: WAGE EMPLOYMENT

- Employees in the enterprises of informal employers.
- Outworkers or Homeworkers: persons working at home, or on premises of his choice other than the employer's, to produce goods or services on a contract or order for a specific employer or contractor.
- Independent wage workers not attached to only one employer, and providing services to individuals, households and enterprises, e.g., maid servants working for households.
- Informal employment in formal sector enterprises: workers whose pay and benefits do not conform to existing labour regulations.

This categorisation is similar to that developed by Sethuraman (1998). The first four categories above are included in the ICLS/SNA definition of the informal sector. Our definition of informal employment is wider and includes other groups of vulnerable workers as well. The need to distinguish the category of independent wage workers can be debated. In many Latin American countries, domestic servants are distinguished in the national surveys and together with independent wage workers are added to the informal sector (ibid.).

INVISIBLE GROUPS OF INFORMAL WORKERS

There has been an international focus on certain groups of workers within the informal sector who are considered more invisible (Chen et al. 1999). Some such groups of workers are the home-based workers, within them the homeworkers or out-workers, and the street vendors. Part of their invisibility stems from the fact that they are often women and work in not very clearly designated 'business places', e.g., within their homes or in the streets. While street vendors are included in the ICLS definition, homeworkers or out-workers are in the informal sector only if their employer is part of the informal sector. Hence, according to the SNA 1993, outworker is an overlapping category as far as the dichotomy of formal and informal goes.

HOMEWORKERS

The ILO adopted a Convention on Home Work in 1996, which refers exclusively to homeworkers, a category not included in the ICSE 1993. It defined homeworker as a person who carried out work for remuneration in premises of his/her own choice, other than the work place of the employer, resulting in a product or service as specified by the employer, irrespective of who provided the equipment, material or inputs used. This is a subcategory of the broader category of home-based workers.

HOME-BASED WORKERS

Home-based workers form a broader category of workers within which the homeworkers are included. They are defined as those own-account workers, unpaid family helpers and homeworkers who pursue economic activities within their home, i.e., their place of work is their home. It may be noted that we have excluded employers working at home from this category.

STREET VENDORS

Street vendors are another category of informal workers that are difficult to capture and measure. There are two kinds of street vendors—those with a fixed location and those without a fixed location who are mobile, such as peripatetic vegetable sellers etc. Besides street vendors there are a number of own-account workers whose place of work is on the street. They include cycle-rickshaw pullers, auto drivers etc.

SIZE OF INFORMAL EMPLOYMENT

It is difficult to obtain empirical data on the size of informal employment and on these specific groups of workers. Conceptually the labour force survey would capture street vendors as persons engaged in trade (industrial classification). Chances of under-enumeration are high due to non-reporting, the seasonal nature of their work etc. However, unless the labour survey asks a question on the 'place of work', it is not possible to estimate the proportion of traders who are also street vendors. The occupational classification at the three digit level, however, has a specific code (431) for street vendors, canvassers and new vendors. Published data at this level of disaggregation are difficult to obtain. It is not very clear how homeworkers and home-based workers are captured in the official data. It is likely that homeworkers are treated as casual workers (employees) and home-based workers, other than the above, as own-account workers (self-employed).

In the GIDR–SEWA study of Ahmedabad district in Gujarat, 1998–99, we made a special effort to separately estimate homeworkers, home-based workers, street vendors, other workers on the street and then estimate the size of informal employment[1] (Unni 2000a). We obtained estimates of the homebased workers and street vendors by cross-classifying the industry divisions and the place of work. In order to estimate homeworkers the survey included an extra question on the nature of contract for persons engaged in home-based manufacturing.

The non-agricultural workers constituted about 98.7 per cent of all workers in urban areas and 24 per cent in rural areas. This proportion was 99.1 per cent for males and 97.5 per cent for females in urban areas and 32 per cent for males and 12 per cent for females in rural areas. Among these non-agricultural workers we present the distribution of all workers, formal and informal in rural and urban areas (see Table 2.1). As per our classification, wage employment constituted about 60 per cent of the workforce in rural and 68 per cent in urban areas, consisting of formal and informal employees and homeworkers. All the self-employed workers, 39 and 32 per cent in rural and urban areas respectively, are considered to be in informal employment. The percentage of self-employment among the non-agricultural workers was 36 per cent for males and 51 per cent for females in rural areas and 32 and 34 per cent in urban areas.

Among women workers, home-based workers constituted about 24 and 51 per cent of the non-agricultural workforce in rural and urban areas respectively, while among males they were only about 9 and 7 per cent. A large proportion of women workers were homeworkers and unpaid helpers, 24 per cent each, in urban areas. In rural areas homeworkers or outworkers was not so important, but unpaid family workers constituted 38 per cent of the workforce. Neither homeworkers nor unpaid workers were important categories

Table 2.1
Distribution of Workers in Formal and
Informal Employment in the Non-agricultural Sector

Derived Work Activity Status	Rural			Urban		
	M	F	P	M	F	P
Wage employment	63.4	49.3	60.5	68.3	65.6	67.7
Employees						
Formal	12.9	12.7	12.9	15.7	14.2	15.3
Informal	49.4	34.7	46.4	50.1	27.3	44.6
Homeworkers	1.1	1.9	1.2	2.5	24.1	7.8
Self-employment	36.5	50.7	39.5	31.7	34.5	32.3
Employer	4.9	–	3.9	2.7	0.1	2.1
Own-account worker	25.8	12.2	23.1	23.7	10.3	20.3
Home-based OAW	6.1	8.3	6.5	3.3	7.9	4.4
Street worker	4.7	1.1	4.0	15.4	2.2	12.1
Street vendors	1.9	1.0	1.7	6.3	2.2	5.3
Others on street	2.8	0.1	2.3	9.1	–	6.8
Own business premises	15.0	2.8	12.6	5.0	0.2	3.8
Unpaid family worker	5.8	38.5	12.5	5.3	24.1	9.9
Home-based worker	8.9	24.2	11.9	7.4	50.7	18.0
Informal employment	87.1	87.3	87.1	84.3	85.8	84.7
All	100.0	100.0	100.0	100.0	100.0	100.0
Number of sample persons	534.0	222.0	756.0	1,095.0	411.0	1,506.0

Source: Unni and Jacob 1999; Unni 2000a.

Note: Home-based worker includes home workers, home-based own-account and unpaid family workers.

among men. The men were mainly employees in formal and informal enterprises and self-employed own-account workers. Obviously the men had a more independent status of work than the women.

About 5 and 15 per cent of the male non-agricultural workers were working on the streets in rural and urban areas. For females, this proportion was relatively small, 1–2 per cent. Street vendors constituted almost all the women workers on the street in urban areas, but only part (6.3 per cent) of the male workers. The rest of the male workers on the street were mainly autorickshaw and cycle-rickshaw drivers and handcart pullers. Self-employed workers with a separate business place constituted only about 15 and 5 percent of all male workers in rural and urban areas and a negligible proportion of women. This lack of a designated place of work is one of the main factors contributing to the vulnerability of informal workers, particularly women.

The formality or informality of the wage workers were determined by the criteria of various economic benefits derived from the job. A small proportion of the workers received all the benefits due to workers in the formal sector such as provident fund, paid leave and medical benefits (Unni and Rani 1999). We finally used the criterion of whether the employee received the benefit of paid leave to judge informality. Only about 13 per cent of the workers in rural areas and 15 per cent in urban areas received this benefit. The rest, that is, 87 per cent in rural and 85 per cent in urban areas formed the category of informal employment, including all self-employed workers, homeworkers and informal employees. There was not much gender difference in the proportion of informal employment in the economy. It is obvious that informal employment is not simply a survival strategy for the marginalised. In fact, there is a heterogeneous informal labour market with a hierarchy of its own.

This estimate of informal employment, as defined above, can be contrasted with the estimate of workers in the informal sector by the official definition of the registration status of the enterprises. According to the National Accounts Statistics, government/semi-government organisations and enterprises registered under the Indian Factories Act, Bidi and Cigar workers Act, Cooperative Societies Act, Provident Fund Act, and recognised educational institutions, are con-sidered to be in the organised or 'formal' sector. By this definition 75 and 71 per cent of the workers were found to be in the informal sector in rural and urban areas respectively. A larger proportion of women, about 84 per cent, were in the informal sector (see Table 2.2).

The estimate of informal employment was about 10–12 per cent higher than the estimate of the informal sector using the official definition, the difference being much higher among men and less so

Table 2.2
Non-agricultural Workers in the Informal Sector by Registration Status

By Registration Status	Person		Male		Female	
	Rural	Urban	Rural	Urban	Rural	Urban
Formal sector	24.7	28.9	27.2	33.1	14.6	16.4
Informal sector	75.3	71.1	72.8	68.9	85.4	83.6
All	100.0	100.0	100.0	100.0	100.0	100.0

Source: Unni and Jacob 1999; Unni 2000a.

among women. Invisibility of enterprises and workers without a designated place of work, and informality of work status within the formal sector enterprises could account for most of this difference by the two concepts.

PLACE OF WORK AND INFORMAL ENTERPRISES

Measurement of the 'place of work' in labour force surveys, informal sector surveys, and population census as a tool for identifying home-workers/outworkers and street vendors emerged as an important issue to tackle at the international level as early as the second meeting of the Expert Group on Informal Sector Statistics (Delhi Group) in 1998. These two categories of workers are not clearly identified in the international definition of the informal sector adopted by the 15th ICLS, 1993. This is either because they overlap the boundaries of the concept of the informal sector ('outworkers') or because they are a subcategory, which the currently and usually collected variables fail to identify separately (the street vendors and street workers). Both categories raise gender issues as women represent a majority of these workers, at least in some regions of the world. Their vulnerability is of special interest for socio-economic security, social protection and child labour.

The concept of the 'place of work' is best applied to the worker in order to identify such invisible groups. However, this concept when applied to the informal enterprises operated by self-employed workers provides interesting insights into the nature of these activities. The distribution of informal enterprises by location (see Table 2.3) showed that in urban areas the majority did not have a separate designated business place to operate from. In rural areas, however, about 50 per cent of the informal enterprises had a designated business place. In urban areas, 67 per cent of the units operated on the streets, in mobile or fixed locations, while in rural areas they were mainly operating from their homes.

In urban areas by industry groups, 60 per cent of the manufacturing activity, excluding homeworkers, and 79 per cent of the services were carried on within the residential premises. Most of the informal sector trading units (60 per cent) and hotels (77 per cent) operated on the streets. The entire transport activity was located on the streets. The type of structure or building from which the

Table 2.3
Informal Enterprises by Gender of Proprietorship
and Place of Work (percentage)

Place of Work	Rural			Urban		
	Male Proprietor	Female Proprietor	Total	Male Proprietor	Female Proprietor	Total
At home	30.8	75.7	34.1	7.6	86.5	23.6
On street	18.8	9.1	17.0	82.1	8.1	67.0
Business place	50.4	39.4	48.9	10.3	5.4	9.3
Total	100.0	100.0	100.0	100.0	100.0	100.0
	(337)	(33)	(370)	(145)	(37)	(182)

Source: Unni and Jacob 1999; Rani and Unni 2000.

Note: Informal enterprises refer to the self-employed units alone. Homeworkers
    are excluded from this distribution of enterprises.

enterprises operate, revealed that only 8 per cent of the enterprises
operate from *pucca* structures. A majority, 22 per cent, work out
of semi-*pucca* buildings while 6 per cent operate from *katcha*
structures. What is striking is the existence of a large proportion,
68 per cent, of enterprises without any structure, 50 per cent being
mobile units. Such enterprises belong mainly to vendors and
others engaged in trade, hotels and transport (Rani and Unni
2000).

GENDER DIMENSION OF
PROPRIETORSHIP AND HOMEWORKERS

The invisibility of the women's work is doublefold. Women propri-
etors operated only 20 and 9 per cent of the informal enterprises in
urban and rural areas respectively (see Table 2.3). And among them,
the majority operated from their homes. The chances of missing the
women workers in any attempt at estimating their number is obviously high.

We found a large proportion of women in our survey in the 'putting
out' system or subcontracting in which women work often in the residential premises, but doing jobs on a contract basis for a parent firm.
They were engaged in making garments, kites, rolling *bidi*s, *agar-
batti*s and manufacturing other products. The household survey

found 24 per cent of the women engaged in such activities. They are categorised as wage workers, 'homeworkers', and not as operating self-employed informal enterprises.

Only a small proportion of the women actually operated an informal enterprise. These women mainly operated enterprises on the residential premises, while the men operated units in a designated business place or on the streets. In the manufacturing sector, while women were involved as outworkers located at home, men operated mainly at a business place. This indicates how the cultural traditional barriers still operate to prevent women from going out of their homes for work or establishing themselves in business places.

This choice of mode of operation may be a manifestation of constraints faced by the women such as the lack of access to markets and resources. The women prefer to operate on a sub-contract basis to bypass the resource and market constraints. The piece-rate job work in the manufacturing sector requires less capital investment, skills and know-how of marketing, accountancy and entrepreneurial skills as compared to petty trade or services.

CONTRIBUTION OF INFORMAL ENTERPRISES AND HOMEWORKERS

A study of the informal economy and informal employment is an attempt to shift the emphasis from a development strategy based mainly on economic growth to one focused on employment as a prime objective. While netting in all workers in the informal economy is important, their contribution to the economy also needs to be emphasised. That is, the correspondence between work and production has to be maintained. In this section we analyse the contribution of informal enterprises and homeworkers. As pointed out in the previous sections, homeworkers or outworkers are not counted as informal enterprises, though a considerable amount of entrepreneurial skills are required to conduct and maintain this activity. We made an attempt to estimate their contribution to value added to the economy. Among wage employment in the informal economy two components are left out of these estimates, the informal employees in formal enterprises and independent wage workers.

Employers operate informal enterprises with the use of hired labour on a regular basis. Own-account enterprises are operated without hired labour and mainly with family labour. These units operate at home, on the street or in a designated business place. The homeworkers also operate at home, engaging in subcontract job work for a shop, contractor or unit. Since a considerable amount of skill and entrepreneurial ability is required to conduct such business they can be considered micro-enterprises of a dependent variety.

In rural Ahmedabad 16 per cent of the informal enterprises were employers, while only 6.5 per cent were so in the urban areas (see Table 2.4). In rural areas 80 per cent were own-account enterprise, with 43 per cent of them having a business premise. The situation was not so good in the informal economy in urban Ahmedabad. About 60 per cent were own-account enterprises, with only 7 per cent operating from a designated business place. As we observed in the case of workers, a large proportion of the informal units were homeworkers in the urban areas, nearly 30 per cent. This form of subcontracting work was less common in the rural areas of Ahmedabad.

The employer in the rural areas contributed nearly half of the gross value added, while in urban areas their contribution was only 11 per cent. The contribution of own account enterprises was

Table 2.4
Distribution of Informal Enterprises/Workers, Gross Value Added (GVA), Average GVA per Unit and per Worker

Type of Enterprise Worker	Rural				Urban			
	Unit/ Worker	GVA	GVA/ Unit (Rs)	GVA/ Worker (Rs)	Unit/ Worker	GVA	GVA/ Unit	GVA/ Worker
Employer	16.7	49.3	1,00,121	21,497	6.5	11.1	62,080	12,694
Own-account enterprise	80.1	49.1	20,679	13,275	63.9	73.4	41,969	31,370
Home-based	22.5	12.0	18,014	11,190	11.5	20.0	63,620	39,848
On the street	14.0	9.1	22,221	15,793	45.5	40.3	32,408	25,766
Street vendor	3.9	3.6	31,698	28,867	16.8	19.3	41,952	28,142
On business premises	43.6	28.0	21,827	13,882	6.9	13.1	68,933	48,118
Homeworker	3.2	1.6	17,114	10,414	29.6	15.5	19,104	13,537
Total	100.0	100.0	100.0	100.0	100.0	100.0	100.0	100.0

Source: Unni and Jacob 1999; Rani and Unni 2000.

Note: The estimate is based on the GIDR–SEWA Survey. It tends to underestimate large units, mainly in manufacturing, trade and private transport.

substantial in the urban areas—73 per cent as seen in Table 2.4. Homeworkers while constituting 30 per cent of the informal enterprises in the urban areas, contributed only about 16 per cent of the value added. This group of workers not generally counted as part of the informal sector, fall between two stools. They are not considered as micro-enterprises, but rather treated as piece-rated workers. Their contribution is not so much in terms generating high value added products, rather they perform a poverty reducing role. However, if they are considered as micro-businesses and provided with the necessary capital and skill training they can undertake higher value added production activities. This would enhance their contribution to the economy as well as to the households. As we had observed earlier most of these workers are women and the restrictions on their mobility and access to resources lead them to engage in homeworking.

Gross value added (GVA) per unit and worker was the highest among the employers in both rural and urban areas, but more so in the rural areas. Own-account enterprises appeared to be doing rather well in the urban areas, particularly enterprises operating from a business premise. The home-based own-account units had slightly lower GVA per unit and worker. Street vendors contributed about 20 per cent of the GVA from informal enterprises in urban areas. While the value added per unit was relatively high, their contribution per worker was slightly lower. A large number of family and even child workers were engaged in these units leading to a lower value added per worker.

A development strategy with emphasis on employment and poverty reduction and not just on economic growth, needs to focus on informal enterprises. Incentives to micro-enterprises should be extended to persons engaged in homeworking. Such persons, with access to resources, credit and skills have all the potential of developing into entrepreneurs engaging in the production of higher value added products.

INCOME AND EMPLOYMENT IN A CITY ECONOMY

An important issue we focus attention on in this chapter, is the contribution of the informal economy and informal employment in a city economy. We bring together the employment and income estimates of the various sectors obtained from different sources and calculate the income and employment generated in the formal and informal sectors of Ahmedabad city. The task of estimating the income and employment of a city is quite difficult, it being an integral part of the much larger economic system. A city, or any spatial unit of a district or state, is small and open. Owing to this, information on many aspects is not available at the city level. Conceptually, the city income consists of the total value of flow of final goods and services that either 'originate' in the city or are 'available' to the city community. Since the city is an open economy, the concepts of 'origin' and 'availability' can differ and in fact they do. The former highlights the production potential of the city whereas, the latter indicates the extent to which the potential is internalised and shared by the city's inhabitants (Kashyap et al. 1984).

For estimating the income for Ahmedabad city we have used both the production and income approaches. The production or value added approach, is used for estimating the income from the manufacturing sector of both the formal and informal segments, and the informal segment of all the industrial sectors. The gross value added is measured by deducting the value of purchased inputs from the gross output. The income approach is used to estimate incomes in the non-manufacturing sectors of the formal segment of the city. In this method all forms of actual and imputed incomes are aggregated, such as income from wage employment and self-employment, profits and rents. The data has been collected from unpublished sources, raw data obtained from official sources, as well as data collected from the GIDR–SEWA informal sector survey. The sources and methodology adopted in the estimation is discussed in Rani and Unni (2000). While our effort has been to be as precise as possible in the collection of data and estimation, certain errors are inevitable. Considering the limitations, the income and employment estimates may be considered as rough estimates and more of an indicator of the situation.

MANUFACTURING SECTOR

Information on income and employment in the manufacturing sector of Ahmedabad city was obtained from three sources. For estimating value added from the organised or formal sector we obtained unpublished data from the Annual Survey of Industries for Ahmedabad city for 1995–96. For the unorganised informal sector we depended on two sources—the National Sample Survey

Organisation's Survey of the Unorganised Manufacturing Sector, 1994–95 and the GIDR–SEWA informal sector survey of Ahmedabad city in 1997–98. These two sources captured two different segments of the informal sector in the manufacturing industry. The National Sample Survey (NSS) Unorganised Sector Survey primarily captured the large and more visible units with fixed and/or mobile premises. The informal sector survey captured mainly home-based workers in the manufacturing sector, who were engaged in processing food, making *bidis*, garments, kites etc. As argued in the previous section such manufacturing activities undertaken by homeworkers are not generally reported to be part of the informal sector.

The manufacturing sector as a whole, organised, unorganised and informal, engaged about 532,000 workers and generated an income of Rs 21,886 million in 1997–98 (Rani and Unni 2000). The organised sector generated nearly 33 per cent of the employment and 57 per cent of the income in the manufacturing sector. The unorganised sector engaged about 19 per cent of the workers and contributed 24 per cent of the income. The bottom tier, the informal segment of the manufacturing sector, absorbed 48 per cent of the workers and generated 19 per cent of the income. The possibility of some double counting in the NSS and informal sector survey cannot be ruled out. However, the differences in productivity and the large number of workers engaged in the bottom tier lead us to believe that this segment of the manufacturing sector is truly invisible to the data collecting agencies (both by definition and during enumeration). There is an urgent need to highlight their role and contribution.

CONTRIBUTION THROUGH EMPLOYMENT AND INCOMES

In 1997–98, the city employed about 1,500,000 persons and generated an income of Rs 60,130 million (Table 2.5). An earlier study estimated the employment in Ahmedabad city in 1976–77 to be 606,000, generating an income of Rs 5,784 million (Kashyap et al. 1984). Employment and income grew exponentially at the rate of 4.4 and 1.1 per cent respectively during these two decades. In 1976–77 the informal economy contributed about 35 per cent of both employment and income in the city.

In 1997–98, the informal economy employed about 1,100,000 persons, i.e., 76.7 per cent[2] of the employment in the city. This sector generated an income of about Rs 28,146 million or 46.8 per cent of

Table 2.5
Formal and Informal Sector Employment,
Income and Productivity in Ahmedabad City, 1997–98

	Employment		Income		Labour Productivity		
	Total	Informal*	Total	Informal*	Formal	Informal	Total
Agriculture	2.3	59.4	0.6	84.8	4,096	15,651	10,958
Manufacturing	35.4	67.4	36.4	43.1	71,658	26,270	41,073
Electricity	0.8	–	2.3	–	110,728	–	110,728
Construction	9.3	100	3.6	100	–	15,424	15,424
Transport	12.7	91.5	11.7	80.5	84,501	32,272	36,693
Storage	0.1	–	0.2	–	100,563	–	100,563
Trade, hotels and restaurants	19.0	90.5	18.9	63.1	155,485	27,733	39,809
Communications, banking and insurance	3.9	–	12.5	–	126,489	–	126,489
Services	16.4	81.5	11.6	48.9	64,454	16,989	24,056
Rentals	–	–	2.2	–	–	–	–
Total	100	76.7	100	46.8	91,344	24,392	39,979
Estimates	1,504,033	–	60,130**	–	–	–	–

Source: Rani and Unni 2000.

Notes: *Share of the informal sector in each industry group.
　　　**In Rs million.

the city income. The contribution of the informal economy to the city in terms of employment and income has grown considerably over the past two decades. Within the informal economy, the manufacturing sector constituted 31.1 per cent of the employment, followed by trade, hotels and restaurants which constituted 22.4 per cent. In terms of income, the bulk of the informal economy's share came from manufacturing, trade, hotels and restaurants. More income was generated in the informal economy in industry groups such as agriculture, transport and trade, while the formal economy did better in the rest.

The formal sector employed 350,000 persons, 23.3 per cent of total employment, and generated an income of about Rs 31,984 million or 53.2 per cent of the total income. Within the formal sector, manufacturing accounted for 49.6 per cent of total employment, followed by the service sector—communications, banking and insurance, with 16.9 per cent and other services at 13.1 per cent.

CONTRIBUTION THROUGH FEES

Since informal employment is created outside the recognised institutional framework, it is assumed that they also do not pay taxes or contribute in any way to the resources of the state. In the informal sector survey we canvassed specific questions on the fees paid by informal enterprises to the authorities to conduct their business. We estimated that about Rs 285 million was collected by the state authorities from the informal enterprises as fees in 1997–98. Of this only 33 per cent was collected legally. The rest, nearly 67 per cent, was collected in the form of bribes. What is interesting is that the state was able to collect Rs 93 million from these enterprises without directly providing any facilities for their activities.

The constraints faced by the informal enterprises in terms of access to resources and markets are also often exacerbated by the prevalence of a hostile policy environment accorded to the informal sector. This is notably in transport, trade and service sector activities which have been subject to a variety of constraints either because they cause traffic congestion, health hazards and illegal use of public spaces or simply because they mar the beauty of the city. These kinds of restrictions, without accompanying positive alternative measures, invariably mean not only a reduction in income opportunities but also induces the enterprises concerned to seek subordinate forms of relationships, say through corruption.

In contrast, the formal sector enterprises not only have free or relatively easy access to resources and markets but also enjoy protection in various forms. But for these restrictive policies, it is argued that the informal sector would have been more efficient. There is also a reluctance in some quarters to take positive measures towards the urban informal sector for fear that it will confer 'legal' recognition on units in unauthorised locations—'illegal' in the eyes of law—and encourage further 'encroachment'. Notwithstanding a general appreciation of the sector's ability to generate employment and incomes for the poor, the fears noted above have often deterred any positive action or even encouraged negative action.

CONCLUSION

In this chapter we have developed a new definition of informal employment within a wider concept of the informal economy. The need to widen the concept of the informal sector to include certain vulnerable groups of workers such as homeworkers, independent wage workers and informal employment within the formal economy, or precarious employment, is brought out. Using a linked household-cum-enterprise survey methodology we arrived at estimates of the employment and incomes generated by the informal economy, disaggregated by the vulnerable groups within them such as home-based workers, homeworkers and street vendors. The contribution of the informal economy in the city economy through employment, value addition and fees paid to the authorities is highlighted.

We estimated that the informal economy generated nearly 76 per cent of the employment and 46 per cent of the income in the city in 1997–98. This effort at documenting the contribution of the informal economy from a micro-perspective is an attempt to draw the attention of policy-makers to the useful role performed by this sector in the society. It is most important to incorporate the needs of the informal economy explicitly in development plans. This would automatically ensure the provision of incentives and distribution of benefits, resulting from development, in favour of the disadvantaged groups. The fact that almost all these enterprises finance their capital requirements through internal sources, suggests that they are capable of generating surpluses and growth. If one takes into account the human capital generated in the informal economy through skill development and apprenticeship training, the case for promoting this sector becomes even stronger. It can be argued further that the elimination of uncertainty and improvement in the policy environment could, by providing an incentive for savings and investment, further enhance the informal economy's ability to generate growth.

NOTES

1. A limitation of the GIDR–SEWA Survey was that it under-enumerated large enterprises mainly in manufacturing, trade and transport industries. The methodology and procedures for the stratification of households used in this study helped in selecting households with female self-employed workers and thus it guaranteed that these groups were not missed out. However, in our design we did not provide for the stratification of enterprises by size. In the enterprise surveys, for example, the NSS Unorganised Sector Surveys, stratification is done on the basis of activity and size of enterprise. This allows for the representation of all types and sizes of enterprises. To some extent the precision of the estimates of the informal sector by activity and type of

enterprise may be affected. However, this is not the limitation of the methodology. A further stratification by activity and type of enterprise will improve the sample design (for details see Unni 2000b).

2. The proportion of workers in the informal economy in Table 2.5 is higher than that obtained in Table 2.2. The estimate in Table 2.2 is based on the informal sector household survey and includes workers who reported working for informal enterprises by the NAS definition of registration of enterprises. The estimate in Table 2.5 is based on the enterprise survey and unpublished secondary data from official sources.

REFERENCES

Chen, M., J. Sebtad and L. O'Connell (1999), 'Counting the Invisible Workforce: The Case of Homebased workers', *World Development*, vol. 27, no. 3.

Fei, J.C.H. and G. Ranis (1964), *Development of the Labour Surplus Economy: Theory and Policy*, Irwin: Illinois.

Hart, K. (1973), 'Informal Income Opportunities and Urban Employment in Ghana', *Journal of Modern African Studies*, March: 61–89.

Holmstrom, M. (1993), 'Flexible Specialisation in India', *Economic and Political Weekly*, vol. 28, no. 35.

Hussmanns, R. (1996), 'ILO's Recommendations on Methodologies Concerning Informal Sector Data Collection', in Bohuslav Herman and Wim Stoffers (eds), *Unveiling the Informal Sector: More than Counting Heads*, Aldershot: Avebury.

ILO (1999), 'Decent Work', Report of the Director General at the International Labour Conference, ILO, Geneva.

Kashyap, S.P., R.S. Tiwari and B.R Veena (1984), *Facets of an Urban Economy: Economic Base Study of Ahmedabad*, SPIESR, Ahmedabad.

Lewis, W.A. (1954), 'Economic Development with Unlimited Supplies of Labour', *The Manchester School*, vol. 22: 139–91.

Lund, Frances and Smita Srinivas (2000), *Learning from Experience: A Gendered Approach to Social Protection for Workers in the Informal Economy*, STEP and WIEGO, ILO, Geneva.

Piore, M.J. and C.F. Sabel (1984), *The Second Industrial Divide: Possibilities for Prosperity*, New York: Basic Books.

Sethuraman, S.V. (1998), *Gender, Informality and Poverty: A Global Review—Gender Bias in Female Informal Employment and Incomes in Developing Countries*, ILO, Geneva.

SNA (1993), *System of National Accounts, 1993*, Commission of European Communities, World Bank, Washington, D.C.

Rani, Uma and Jeemol Unni (2000), 'Urban Informal Sector: Size and Income Generation Processes in India, Part–II', SEWA–GIDR–ISST–NCAER, *Contribution of the Informal Sector to the Economy, Report No. 3,* National Council of Applied Economic Research, New Delhi.

Unni, J. (2000a), 'Urban Informal Sector: Size and Income Generation Processes in India, Part–II', SEWA–GIDR–ISST–NCAER, *Contribution of the Informal Sector to the Economy, Report No. 2,* National Council of Applied Economic Research, New Delhi.

——— (2000b), 'Informal Economy: Definition and Survey Methods', Paper Presented at the *Fourth meeting of the Expert Group on Informal Sector Statistics* (Delhi Group), at ILO Headquarters, Geneva.

Unni, J. and Paul Jacob (1999), 'Informal Sector Activities in Rural Areas: A Methodological Study', Gujarat Institute of Development Research and Self-Employed Women's Association, Ahmedabad, Mimeo.

Unni, J. and Uma Rani (1999), 'Informal Sector: Women in the Emerging Labour Market', *Indian Journal of Labour Economics,* Conference Issue, vol. 42, no. 4.

❸

Income and Employment in Informal Manufacturing: A Case Study

KESHAB DAS

INTRODUCTION

Close to three decades now, the term 'informal sector' has lost much of the ignominy, attributed or otherwise. This sector is recognised as having contributed immensely towards employment and income generation in most economies, especially developing economies, and in containing regional disparities. The growing role and importance of the informal sector has received much attention, especially since the publication of the ILO reports on this sector during the early 1970s (Lubell 1991; Swaminathan 1991).

Till the early 1990s, the dichotomy between the formal and informal sectors was considered to reflect the divide between the modern and traditional sectors, whereby the latter absorbed the excess labour of the former. However, in the era of globalisation, the informal sector has become an integral part of the formal sector, even in developing countries. The most recent definition by the ILO delineates the informal sector in terms of its intrinsic role and characteristics. It states,

The informal sector consists of small-scale, self-employed activities (with or without hired workers), typically at a low level of organization and technology, with the primary objective of generating employment and incomes. The activities are usually conducted without proper recognition from the authorities, and escape the attention of the administrative machinery responsible for enforcing law and regulations (ILO 1999).

Indeed the failure of the informal sector to conform to a regulatory framework has often been a point of criticism.

The informal sector creates a decentralized model of economic organization, which makes formal coordination and planning difficult and problematic. Informal activities distort the factor, resource, and product markets variously; consequently, competition and the official measures of economic performance are also distorted (Briassoulis 1999: 221).

Occasional negative characterisations of this sector as 'clandestine', 'illegal' and 'unregistered' apart, its relevance and potential in generating large-scale employment, including self-employment, have not been questioned (Castells and Portes 1989; Llosa 1990). And the dominant concern of policy-makers, development practitioners and academics has been the need to promote this sector through legitimate means and reorient policy in order to see that the workers do not get marginalised.

THE CONTEXT: TOWARDS A MEANINGFUL SOCIAL STATISTICS

Despite the recognition of the potential of this sector, there is no agreement or clarity over its definition. This absence of a universally acceptable definition, which stems from the complexity and diversity of the informal sector, has been a major limitation of the discourse on this sector. Fortunately in India, ongoing debates about the informal sector have contributed significantly towards building a robust theoretical foundation for analysing informal production regimes. However, the empirical base, as obtained through published official statistics, leaves much to be desired. As the quality of data generated depends on both the methodology of data collection and the content of data-gathering instruments, one needs to look closely into these aspects. The delay in publication of data is another source of anxiety, with even authorities responsible for the task expressing concern over their incomparability, inadequacy and, often, irrelevance. These limitations have resulted in imprecise estimates of this sector's size, in terms of employment as well as contribution to the national income.

In a social statistics framework, the purpose of data collection and subsequent analyses goes beyond the statutory requirement. This has significant policy implications for certain sectors and workers, both at the level of the government as well as non-government organisations. In the Indian context, the extensive surveys conducted at high cost using sophisticated scientific techniques are extraordinary exercises. Unfortunately, their validity and usefulness is limited because the data suffers from various limitations such as lack of comparability over time, inadequate coverage and delayed publication (Paul 1989). More importantly,

> the estimates on the size of the (informal) sector and its correlates vary widely and irreconcilably so much so that they suggest opposite trends and directions. This often has led researchers and planners to come out with policy prescriptions that are equivocal and even contradictory (Kundu 1998: 439).

An equally important dimension is the sensitivity of the statistics to the emerging issues in the sector. If the available database captures the dynamism of a sector, much of its social purpose is served. The need for informed social statistics cannot be overstressed, especially in the case of the informal sector. But the official statistics on unorganised manufacturing (often equated, erroneously, with informal manufacturing) have not only been severely limited in their coverage, but have also continued to gather information on variables that can hardly distinguish between formal and informal units.

The enormity of the task of organising systematic data-collection in order to get the real picture about this sector is recognised. However, an immediate concern is the usability of the collected data in framing policy which is wage or sub-sector specific. It is also important to see whether the data adequately reflect the specificities of the social and economic relationships that characterise the given sector.

APPROACH TO INFORMAL SECTOR: OFFICIAL STATISTICS IN INDIA

Studies on Indian economic development, especially labour, have recognised the significance of the informal sector. Besides a plethora of empirical micro-studies, presenting information on a variety of aspects relating to this sector, the national official statistical apparatus has also been publishing data on a set of variables from time to time. However, formally, neither the National Accounts Statistics (NAS) nor other official statistics use the term 'informal' per se (Kulshreshtha and Singh 1999: 219). The categories 'organised' and 'unorganised' sectors are often, though inexactly, used synonymously with 'formal' and 'informal' sectors. The term 'informal sector' has a wider, global connotation, whereas 'unorganised sector' is largely an Indian usage. There is a distinction between informal and unorganised sectors, though the dividing line is not very sharp. Though the term, unorganised sector, is used extensively, it 'still retains its ambiguous character' (Singh 1990: 11).

The Fifteenth International Conference of Labour Statisticians (ICLS) passed a resolution on the nature and characteristics of the informal sector. The resolution, the implementation of which 'requires considerable experimentation in a variety of settings' (Visaria and Jacob 1996: 157), has found broad acceptability with the System of National Accounts (SNA). The concept of the informal sector as outlined in the resolution is reproduced in Box 3.1.

Even as Indian statistical agencies are being prevailed upon to adopt the recommendations of the SNA (1993), the unorganised sector continues to represent the informal domain. According to the Central Statistical Organisation (CSO), the unorganised sector comprises 'All unincorporated enterprises and household industries—other than organised ones and which are not regulated by any of the Acts, and which do not maintain annual accounts and balance sheets' (CSO 1980: 135). In another sense, from the point of view of employment, the informal sector refers to that part of the economy wherein 'the employed persons did not enjoy the advantages of unionization, social security and/or other associated benefits, or any assurance of regular employment. A large majority of the self-employed and unpaid family workers constitute part of the informal sector' (Visaria and Jacob 1996: 138). In contrast, in the organised sector 'tasks as well as likely returns of each person

Box 3.1: Concept of Informal Sector

5.(1) The informal sector may be broadly characterized as consisting of units engaged in the production of goods or services with the primary objective of generating employment
and incomes to the persons concerned. These units typically operate at a low level of organization, with little or no
division between labour and capital as factors of production and on a small scale. Labour relations—where they
exist—are based mostly on casual employment, kinship or
personal and social relations rather than contractual
arrangements with formal guarantees.

(2) Production units of the informal sector have the characteristic features of household enterprises. The fixed and
other assets used do not belong to the production units as
such but to their owners. The units as such cannot engage
in transactions or enter into contracts with other units, nor
incur liabilities, on their own behalf. The owners have to
raise the necessary finance at their own risk and are personally liable, without limit, for any debts or obligations
incurred in the production process. Expenditure for production is often indistinguishable from household expenditure. Similarly, capital goods such as buildings or vehicles
may be used indistinguishably for business and household
purposes.

(3) Activities performed by production units of the informal
sector are not necessarily performed with the deliberate
intention of evading the payment of taxes or social security
contributions, or infringing labour or other legislations or
administrative provisions. Accordingly, the concept of
informal sector activities should be distinguished from
the concept of activities of the hidden or underground
economy.

Source: SNA (1993: 111)

involved in the productive activity are clearly defined and are
subject to previously agreed contracts ... Moreover, all contracts,
including those with workers, are protected by State machinery'
(Banerjee 1988: 73).

Despite the characterisation of the 'unorganised' sector as a residual category, it does not include activities which are not economically productive. Also, as the CSO definition distinguishes between the organised and unorganised sectors in terms of the way enterprises are structured, implying thereby that the two sectors may have similar products, techniques or markets.

Going by the implications of these definitions, the unorganised sector has a significant presence in the Indian economy. As per the NAS, at least up to 1995–96 this sector accounted for above 90 per cent of total employment and about 60 per cent of net domestic product (NDP) generated in the economy (CSO 1998; Das 2000a: 122).

OFFICIAL SOURCES OF DATA AND NEED FOR A CASE STUDY

The most widely used and comprehensive data source for the Indian manufacturing sector is the Annual Survey of Industries (ASI). While National Industrial Classification (NIC) two-digit level data are published in the *ASI, Summary Results: Factory Sector*, a further disaggregated NIC three-digit state level data are published in the *Supplement to the ASI, State-Industry* volumes. The ASI units registered under the Factories Act, 1948 are categorised as belonging to the organised sector, the reason being that these units comply with the existing rules and regulations of industrial production. Therefore, they need to come under the purview of labour laws including those concerning minimum wages, Employees' State Insurance and Provident Fund. The registered sector comes under the inspection/control of some 30 odd departmental agencies.

As mentioned before, the informal sector is often envisaged as a residual category rather than an independent one. Thus, all those units not registered under the Factories Act, are taken as constituting what might be called the unorganised/informal sector. It is important to consider two general points here. First, as argued by Kundu, the present statistical system has a strong bias in favour of the organised sector, possibly due to its importance in terms of contribution to the national income. He further points out that

The survey organised for gathering information on unorganised activities or informal sector—the two terms being generally used interchangeably in the literature—have often lacked temporal comparability due to non-standardisation of concepts, changes in the format of tabulation, etc. Sometimes, paucity of staff and other resources, made available for this purpose, have also become important hindrances (Kundu 1998: 439–40).

The second point emerges from the first and relates to the existing methods of enquiry. According to Breman, until recently, even the leading professional journals, such as *The Indian Journal of Industrial Relations* and *The Indian Journal of Labour Economics*, demonstrated their one-sided interest in formal sector employment. He attributes this neglect of the unorganised sector

> both to lack of knowledge regarding the lower levels of the urban economy and to lack of affinity with methods of research that could increase that knowledge. The informal sector included a rag-bag of activities for which no statistics were available and to which customary measuring and counting techniques were inapplicable (Breman 1999: 409).

DATABASE AND METHODOLOGY: A NOTE

The National Sample Survey Organisation (NSSO) publishes the primary source of data on the unorganised manufacturing sector in India. This data is classified across three categories of enterprises, namely, Directory Manufacturing Establishments (DMEs), Non-Directory Manufacturing Establishments (NDMEs) and Own-Account Enterprises (OAEs). Establishments employing between six and 10 people as hired labour are categorised DMEs; those hiring up to five workers are called an NDMEs; and those not employing any hired worker are labelled OAEs.

The NSSO follows a two-stage sampling frame. The first stage units (FSUs) are derived from the list of enterprises compiled through the Economic Census, which enumerates all the enterprises, irrespective of premises and legal status, once every decade under a massive nationwide data collection drive. The samples at stratum/sub-stratum level, for both rural and urban areas, are selected with probability proportioned to size (PPS), where size refers to the number of OAEs, NDMEs and DMEs belonging to the three respective sub-stratum levels. The important point to note, however, is that once the FSUs are chosen, on the basis of the Economic Census frame, the NSS does a fresh round of listing of units for its second stage units (SSUs). The 'discarding' of the Economic Census data on unorganised units midway creates confusion and raises the basic issue of their utility. It needs to be recognised that non-sampling errors could occur at the levels of both the Economic Census and NSS SSUs.

The data obtained through the NSS reports of the OAE, NDME and DME sectors could grossly underestimate the unorganised sector since there does not exist a clear-cut method for including/excluding specific sub sectors, i.e., below the NIC two-digit level. We have made an attempt to assess the nature and coverage of official statistics on the unorganised manufacturing sector in Gujarat by using an indirect and somewhat unusual method (see Table 3.1). ASI data at NIC three-digit level have been compiled for three selected reference years, 1978–79, 1984–85 and 1994–95, the years for which NSSO data on the unorganised manufacturing sector are available. For purposes of comparison, NIC three-digit data on organised/registered manufacturing, relating to these three years, have also been collected from the *Supplement to the Annual Survey of Industries*. In column two we have noted those three-digit industry groups which have been covered by the NSSO survey of the unorganised/unregistered manufacturing enterprises (DMEs/NDMEs/OAEs), but do not appear in the ASI database in each given year. The data indicates that none of the units belonging to these industry groups is in the organised sector, or, in other words, are not registered under the Factories Act. Interestingly, the number of industry groups in this 'exclusively' unorganised category has risen from a mere eight in 1978–79 to 22 in 1994–95. Either these additional groups did not exist during the 1978–79 survey, or (and this is a more likely explanation) they were missed out by the survey.

Column three lists those NIC three-digit industry groups which have been reported in the corresponding year's *Supplement to the Annual Survey of Industries*, but not by the NSSO's survey of unorganised enterprises. Clearly, all the units in these industry groups are registered with the Factories Act. In other words, there were no or few unorganised units in these industry sub-sectors for the reference year. Such data can be grossly misleading. For instance, for the years 1978–79 and 1984–85, the list includes such industries as manufacturing or processing of cotton textiles (230, 231, 232 and 236); bleaching, dying and printing of artificial synthetic textile fabrics (248), drugs, cosmetics and washing and cleaning

Table 3.1
Missing Sub-sectors in the Official Database on Unorganised and Organised Manufacturing in Gujarat

Year	Does Not Figure in ASI*	Does Not Figure in NSS (DME–NDME–OAE)**
1978–79	322, 390, 391, 392, 393, 394, 395, 399 **(8)**	202, 203, 206, 207, 208, 210, 213, 215, 216, 217, 225, 228, 229, 230, 231, 232, 236, 239, 240, 241, 248, 249, 260, 266, 267, 269, 270, 280, 281, 283, 285, 288, 290, 293, 299, 300, 301, 302, 304, 305, 307, 310, 311, 312, 313, 314, 315, 316, 319, 321, 323, 324, 326, 327, 328, 329, 330, 332, 333, 334, 335, 339, 341, 345, 349, 351, 354, 355, 356, 357, 358, 359, 360, 361, 362, 363, 364, 366, 367, 369, 370, 372, 374, 375, 376, 379, 380, 381, 382, 387, 400, 410, 420, 741, 973, 979 **(96)**
1984–85	200, 214, 223, 243, 265, 266, 277, 322, 327, 332, 378, 385, 390, 391, 392, 393, 394, 395, 379 **(19)**	202, 203, 206, 207, 208, 210, 212, 213, 216, 217, 228, 240, 245, 248, 249, 260, 267, 275, 280, 284, 287, 304, 305, 307, 310, 311, 313, 315, 316, 319, 323, 330, 335, 336, 357, 358, 361, 366, 367, 370, 375, 376, 381, 382, 386, 387, 400, 410, 420, 741, 972, 973, 979, 990 **(54)**
1994–95	200, 212, 221, 233, 241, 257, 266, 275, 277, 287, 292, 294, 299, 372, 378, 386, 392, 393, 394, 970, 971, 975 **(22)**	203, 206, 213, 214, 218, 220, 222, 235, 242, 301, 314, 315, 319, 363, 365, 376, 385, 400, 410, 420, 741, 749 **(22)**

Notes: * But appears in NSS (DME–NDME–OAE).
** But appears in ASI.
Figures in brackets are total number of sub-sectors in respective blocks.

preparations (304 and 305); plastic products not elsewhere classified (313) and machine tools, parts and accessories (357). As is well known, these include most of the prominent industries in the state which have a significant component of the unorganised sector.

The data collection practices appear to have improved over the years. The table shows a notable decline in the number of units missing from the NSS survey from 96 in 1978–79 to only 22 in 1994–95. The moot point, however, is that once a certain three-digit level industry group is left out in the so-called 'comprehensive' database, information on the number of units, which could actually be large, and related variables will be lost. In the present case, the number of 'missing' units seems substantial since the number of corresponding three-digit industry groups is quite large. The obvious conclusion would be that there are either no units at all in the missing sub-sectors or the number is so small that they are insignificant from the sampling point of view. Nevertheless, the extent of coverage in the Economic Census would continue to be crucial in determining the likelihood of a certain sub-sector being covered in the NSSO frame. This means that there is scope for closer examination of the validity of the enterprise list provided by the Economic Census.

There is also a problem in the method of estimating the contribution of the reported sub-sectors. In Gujarat, the estimates of manufacturing gross value added (GVA) are based on results of the Enterprise Survey of 1984–85 for OAEs, NDMEs and DMEs separately. The gross product obtained for 1984–85, by multiplying the GVA per enterprise with the total number of enterprises, is taken as the benchmark estimate. As regards the estimates of GVA for the benchmark year 1984–85, separately for DMEs and NDMEs plus OAEs, the results of the Enterprise Survey 1984–85 have formed the base. The data on number of enterprises and value added per enterprise as obtained from this survey have been used for evaluating the gross product for the year 1984–85 (Government of Gujarat 1997: 92; Government of Gujarat 1998: 90–91). For the subsequent years, at least up to 1997–98, the estimates at current prices have been obtained by moving forward two-digit industry-wise estimates for the year 1984–85, with the help of certain indicators, as detailed in Table 3.2. It may be noted, however, that the aforesaid method of estimating income from unregistered manufacturing (using GVA per enterprise as the variable) is an important departure from the earlier practices, where income estimates of unregistered manufacturing were prepared by 'taking the product of value added per worker and the working force estimates of the sector' (Government of Gujarat 1989a: 42).

The CSO made major changes in the methodology for estimating SDP in 1988 as part of which the base year was shifted from

Table 3.2
Indicators used for Estimating GVA of Unorganised
Manufacturing for the Benchmark Year 1984–85 in Gujarat

Industry Group	Indicators
Food and food products (20–21)	Value of output of paddy, wheat, sugarcane, oilseeds and pulses.
Beverages and tobacco etc. (22)	Value of output of tobacco, mangoes and citrus fruits.
Textiles (23–26)	Value of output of cotton and silk and wool (obtained from Khadi and Village Industries Commission, Bombay).
Wood furniture etc. (27)	Value of output of industrial wood being used in the construction sector.
Leather and fur products (29)	Value of output of hides and skins.
Remaining industry groups (i.e., 28 and 30–39)	Gross value added of Registered Manufacturing sector.

Source: Government of Gujarat (1998: 91).

1970–71 to 1980–81, 'to take into account the structural changes in the economy as well as the availability of more current data' (Government of Gujarat 1989b: 57). The state adopted this change in order to retain the comparability of the series of estimates of SDP with that of the national gross domestic product (GDP). Consequently, the Directorate of Economics and Statistics (DES) of the Government of Gujarat published two different sets of statistics in 1989, covering the period up to 1987–88 using 1970–71 and 1980–81 as base years. This data set also made use of some newly available information on a few critical variables such as workforce. A note on the details of the methodology and changes has been presented in the Appendix.

For our present purpose, as indicated in Table 3.2, the GVA of the registered manufacturing sector has been used for industry groups 28 and 30–39. The number of enterprises reported in the 1984–85 survey would largely decide the GVA. Further, the recent proposal of using the Index of Industrial Production (IIP) of selected three-digit groups for carrying forward the GVA, would not include the effect of technology change (often remarkable in specific sub-sectors) in the excluded sub-groups. Also the quality of IIP data itself has been challenged in recent times, with the 'deterioration' of the quality of such data since the 1980s being a cause for concern (Nagaraj 1999: 354).

NEED FOR A CASE STUDY

Given the inadequacies and complexities of the official database, we had to choose a sub-sector, the size and contribution of which could be amenable to comparison with the available estimates. Quite apart from the resource constraints in covering the relatively prominent sectors, the central concern was to attempt a realistic estimate of the informal manufacturing sector, through capturing the various layers of functioning of the sector. Despite serious problems of the database, it is well established that the informal units are often part of the less 'prominent' (in terms of size and contribution) industry sub-sectors. An enquiry into informal manufacturing must go beyond the size of the sector. We thought it most pragmatic to choose an industry group that reflected the typical characteristics of the informal sector, and at the same time, be manageable from the resource and logistics point of view. Based on both published and unpublished information/literature and our field experience, we decided to focus on the ceramic ware sub-sector (NIC code 323) in Gujarat.

An important point of departure of the present micro-level study, focusing on an NIC three-digit industry sub-sector (non-structural ceramic ware industry) at a state (Gujarat) level, is that it attempts to link its findings with the NAS. The study has two broad objectives: (i) to arrive at a tentative estimate of the selected manufacturing sub-sector's size, both in terms of employment and contribution, in terms of GVA, to the state income; and (ii) to unravel the various layers of functional dynamics of this sub-sector that would help improve the data collection instruments to be used by the concerned government machinery. Essentially, this study concerns methodological issues and the empirical core of the study is derived from detailed enterprise surveys.

SAMPLE SELECTION AND DESIGN OF THE SURVEY

This section discusses the processes followed in this study to select the sample. Although the ceramic ware industry is spread across

most districts of Gujarat, a majority (81 per cent) of the units are
concentrated in three districts, namely, Surendranagar, Ahmedabad
and Sabarkantha (see Table 3.3). Moreover, these units, both registered and unregistered, were clustered in three regions, namely,
Than, Naroda and Himatnagar respectively of these districts. In
terms of product range, 87 per cent of all the units are engaged in
producing just three broad categories—tableware/kitchenware; sanitaryware, including tiles; and insulators for electrical appliances and
equipments. The ceramic ware industry of Than, Naroda and
Himatnagar accounted for 84 per cent of all the units in the above
three categories in the state. It was in the light of these facts that we
decided to focus on these three locations.

The next step was to gather secondary information on the ceramic ware industry. It was essential to cover both the registered and

Table 3.3
Distribution of the Ceramic Ware Industry (Registered Units)
in Gujarat by District, as on December 1996

District	No.	Percentage	Products
Surendranagar	181	53.5	1, 2, 3, 4, 9
Ahmedabad	61	18.0	1, 2, 3, 9
Sabarkantha	32	9.5	1, 9
Mahesana	19	5.6	1, 2, 3, 9
Rajkot	16	4.7	2, 9
Vadodara	9	2.7	1, 9
Kutch	6	1.8	2, 3, 9
Panchmahals	5	1.5	2, 3
Kheda	4	1.2	1, 3
Surat	2	0.6	3, 4
Bhavnagar	1	0.3	2
Bharuch	1	0.3	9
Valsad	1	0.3	2
Gujarat state	338	100.0	

Source: Office of the Chief Inspector of Factories, Ahmedabad.

Notes: Products:
    1 = Tableware and kitchenware
    2 = Sanitaryware
    3 = Insulators and fittings for electrical appliances
    4 = Laboratory equipment
    9 = Other non-structural ceramic ware, n.e.c.

unregistered units in order to capture the dynamics and the 'informality' of the production in the sub-sector. There are three major sources of industry data in the country—Directorate of Industries (DI) or District Industry Centres (DICs), Small Industry Development Organisation (SIDO) and NSSO. In the case of the ceramic ware industry, the SIDO does provide a list of units, excluding those registered under the Factories Act, but the information is highly inadequate as it contains details of only those units which it has assisted in some form or the other. Also, this data is available for a few recent years. For instance, in Gujarat, the SIDO data is available on a yearly registration basis only from 1992 onwards. The problems of outdated data and the inclusion of units which may have shut down, render such data practically unusable. The DIC database also suffers from various limitations such as the inclusion of non-functioning and fictitious units (NCAER 1993; Morris et al. 1998). Though the sub-sector 323, appears in the NDME list of the NSS (51st Round 1994–95), it reports only one urban sample unit. The total estimated number of units was given as eight. There was no rural sample.

SELECTION OF SAMPLE UNITS

REGISTERED UNITS

At the time of the field survey, the most recent and complete list of addresses of registered units, classified at the four-digit NIC level, was available only with the office of the chief inspector of factories (CIF). Eventually, this formed the universe for selecting the sample for the registered units. A list of units located in the three selected regions was prepared. We decided to take a sample of 15 per cent of the total 274 units thus listed. Following systematic circular sampling with a random start we netted 41 sample units. Finally, with a single schedule being rejected due to incomplete data, a total of 40 units were covered.

UNREGISTERED UNITS

The most formidable problem we faced while finalising a sampling frame for the unregistered units was to decide on the universe. To arrive at a universe for sample selection became essential as no reliable official database, specifically the Economic Census, was available on the sub-sector. Given this situation, we made every

Table 3.4
Distribution of Unregistered Units in the Ceramic Ware Industry

Products	Than	Ahmedabad
Lustre kilns	12	35 (25)
Heater plates	63 (40)	–
Toys and decorative pieces	26	–
Insulators, fuses and carbodems	15	–
P-trap	10	–
Mould	1	–
Cups and saucers	1	–
Other	1	–
All	129 (169)	35 (60)
Confirmed total	164	
Unconfirmed total	229	

Source: Field Survey.

Note: Figures in brackets indicate number of additional units whose detailed
      addresses could not be confirmed during the survey period.

possible effort to build up a list of 'informal' enterprises in the survey locations. This exercise necessarily involved undertaking repeated trips to these areas and developing a rapport with local key persons, such as members of industry associations, labour welfare agencies, traders, bankers and workers. In Himatnagar, we did not come across any unregistered units. However, in Than and Naroda, we could prepare a list of 164 units, which we call the 'confirmed' list as we managed to obtain the complete addresses and other details of these units (see Table 3.4). Additionally, we managed to get partial information on another 65 units (40 heater plate-makers in Than and 25 lustre kilns in Ahmedabad). By adding these units to the 'confirmed' list, we made a second list of unregistered units numbering 229; this we have termed the 'unconfirmed' list. For purposes of the survey, we have taken into account the confirmed list only.

Following detailed deliberations at the First Review Meeting on the project, held at NCAER in May 1998, we decided to draw a 20 per cent sample on this universe. Here again, systematic circular sampling with a random start method was followed. Unlike in the case of registered units, it was either impossible to obtain information from unregistered units or the available information was sketchy, particularly in Than. We could finally manage to collect data from 35 units, more than the required sample size. Information on the number of

Table 3.5
Number of Ceramic Ware Units Surveyed

Type of Units	Naroda	Himatnagar	Than	Total
Registered units	11	18	11	40
Unregistered units	18	–	17	35
Total	29	18	28	75

Source: Field Survey.

units surveyed in different locations and the types of units covered is given in Table 3.5.

CERAMIC WARE INDUSTRY IN GUJARAT: GROWTH AND DYNAMICS

EMERGENCE AND GROWTH

The emergence of a fairly large ceramic ware industry base in Gujarat, especially in the Saurashtra region, has to do with the availability of raw materials and skilled labour. Almost all the required raw materials such as china clay, ball clay, fire clay, quartz, limestone and sandstone are found in abundance in the vicinity of Than. 'The deposits of clay in and around Thangadh are of plastic ball clays and burns white after firing. This clay is suitable as *batch* constituents in the manufacture of all types of white wares, stonewares, refractories, etc' (Government of Gujarat 1977: 340). Local labour is both skilled and inexpensive.

Before Independence, the ceramic, or pottery, industry was largely confined to a few relatively big units dotted around the country, especially, Bengal and Saurashtra. The products included common crockery, stoneware jars and ordinary firebricks. Much of the domestic demand was met through imports from Japan and European countries (ibid.: 340–41).

The history of the modern ceramic ware industry in Gujarat can be traced back to 1914, when a Parsi entrepreneur from Bombay (originally, a grass contractor to the government) started a factory to manufacture roofing tiles and, later, ceramic flooring tiles. In 1934, following a change of ownership, the factory came to be known as the Parshuram Pottery Works. After 1940, there was a drop in the demand for ceramic tiles, and units diversified into cement tiles and ceramic products like stoneware jars, used for storing pickles and acids. By 1972, jar manufacturing had to be stopped in order to expand the sanitaryware division, following a rise in the demand. The industry was largely located in the Saurashtra region (Than, Wankaner and Morbi), North Gujarat (Himatnagar, Mehsana, Vijapur, Kalol and Chhatral) and Ahmedabad (Naroda).

The industry grew at a very slow pace. From a couple of prominent units before Independence, the number of units registered under the Factories Act, 1948 increased to nine in 1965 and to only 12 by the early 1970s. The growth of small-scale pottery units picked up only from the late 1970s.

The rapid growth of the sector came only in the late 1970s and by 1980–81, the number of registered units had shot up to 144 units (see Table 3.6). The industry suffered a temporary setback during the mid-1980s when the crockery market was flooded with durable and cheap plastic and melamine products. By December 1996 however, the number of units registered under the Factories Act had risen to 338. Gujarat is now second only to Uttar Pradesh in terms of the number of ceramic ware units. In 1994–95 it accounted for about two-fifths of the total number of units in the country, one-fourth of fixed capital and employees and one-fifth of net value added.

PROFILE OF THE INDUSTRY

Though there were a large number of unregistered units during the late 1970s and early 1980s, these units mushroomed during the late 1980s and the 1990s. However, it needs to be remembered that several small units in the kitchenware sector had closed down particularly during the mid-1980s. Also, units illegally tapping electricity had to cease operations when they were caught. The number of registered units has also steadily risen over the last two decades. These units are larger in both size and turnover compared to the unregistered ones. Table 3.7 shows that while 91.4 per cent of unregistered units had a turnover less than Rs 500,000 72.5 per cent of the registered units had turnover above Rs 1 million.

Both registered and unregistered units have distinct patterns of ownership. The 40 registered units surveyed were more or less evenly divided between proprietory (16) and partnership (24) units. On the one hand, 31 out of 35 unregistered units were single proprietory concerns. Ownership of registered and unregistered units also has a

Table 3.6
Status of Ceramic Ware Industry in Gujarat, 1980–81 to 1994–95

Variables	1980–81	1984–85	1987–88	1990–91	1994–95
No. of units	144	172	191	186	239
	(33.9) [12.36]	(35.17) [12.77]	(36.04) [14.03]	(36.05) [14.13]	(39.64) [18.53]
Fixed capital	721.87	2,522.91	3371.42	4,394.23	1,1703.32
	(20.8) [14.21]	(22.05) [12.73]	(22.87) [11.47]	(17.90) [7.46]	(25.38) [7.39]
Total employees	5,742	6,352	7,864	7,476	6,631
	(19.42) [12.42]	(21.33) [11.36]	(25.35) [16.05]	(27.55) [14.49]	(26.45) [10.87]
Net value added	382.22	698.82	1,656.22	1,704.13	2,904.68
	(10.27) [9.41]	(13.42) [10.42]	(23.96) [19.53]	(18.44) [9.07]	(16.63) [5.62]

Source: Annual Survey of Industries and Supplement to Annual Survey of Industries, relevant volumes.

Notes: Figures in ( ) are percentages corresponding to All India figures and those in [ ] are percentages corresponding to state level two-digit 32, non-metallic mineral products group. Values in Rs. lakh; others in numbers.

Table 3.7
Turnover in the Ceramic Ware Industry

Turnover	Registered		Unregistered	
	No. of Units	Percentage of Units	No. of Units	Percentage of Units
<5 lakh	4	10.0	32	91.4
5.1 to 10 lakh	7	17.5	3	8.6
10.1 to 30 lakh	25	62.5	–	–
30.1 to 50 lakh	3	7.5	–	–
50.1+	1	2.5	–	–
Total	40	100	35	100

Source: Field Survey.

Table 3.8
Ownership Profile of Ceramic Ware Units by Caste

Caste	Registered Units		Unregistered Units	
	No. of Units	Percentage of Units	No. of Units	Percentage of Units
Patel	20	50.0	1	2.8
Prajapati	7	17.5	10	28.6
Harijan	4	10.0	9	25.7
Brahman	3	7.5	1	2.8
Sindhi	–	–	3	8.6
Koli	–	–	3	8.6
Others*	6	15.0	8	22.9
Total	40	100	35	100

Source: Field Survey.

Note: *'Others' include primarily individual cases from different caste groups.

caste dimension (see Table 3.8). The Patels own 50 per cent of the registered units, with the Prajapatis trailing behind with 17.5 per cent. The Prajapatis, however, dominate the unregistered units, own-ing 28.6 per cent of these units. The Harijans follow close behind with 25.7 per cent.

Traditionally, pottery was predominantly an activity of the Prajapati community. However, the Patels and other better-off communities like Marwaris and Banias invested large sums in this industry. The construction boom of the 1980s, in the state and the country as a whole, gave a major fillip to the ceramic ware industry, especially the sanitaryware and tiles sector. The Patels, particularly, reinvested their agricultural surplus in the industry.

TECHNOLOGICAL CHANGE AND DIVERSIFICATION

The technology used by a unit has a bearing on both the value addition and labour processes. Understanding the technological changes occurring within an industry helps in appreciating the dynamics of the production process.

The ceramic ware industry manufactures a range of products using different technologies and through varying production processes. The registered units have focused on high-value products, such as kitchenware and sanitaryware (see Table 3.9). The unregistered units, for their part, have been confined to low-value work like decoration of cups and saucers, and manufacturing toys and heater plates. Though the registered units have an advantage in terms of better technology, the actual production process is still highly manual in nature.

Till the early 1970s, the technology used in the registered units was fairly commonplace and simple.

Some units started their works with a few machines such as small ball-mills and jigger and jally equipments with a down (draught) furnace. Workers crushed their stony matter into small lumps by

Table 3.9
Product Profile of Surveyed Ceramic Ware Units

Product	Registered Units*	Unregistered Units
Kitchenware (cups, saucers, bowls, etc.)	25	–
Ceramic decoration (lustre kilns)	–	18
Sanitaryware (incl. tiles)	8	–
Artware/toys	5	9
Electric fuses	7	2
Heater plates	–	6
Others (firebricks and cassettes for tiles)	2	–

Source: Field Survey.

Note: *Includes some units manufacturing more than one product group.

breaking the big lumps manually with hammer and then achieving the final grinding in the ball-mills by a period of operations longer (than) that could be ordinarily needed in the grinding of raw materials and shaping on jigger and jallies. Most of the work was done by manual methods (Government of Gujarat 1977: 341).

A select list of machinery frequently used in both registered and unregistered units is provided in Table 3.10. Except for the furnaces, the rest involve substantial manual work. The only noteworthy

Table 3.10
Type of Main Machinery used in Ceramic Ware Units

Machinery	No. of Units	
	Registered	Unregistered
Ball-mill	33	–
Tunnel furnace	27	9
Chakda	19	17
Pad-mill	12	–
Filter press	10	–
Fire shuttle	4	4
Power press	3	6
Compressor	2	8
Down draught furnace	2	5
Surki machine	1	6

Source: Field Survey.

Table 3.11
Main Reasons for Preference for New Furnace Technology

Respondents	Reason
Registered units (30) and unregistered units (12)	1. Unreliable quality and high price of coal procured from Bihar through rail. Coal had to be abandoned.
	2. Coal could be substituted as the main fuel by high speed diesel, which could be procured from the central government at a reasonable price and of an assured quality.
	3. Electricity consumption is much less.
	4. Product quality has also improved substantially as has the pace and volume of production.

Source: Field Survey.

change in technology has been the switch-over to tunnel furnaces in 1957. The reasons for this change are given in Table 3.11. There are practically no functioning traditional kilns, which use coal as the main fuel, in the present day. Even the unregistered units prefer to use the tunnel furnace of the larger units for 'firing' and glazing their products, paying a nominal rent.

EMPLOYMENT AND MANUFACTURING VALUE ADDED: ESTIMATES AND ISSUES

The main argument in favour of the informal sector is its capacity to absorb the growing mass of the unemployed and underemployed whom the formal sector has failed to accommodate. The expansion of the urban informal sector, which comprises a large proportion of migrant labour, has particularly been justified on the grounds that it provides employment and income for a mass of population who have little or no opportunity in the deprived rural areas they hail from. But there is a downside to all this, as the growing literature on casualisation of the workforce shows. In addition to the uncertainty about jobs, labour finds itself systematically excluded from certain minimum social benefits which have legislative sanction, such as employees' state insurance, workmen's compensation, minimum wages, provident fund, gratuity, pension and maternity leave. The typical problems faced by workers in informal enterprises are poor working environment, long hours of work and unprotected handling of hazardous substances. A problem specific to the labour in this sector is the 'invisibility' of their actual work status and contribution; this reaffirms the social exclusion that they are subjected to. The ramifications of this exclusion need close scrutiny.

As noted earlier, the available published data on the unorganised manufacturing sector misses out on many vital aspects of the production organisation, labour process, terms of employment and mode of payment. We have attempted to address these aspects in our case study.

DISTRIBUTION OF EMPLOYEES

Not surprisingly, nearly half the employees in the small unregistered units were family members (see Table 3.12). The contribution of the family members in the informal enterprises is often

Table 3.12
Distribution of Employees in Ceramic Ware Units

	Registered Units		Unregistered Units	
	No. of Employees	Percentage	No. of Employees	Percentage
Male	618	69.7	135	61.9
Female	267	30.1	76	34.9
Child	2	0.2	7	3.2
Family members	73	7.9	110	49.8
Total workers	887	–	218	–
Workers per unit	22.2	–	6.2	–
Supervisors	42	–	3	–
Employees per unit	23.2	–	6.3	–
Total employees	929	–	221	–

Source: Field Survey.

crucial to their very existence and growth. The savings in labour costs often gives them a competitive edge. In the registered units, on the other hand, most of the family members worked in the supervisory capacity.

The average number of workers per unit in the registered units (22.2) is more than three times that of the unregistered units (6.2). The male–female ratio among workers in both categories of units was more or less similar. Although our survey showed the existence of child labour to be negligible (0.2 per cent in registered units and 3.2 per cent in unregistered units), an earlier study on the status of labour in registered ceramic ware units had noted the prevalence of child labour to a significant extent (Parmar 1994). The insignificant number of child workers probably indicates the skill-intensive nature of the labour process. Table 3.13 shows the high skill requirements of the industry; skilled workers account for 85 per cent of the labour in unregistered units and 69 per cent in registered units. The figure is higher in the case of the unregistered units because the labour processes are largely manual in nature.

Although local workers, especially those from the Prajapati community, dominate the labour force, the larger registered units do employ workers from outside Gujarat (see Table 3.14). These workers are mainly from Uttar Pradesh, Bihar, Orissa and West Bengal.

Table 3.13
Distribution of Workers by Skill

	Registered Units		Unregistered Units	
Skill Level of Worker	No. of Workers	Percentage	No. of Workers	Percentage
Skilled worker	519	58.5	90	41.3
Multiple skilled worker	90	10.2	95	43.6
Unskilled worker	278	31.3	33	15.1
Total	887	100.0	218	100.0

Source: Field Survey.

Table 3.14
Local and Migrant Workers

	Registered Units		Unregistered Units	
Origin of Worker	No. of Workers	Percentage	No. of Workers	Percentage
Local worker	683	77.0	214	98.2
Migrant worker	204	23.0	4	1.8
Total	887	100.0	218	100.0

Source: Field Survey.

Since registered units have to conform to certain rules and regulations, it is reasonable to assume that their workers are given basic facilities/benefits, as stipulated in various labour laws. This, in fact, is what distinguishes them from their unorganised sector counterparts, who are deprived of these entitlements. But various studies have highlighted the existence of informal working arrangements in the organised sector, or contract labour. In most cases, it is difficult to get a clear picture of the size of the contract labour force, as such a labour arrangement is recorded only as a cost. Not only does this conceal the number of 'informal' workers in the formal sector, it also hides the wages paid to these workers and, finally, their contribution to the value addition.

REPORTED FUNCTIONAL STATUS OF WORKERS

To look into the functional status of labour in ceramic ware units, workers were classified under three categories—regular, temporary

Table 3.15
Distribution of Reported Status of Workers

| | Registered Units | | Unregistered Units | |
Status	No. of Workers	Percentage	No. of Workers	Percentage
Regular	492	55.5	82	37.6
Temporary	225	25.4	95	43.6
Casual	170	19.1	41	18.8
Total	887	100.0	218	100.0

Source: Field Survey.

and casual (see Table 3.15), as reported by the entrepreneurs. These categorisations are made on the basis of length of service rather than any fixed job arrangement or a formal contract. A regular worker, for example, is someone who has been working in a unit for more than three to four years, even if he does not get benefits stipulated under labour laws. Similarly, a temporary worker is one who gets work for a reasonable period of time, say, for about two to three months at a stretch, or for as much time is required to produce a certain quantity of goods, depending on demand. Such workers may receive occasional favours from the owners, such as consumption loans, a place to stay in the factory premises, some food and beverages, typically, buttermilk during summers. Significantly, the 'temporary' worker category is slightly vague, as the factory owners would not distinguish between the criteria of length of time for which work is undertaken and what benefits are given.

The third category of casual workers do not enjoy even a semblance of job security, no written contracts and no obligation on the part of the employer. Clearly, both the so-called temporary and casual categories essentially indicate informal work arrangements; the nomenclature is an unsound base to distinguish the actual terms of employment. We shall return to this point soon.

Two observations need be made here. First, the registered units did report the fact that about 45 per cent of workers were temporary or casual workers. Second, 37 per cent of the workforce in the unregistered units were regular employees. The fairly high number of non-regular workers in the registered units is important because it raises the issue of the reliability of available official statistics on employment in the organised manufacturing sector. Clearly, we have very little knowledge of the magnitude of such casual workforce in the registered sector. This issue, if pursued in earnest by the national statistical authorities might present a significantly different picture of the industrial workforce in India. Similarly, the 'regular' workers in the unregistered sector can also be a misplaced category. Despite these figures not being usable, it is indicative of the reporting practices in labour employment by small firms.

CLASSIFICATION OF WORKERS BY BENEFITS PROVIDED

Given these ambiguities in categorisation, we have tried another classification through which a better estimate is possible. Workers have been classified as regular or irregular depending upon their access to benefits like provident fund, employees' state insurance, leave and bonus (see Table 3.16). Workers who are not to get these benefits are categorised as irregular. We have avoided using terms like 'temporary' or 'casual' to avoid confusing the criterion of benefits with that of the length of contract. The irregular workers are subdivided into two categories. Type I category workers might receive, as

Table 3.16
Status of Workers by Benefits/Facilities Provided

	Registered Units			Unregistered Units		
	Workers		Units	Workers		Units
Status of Workers	Number	Percentage		Number	Percentage	
Regular	166	18.7	7	–	–	–
Irregular						
Type I	701	79.0	32	144	66.1	19
Type II	20	2.3	1	74	33.9	16
Total	887	100	40	218	100	35

Source: Field Survey.

Notes: Regular: Those who are provided at least the benefits, viz., PF; ESI; Leave.
Irregular I: Those who are provided bonus, personal loans and some arrangement for stay and food, but no benefits as in the 'regular' category.
Irregular II: None of the aforesaid benefits/facilities.

a 'favour' some benefits like bonus, personal loans, space to stay within the factory premises and food. Type II workers, however, do not receive any benefits at all.

An analysis of the distribution of workers along these lines shows that over 80 per cent of the employees in the registered/formal units are irregular workers. This raises some important questions: Does this represent a widely prevalent practice in most industries, or at least the small and medium enterprises? If so, which industries and where? Are there any estimates of this apparently large body of irregular workers in the organised sector? These questions need to be addressed urgently.

Moreover, the number of regular workers in our survey could be an overestimate, as we have assumed that all the workers actually receive the benefits which the units employing them reported as having provided. The discussions regarding actual payments or provision of benefits revealed quite a different picture. Several units maintained registers which showed their family members, who never worked there, as their employees. Payment of benefits were shown as having been made to these persons while the actual workers, whose names were not in the registers, did not get anything.

There were no regular workers in the unregistered units. Of the irregular workers, a high 66 per cent belonged to the Type I category. And since, in many cases, these workers were family members, these benefits given as 'favours' were very limited. The Type II irregular workers, of course, never received any benefits.

The workers in this industry are predominantly from socially deprived communities (see Table 3.17). The factory owners lured skilled labour, preferably from Than, by extending long-term 'interest free' consumption loans up to Rs 20,000. This was a tempting offer

Table 3.17
Caste/Community of Workers

Caste/Community	Percentage
Baxi panch	44
Scheduled castes	28
General	20
Scheduled tribes	7
Muslim	1

Source: Field Survey.

as the cash could be used for major household consumption purposes, like house construction, marriage and even repayment of older loans. Interestingly, often factory owners compete with each other at offering attractive loans, to pull in more skilled workers. The loan could be repaid through regular deductions from the daily/monthly earnings. However, in some cases not only was an interest of 2 per cent per month charged, no worker could leave without settling the loan. As described in an earlier report,

> The practice followed by the employer is as follows: He brings the workers, along with their families, from the scarcity-prone villages of Saurashtra, notably Surendranagar district, after 'freeing' them of the local debt by giving a certain advance. This advance is the beginning of a new vicious circle from which the workers never emerge. They can shift their loyalty only if the incumbent employer is ready to pay the past debt. This keeps the workers perpetually in debt (Shah 1996).

Additionally, the health hazards arising out of the particular nature of labour processes and substances handled, not only reduce their working life but also increase medical expenses (Saiyed et al. 1995; also number of reports in the local press in recent years).

The status of workers, as in the case of the ceramic ware subsector, raises interesting issues. Clearly, the contract labour phenomenon is not limited to the large manufacturing sector; small scale units are also largely dependent on temporary workers. Also, subcontracting of production is not the only reason for the use of temporary workers. In several sub-sectors dominated by small enterprises the entire production process is carried out within the unit itself. The conventional notion that small firms are essentially dependent upon large firms can be quite misleading and can hide the phenomenon of registered small firms employing few or no regular workers even though they do not take or give jobs on contract. The employment registers in formal small units may present a picture which is in complete contrast to reality.

MODE OF PAYMENT AND EARNINGS

One area which has not received any attention in official statistics on employment and in various studies relates to the mode of payment. Information on this is important because it not only helps in arriving at a better estimate of the income of workers, but also serves as a record of the terms of employment. Such information will have significant policy implications, especially in case of the unorganised manufacturing sector.

Two kinds of mode of payment have been identified: time-wages and piece-wages. Time-wages are paid on a daily, weekly or monthly basis, depending upon the value of labour that is spent and the nature of work during a given time period. Given the large numbers of irregular workers and also the kind of work involved, especially, in the kitchenware and sanitaryware units (breaking different mineral blocks into small pieces, mixing mortar, attending to machines and odd jobs like sweeping, etc.) the practice of daily wage payment seems more prevalent in the relatively large registered units than in the unregistered units. Table 3.18, presents prevailing daily wage rates across sex and skill categories in registered and unregistered units. The minimum wage levels in the registered units is invariably below those prescribed under the Minimum Wages Act. Further, the wages paid in the unregistered units are often much lower than in the registered units.

Table 3.18
Daily Wages and Earnings in the Ceramic Ware Industry, Gujarat
(in rupees)

	Male		Female		Child	
	Reg.	Unreg.	Reg.	Unreg.	Reg.	Unreg.
Skilled						
Minimum wage						
per day	59	40	52	50	–	–
per month	1,770	1,200	1,587	1,500	–	–
Maximum wage						
per day	70	60	65	50	60	–
per month	2,100	1,800	1,950	1,500	1,800	–
Unskilled						
Minimum wage						
per day	53	40	50	50	–	20
per month	1,590	1,200	1,500	1,500	–	600
Maximum wage						
per day	62	60	61	50	30	20
per month	1,860	1,800	1,830	1,500	900	600

Source: Field Survey.

A prominent mode of payment of wages is the piece rate system. A detailed discussion on the nature and implications of this system can be found in Marx (1983: 516–23). The following extract sums up the nature of the piece wage system:

> The quality of the labour is here controlled by the work itself, which must be of average perfection if the piece-price is to be paid in full. Piece-wages become, from this point of view, the most fruitful source of reduction of wages and capitalistic cheating ... Since the quality and intensity of the work are here controlled by the form of wage itself, superintendence of labour becomes in great part superfluous (ibid.: 518).

The piece rate system, which reflects the confused status of labour as both 'free' (in being able to choose working hours and the employer) and 'unfree' (in not being able to influence the rate of payment and losing out on the collective bargaining front), is hardly reflected in the available database. Also, the existence of such a mode of payment restricts meaningful analyses of the labour market situation, including issues relating to discrimination based on gender, age and social security (Sparke 1994).

The piece rate system is widely prevalent among unregistered units, with 88 per cent of them opting for it (see Table 3.19). Interestingly, nearly half (47.5 per cent) of the registered units followed this system. The piece wages system may not be practicable where processes/activities are highly integrated. Also, the nature and extent of mechanisation can largely determine if this mode is feasible. In the ceramic ware industry, a number of activities are still

Table 3.19
Prevalence of the Piece Rate System of Wages in the Ceramic Industry

Type of Units	No. of Units	Percentage
Registered	19	47.5
Unregistered	22	88.0*

Source: Field Survey.

Note: *Percentage based on a total of 25, instead of 35, as 10 units did not report hiring any worker.

amenable to payment on a piece basis, given the level of technology in different manufacturing processes.

The rate and mode of payment eventually determine the level of earnings by the workers. Two points need to be made here. First, as the wage paid is based upon the number of items made or number of times a certain activity has been performed, the natural inclination of the worker is to squeeze in more pieces into his/her working time. As there is always a physical limit to how much one can work, the number of extra pieces made might actually decline, over time, following an initial rise. So, the level of average daily earnings over a period of time would remain low, if not decline substantially. Second, the only way the earnings could rise is if there is an increase in the rate per piece. But as mentioned earlier, the very dynamics of the piece wage system is such that, though it allows the freedom to choose the hours of work, it has little or no scope for demanding a hike in the rate per piece. The basic purpose of emphasising the mode of payment aspect goes much beyond making a case for another variable. Such information could be used to address complex labour issues in the informal sector and to influence policy interventions. Moreover, it could obtain a much better estimate of the factor incomes.

Based on the primary survey, an attempt has been made to compile information on prevailing piece rates across product types and the average number of items that can be made by a worker under normal physical conditions (see Table 3.20). That, in general, the average daily earnings are low (as compared to the statutory daily minimum wages of Rs 50 for females and Rs 62 for males) in both registered and unregistered units is fairly obvious. The average daily earnings are relatively higher for certain items manufactured in the registered units, namely, the large-sized electrical insulating equipment and the washbasin and toilet pans.

A number of activities are assigned almost exclusively for female workers, especially in the unregistered units. Women are generally given jobs which are extremely strenuous and demand utmost care and attention such as fixing decorative stickers and drawing lines on the white glazed cups and saucers, packing the fragile cups and saucers with straw in poorly lit and unclean surroundings. What is of concern here is that despite such working conditions, the average daily earnings are far below the stipulated minimum wages. The utility of official statistics would be enhanced by including gender disaggregated information on mode of payment and daily earnings in the unorganised manufacturing sector.

Table 3.20
Average Daily Earnings of Workers: Ceramic Products

Item	Piece Rate (Rs)	No. per Day	Daily Earnings per Capita (Rs)
Toys	Small: 0.25	100–150	25–40
	Big: 1.00	40–50	40–50
Electric equipment (press)	Big:* 2.25	40–50	80–90
Heater	Plate: 0.60	100 doz	55–60
	Finishing (F) 1 doz: 0.25	15 doz	35–40
Cup and saucer	Cups and saucers* 1 piece: 0.05–0.06	1,000	45–60
	Glazing (F) 1 piece: 0.05–0.04	1,000	25–40
	Trolley fillings* 1 piece: 0.01–0.02	2,500–3,500	25–70
	Sticker (F) 1 doz: 1.25	25–40 doz	40–50
	Line draw (F) 1 doz: 2.00	35–40 doz	70–80
	Packing (F)** 1 doz: 0.25	160 doz	40–50
Sanitaryware	Washbasin/toilet pan:* 3.00–4.00	40	120–160
	P-trap: 2.00**	20–25	40–50

Source: Field Survey.

Notes: *Concerns registered units.
**Concerns both registered and unregistered units.
'F' Indicates that the activity almost entirely engages female workers.

ESTIMATES OF SIZE AND CONTRIBUTION

EMPLOYMENT

The actual status of employment in manufacturing units is often unclear and also goes unrecorded. Where records are kept, they do not necessarily reflect the reality. As a result, the data generated on the sector is often unreliable. Through the case study, we have demonstrated the typical problems associated with the reporting practices as also the inadequacies of the data collection instrument. Keeping these limitations in mind, we have estimated the employment size of the ceramic ware industry in Gujarat.

The method followed in estimation is as follows: for both registered and unregistered sectors, the total number of units in the state have been multiplied with the employees per surveyed unit of the respective sector. The CIF list for December 1996 has been used to get the total number of registered enterprises. In the case of the unregistered sector, in the absence of a reliable official figure on the number of units, we have used two sets of estimated totals, based on the 'confirmed' and 'unconfirmed' lists. By assuming the number of units in the unregistered sector in Than, Ahmedabad and Himatnagar as 81 per cent of the number of units in the state, the state totals have been estimated to be 205 as per the confirmed list and 286 as per the unconfirmed list. The calculated figures for employees per surveyed unit in both registered and unregistered sectors have been taken from Table 3.12.

Using this method, the total estimated employee figure for the registered units turns out to be 7,842. Except for the ASI figure of 6,631 (total number of employees in the sub-sector in 1994–95) no other reliable and comparable data were available. In the case of the unregistered units, the total employment was estimated as 1,292 (as per the confirmed list) and 1,802 (as per the unconfirmed list). The NSSO (51st Round, 1994–95) survey of unorganised manufacturing, provides an abysmally small number of only 24 workers in the ceramic ware industry for Gujarat.

MANUFACTURING VALUE ADDED

Based on our survey data, an estimate of the sub-sectoral contribution to GVA has been arrived at (see Table 3.21). The product of value added per surveyed enterprise and the total number of ceramic ware units in the state has been taken as the estimate of the GVA. As regards the total number of units in the registered and unregistered sectors, we have taken the same information used for the calculation of employment size. The GVA of the registered sector, according to this estimate, is about seven to 10 times that of the unregistered sector. We, however, have a specific point concerning the reliability of the GVA per se. In a number of industries, below the two-digit level, significant technological changes from the mid-1980s onwards have led to increased value addition in the specific sub-sector. To the extent that any two-digit industry group does not include one or more constituent three-digit categories for arriving at its GVA, any technological change in the excluded sub-sectors will not be reflected. This may ultimately result in underestimation of the GVA.

Table 3.21
Estimated GVA in the Ceramic Ware Industry in Gujarat

	GVA (Rs)	Percentage
Registered Unit		
As per survey	277,543,437	–
Unregistered Unit		
As per confirmed list (205 units)	19,002,383	6.8
As per unconfirmed list (286 units)	26,510,641	9.6

Source: Field Survey.
Note: Percentages in the last column are to GVA as per surveyed registered units.

The case of the ceramic ware industry illustrates this amply. During the 1990s, there has been substantial advancement in the technology—a shift from coal-based batch production kilns to continuous-process tunnel furnaces using high speed diesel. This technological transformation has been an important reason for the growth of this sub-sector during the last one-and-a-half decades. The effect of substantial technology change, as captured through capital-value added and capital-labour ratios, is quite obvious (see Table 3.22).

Table 3.22
Indicators of Technological Change in Gujarat's Ceramic Ware Industry

Year	Gujarat		India	
	FK/NV	FK/WK (Rs)	FK/NV	FK/WK (Rs)
1980–81	1.89	15,751	0.93	15,097
1984–85	3.61	43,926	2.20	44,329
1987–88	2.04	35,415	2.13	41,208
1990–91	2.58	44,387	2.66	71,399
1994–95	4.03	109,272	2.64	120,223

Source: Annual Survey of Industries and Supplement to Annual Survey of Industries, RBI Bulletin and Chandhok and The Policy Group (1990), relevant volumes.

Notes: FK = Fixed Capital; NV = Net Value Added; WK = Total Workers.

Moreover, there are various interactions between formal and informal units, particularly those concerning the production organisation, which often go unnoticed when compiling the official database. For instance, in this sub-sector, while we found the formal sector contracting out part of its production activities, such as making moulds, to the informal sector in order to take advantage of low costs, there were also cases where the informal units used the firing technology facilities of the formal units. The usefulness of the available estimates of GVA in capturing the interrelationships between formal and informal sectors needs to be seriously considered.

MISSING UNITS AND IMPLICATIONS FOR NAS

The quintessential objective of the national level project, of which the present study forms a part, was to assess the contribution of the informal sector to the national income. As comparable data below the NIC three-digit industry level and also below the state level were not available, we chose a certain sub-sector in Gujarat and, through primary surveys, ascertained values of variables such as the number of units, employment size and the value added. In this section, we examine the issue of validity of official statistics on the number of units in the unorganised/unregistered ceramic ware industry.

We have two sets of estimates for the number of units. The estimate based on the 'confirmed' list suggests the total number of units in Gujarat to be 205 (see Table 3.23), while the other, based on the 'unconfirmed' list, suggests a figure of 286. We have also included in the table the only available data on this industry's unregistered component from the NSSO report of 1994–95. As indicated earlier, this is the only instance, where an entry on this sub-sector appears. The number of units as recorded in the official database—eight—is not only a gross underestimation, but also has no entry of 'rural' units.

A reference to the Enterprise Survey of 1998 (which, conventionally would have been done in 2000, a decade following the same in

Table 3.23
Number of Ceramic Ware Manufacturing Units in
the Unorganised/Unregistered Sector, Gujarat

Source	Location	Number*
Author's field survey (1998)	Rural and Urban	
Confirmed		205
Unconfirmed		286
NSSO 51st Round (1994–95)	Urban	8

Note: *Estimated figures.

1990) is in order here. Coincidentally, the Enterprise Survey for the fourth Economic Census had been undertaken by the DES in Gujarat almost at the same time as when the survey for the present study was conducted. The DES, following communication from the Director General of Economic Census has agreed to share the data on the number of units and other information collected on the ceramic ware industry in Gujarat (cf letter from the Joint Director, DES, Gandhinagar, No. AGM/98/23521, dated 7 June 1999). Though the results of this Census has already been published by now, the required data on the ceramic ware industry are yet to be made available to us; such data would have been an excellent and unique information for comparison.

Irrespective of our getting access to this information, the important point still remains: if the coverage of the unorganised units in the official statistics is grossly inadequate, the magnitude of related variables such as employment, income, etc., essentially become unreliable for use in any analysis. The tendency to dismiss the substantial number of missing units as a mere case of non-sampling error, requires serious reconsideration and in-depth probing.

CONCLUDING OBSERVATIONS

There has been an increasing appreciation at the theoretical level of the nature, role and contribution of the informal sector to national economies. However, there has been no corresponding improvement in the quality of the instruments and method of collection and reporting of official statistics. As a result, there is a serious mismatch between the issues deliberated upon in literature and the data made available by official agencies.

The data gathering and reporting system in India suffers from inadequacies arising mainly out of (1) the omission of production sectors (as 'non-sampling error') which significantly contribute to the national income; and (2) non-recognition of the 'informal' aspects of the production organisation. This case study attempted to highlight the possible implications of these inadequacies for the income and employment estimates in the ceramic ware industry at the state level.

The issue of omission in the unregistered sector has been found to be quite serious with only about 3 per cent of the total number of units getting reflected in the official statistics. Similarly, the official data on employment was less than 2 per cent of our estimate. The case study also found that there is a fairly high degree of informality in the production organisation even within the registered sector. One indication of this is the existence of a large number of temporary/casual and irregular workers in the registered sector. The second indication, which is hardly addressed in official statistics, is the widespread prevalence of the piece wage system in both registered and unregistered units. Further, the study demonstrated that the use of contract labour is not restricted to situations where production is subcontracted. Non-contracting registered small firms also relied largely on irregular workers.

In the light of all this, it is important to recognise that informal labour arrangements are an integral part of the production process in both registered and unregistered sectors, and blur even the otherwise clearly defined official boundaries between these two sectors. This recognition should be central to any effort to eliminate the ills of informalisation. Along with this, the quality and utility of data gathering instruments and the methodology of data collection need to be improved by incorporating issues like mode of payment, formal-informal interrelationships and technological change, and by ensuring a realistic coverage of sectors and sub-sectors.

It has been shown time and again that most of the registered sector units in India build their competitiveness by flouting basic norms and laws. In other words, there is little to ensure security of work and earnings to a large proportion of labour. This situation will continue unless the enterprises are motivated to conform to the legal and regulatory systems. The rules and regulations should be rationalised in a manner that they are followed. Unfortunately, the ongoing debates on industry and economic reforms are directed almost exclusively by the interests and concerns of the entrepreneurs, and are practically silent on the right of workers to safety and security.

APPENDIX 3

NOTE ON METHODOLOGIES FOR ESTIMATING INCOME FOR UNREGISTERED MANUFACTURING SECTOR, WITH 1970–71 AND 1980–81 AS BASE YEARS

STATE DOMESTIC PRODUCT WITH 1970–71 AS THE BASE YEAR

'Estimates of income from this (Unregistered Manufacturing) sector is prepared by taking the product of value added per worker and the working force estimates of the sector.

The estimates of the working force have been prepared for the year 1971 from the information available from the 1971 population census for rural and urban areas. Since 1971 census working force comprise principal workers only, the estimated number of secondary workers are added to the principal workers. From this estimate the employment in the registered sector as thrown up by ASI has been deducted to arrive at the working force for the "Manufacturing: Unregistered Sector". The working force estimate, thus prepared for 1970–71, is then carried forward for subsequent years on the basis of the growth rate observed in workers employed in working factories. The number of workers employed in working factories is available from "The Chief Inspector of Factories" of the State.

The estimates of product per worker for rural and urban areas have been obtained for the year 1974–75 from the results of NSS 29th round given in the NSS draft report 280/1. (Tables with notes on survey of self-employed households in non-agricultural enterprises.) For other years value added per worker has been adjusted with the index of daily wages of rural skilled workers, while that for the urban worker is adjusted with index number of consumer prices for industrial workers.

The net product at constant (1970–71) prices has been prepared by applying the estimated value added per worker in the base year (1970–71) to the working force estimates for subsequent years' (Government of Gujarat 1989a: 42–43).

STATE DOMESTIC PRODUCT NEW SERIES
WITH 1980–81 AS THE BASE YEAR

'At the national level, the CSO has introduced a major change during 1988 in preparing the estimates (of) National Product by shifting the base year from 1970–71 to 1980–81 for the constant price estimates with a view to take into account the structural changes in the economy as well as the availability of more current data. The DES has also now revised the constant price series of SDP by adopting on similar considerations, 1980–81 as the base year in place of 1970–71, the base year hitherto, in order to have the series of estimates of State Domestic Product comparable with the estimates of National Product.

In the new series, apart from the changes of base year, other significant changes either relating to the data base and/or to the methodology of deriving estimates have also been introduced broadly on the lines adopted by the CSO at the national level. The comments and suggestions of the CSO on the estimates were also taken into account. Some of the important methodological improvement incorporated in the new series are ... estimation of Consumption of Fixed Capital (CFC), based on estimates of Fixed Capital Stock and estimated working life of assets ... and estimation of working force. In preparing the new series all efforts have also been made to make use of as much current data as possible replacing the results, rates, ratios, etc., based on old surveys and studies. The important source data used in preparing estimates of new series are as follows:

Working force estimates using data of latest 1981 Census population ... survey results of 33rd (1978–79) and 40th (1984–85) round of NSS (State Sample) in respect of unorganised manufacturing sector ...' (Government of Gujarat 1989b: 57).

REFERENCES AND
SELECT BIBLIOGRAPHY

Banerjee, N. (1985), *Women Workers in the Unorganised Sector*, New Delhi: Sangam.

——— (1988), 'The Unorganised Sector and the Planner', in A.K. Bagchi (ed.), *Economy, Society and Polity: Essays in the Political Economy of Indian Planning, in Honour of Professor Bhabatosh Datta*, Calcutta: Oxford University Press: 73.

Breman, J. (1999), 'The Study of Industrial Labour in Post-colonial India—The Informal Sector: A Concluding Review', *Contributions to Indian Sociology* (New Series), vol. 33, nos 1 and 2: 409.

Briassoulis, H. (1999), 'Sustainable Development and the Informal Sector: An Uneasy Relationship?', *The Journal of Environment and Development*, vol. 8, no. 3: 221.

Castells, M. and A. Portes (1989), 'World Underneath: The Origins, Dynamics and Effects of the Informal Economy', in A. Portes, M. Castells and L. Benton (eds), *The Informal Economy: Studies in Advanced and Less Developed Countries*, Baltimore: Johns Hopkins University Press.

Central Statistical Organisation (1980), *National Accounts Statistics: Sources and Methods*, Department of Statistics, Ministry of Planning, Government of India: 135.

——— (1989), *National Accounts Statistics: Sources and Methods*, Department of Statistics, Ministry of Planning, Government of India.

——— (1998), *National Accounts Statistics 1998*, Department of Statistics, Ministry of Planning, Government of India.

Chandhok, H.L. and The Policy Group (1990), *India Database: The Economy, Volume II*, New Delhi: Living Media India Ltd.

Das, K. (2000a), 'The Informal Sector', in Alternative Survey Group, *Alternative Economic Survey 1998–2000: Two Years of Market Fundamentalism*, Delhi: Rainbow Publishers: 122.

——— (2000b), *Issues in Estimating Income and Employment in Informal Manufacturing: Study of Ceramicware Industry in Gujarat*, Contribution of the Informal Sector to the Economy; Report No. 4. New Delhi: National Council of Applied Economic Research.

Government of Gujarat (1977), *Gujarat State Gazetteers: Surendranagar District*, Ahmedabad: Government Printing, Stationery and Publications: 340–41.

——— (1989a), *State Domestic Product (1970–71 Series), Gujarat State 1987–88*, Directorate of Economics and Statistics, Gandhinagar: 42–43.

Government of Gujarat (1989b), *Socio-Economic Review, Gujarat State 1988–89*, Directorate of Economics and Statistics, Gandhinagar: 57.

—— (1997), *State Domestic Product, Gujarat State 1995–96*, Directorate of Economics and Statistics, Gandhinagar.

—— (1998), *State Domestic Product, Gujarat State 1996–97*, Directorate of Economics and Statistics, Gandhinagar: 91.

International Labour Organisation (1999), 'The Informal Sector', from their website: *http://www.ilo.org*.

Kulshreshtha, A.C. (1998), 'Informal Sector in India: Conceptual and Estimational Issues in the Context of the U.N. System of National Accounts', *The Indian Journal of Labour Economics* (Special Issue on Informal Sector), vol. 41, no. 3.

Kulshreshtha, A.C. and G. Singh (1998), 'Contribution of Unorganised Sector in the Indian Economy', *Manpower Journal* (Special Issue on Impact of Structural Reforms on Employment Scenario), vol. 34, no. 3.

—— (1999), 'Gross Domestic Product and Employment in the Informal Sector of the Indian Economy', *The Indian Journal of Labour Economics*, vol. 42, no. 2: 219.

Kundu, A. (1998), 'Introduction', *The Indian Journal of Labour Economics* (Special Issue on the Informal Sector), vol. 41, no. 3: 439–40.

Lewis, A. (1954), 'Economic Development with Unlimited Supplies of Labour', *The Manchester School*, vol. 22: 139–91.

Llosa, M.V. (1990), 'Foreword' to H. de Soto, *The Other Path: The Invisible Revolution of the Third World* (reprint), Perennial Library: Harper & Row.

Lubell, H. (1991), *The Informal Sector in the 1980's and 1990's*, Paris: OECD Development Centre.

Marx, K. (1983), *Capital, Vol. I*, Moscow: Progress Publishers: 516–23.

Morris, S., R. Basant, K. Das, K. Ramachandran and A. Koshy (1998), *Overcoming Constraints to the Growth and Transformation of Small Firms*, Report submitted to the DC(SSI), Ministry of Industry, Government of India (Mimeo, Unpublished).

Nagaraj, R. (1999), 'How Good Are India's Industrial Statistics?: An Exploratory Note', *Economic and Political Weekly*, vol. 34, no. 6: 354.

National Council of Applied Economic Research (1993), *Structure and Promotion of Small Scale Industries in India: Lessons for Future Development*, New Delhi: NCAER and FNSt (Mimeo, Unpublished).

Parmar, R. (1994), *An Exploratory Study on Educational and Health Status of the Children Engaged in Ceramic Industries in Gujarat*, Ahmedabad: Janpath (Mimeo, Unpublished).

Paul, S. (1989), 'A Note on Social Statistics in India', *Indian Economic Journal*, vol. 36, no. 4.

Saiyed, H.N., N.B. Ghodasara, N.G. Sathwara, G.C. Patel, D.J. Parikh and S.K. Kashyap (1995), 'Dustiness, Silicosis and Tuberculosis in Small Scale Pottery Workers', *Indian Journal of Medical Research*, vol. 102, September.

Shah, Rajiv (1996), 'Potteries Regress into Feudalism', *The Times of India*, Ahmedabad, 14 April.

Singh, M. (1990), *The Political Economy of Unorganised Industry: A Study of the Labour Process*, New Delhi: Sage: 11.

SNA (1993), *System of National Accounts 1993*, Commission of the European Communities, World Bank, Washington, D.C.: 111.

Sparke, Matthew (1994), 'A Prism for Contemporary Capitalism: Temporary Work as Displaced Labor as Value', *Antipode*, vol. 26, no. 4.

Suryanarayanan, S.S. (1998), 'Information Base for the Informal Sector', *The Indian Journal of Labour Economics* (Special Issue on Informal Sector), vol. 41, no. 3.

Swaminathan, M. (1991), 'Understanding the "Informal Sector": A Survey', *Working Paper No. 95*, WIDER, Helsinki.

Visaria, P. and P. Jacob (1996), 'The Informal Sector in India: Estimates of Its Size, Needs and Problems of Data Collection', in B. Herman and W. Stoffers (eds), *Unveiling the Informal Sector: More than Counting Heads*, Aldershot: Avebury: 138, 157.

4

Informal Economy: Gender, Poverty and Households

Anushree Sinha, N. Sangeeta and K.A. Siddiqui

This paper presents some of the findings of a multi-sectoral study of the Indian economy. By constructing a social accounting matrix with a formal-informal breakdown of the production sectors of the economy, it is possible to bring out the high degree of overlap that exists between informal households, gender and poverty.

In this study, the major concern is of understanding the informal economy in terms of a production sector and also in terms of the people involved in it. We then attempt to trace the interrelationship this sector has with other sectors. On the production side, we have used information from the Central Statistical Organisation (CSO) to break up each sector into formal and informal parts. The formal sector or the registered sector as defined by the CSO consists of establishments that employ 10 or more workers and use power, or employ 20 or more workers without using power and are registered in accordance with the Factories Act. These establishments come under the coverage of the Annual Survey of Industries (ASI). The rest of the manufacturing establishments form the unorganised sector. The information about the organised and unorganised sectors from the ASI and the Enterprise Follow-up Surveys were used to break up the 115 sectors of the CSO's input-output table. These sectors are aggregated to 24 sectors on the basis of their usefulness in providing information about the informal part of the sectors. The National Accounts Statistics (NAS) also provided the information about value added generated from manufacturing sectors and net domestic product (NDP) for agriculture and other sectors and further, their break up into registered and unregistered parts. As information regarding household members can be extracted from the raw data collected by the National Sample Survey Organisation (NSSO) and it is possible to see the worker composition in a household, on the basis of such information, we have attempted to get to the households that earn their income primarily, from informal activities.

In this study the registered and the unregistered parts of value added by sectors as obtained from NAS, are distributed to the formal and informal workers respectively, using sector-wise factor owner- ship information from the NSSO survey data. Here we state the assumptions used to relate National Accounts value added, workers and the information retrieved from household survey. From sample survey data we can identify a worker as formal or informal on the basis of whether (s)he is regular or casual. National Accounts Statistics (NAS) provides value added (wages, operating surplus and mixed incomes separately) and NDP generated in the formal sector (registered) and the informal (unregistered) sector. We use estimated earning rates (from NSSO) and value added (from NAS) to break up workers in formal and informal parts of a sector. We assume that the formal sector wages get distributed to both formal and informal labourers in the proportion as obtained by sample survey data according to differential wage rates (average wage rates separately for formal and informal labourers). So we estimate the number of for- mal workers and the number of informal workers that generate the total wage in the formal part of a sector. For the informal part of the sector the informal earning rate is used to estimate the informal labourers. Similarly, using an estimated profit earning rate and capi- tal part of value added, we obtain formal and informal capitalists in the formal and informal parts of the sector.

We impose the formal/informal proportions on the actual number of workers as given by National Accounts. Per worker wage rates can be thus obtained using NAS wages and NAS workers broken up into formal and informal parts (Appendix 4.6). This methodology at pre- sent allows us to break up informal workers and informal households from their formal counterparts, while adhering to the overall national accounting as given by NAS. In the following section we describe how the informal households are conceptualised.

INFORMAL HOUSEHOLDS

The concept of the informal sector covers a number of different issues. The experience in informal sector studies has made it obvious that the informal sector is not easily captured through statistical measurement (Hussmanns 1996). The wide range of activities that can be termed as informal has made this concept a difficult one to be quantified. In this exercise the core concern is to study the informal sector in terms of the people involved in it. The data for such information is better obtained from household surveys. It is not possible to have complete coverage of informal sector workers by undertaking enterprise surveys. Many informal sector businesses are difficult to identify, as they are located in premises that cannot be easily recognised as business centres. Home-based work, such as tailoring and food processing, are usually not identifiable. Further, the casual relationship that an employee might have even in a formal or modern sector cannot be captured from an enterprise survey. In capturing data about the informal sector, it may be recognised that the household would be a composite unit providing such information through member activity. Households can be involved in any kind of economic activity in addition to being units demanding final goods as consumers. In this respect, households will be more varied than any other institution whose activities would be restricted to the purpose for which they are created. Members of households play a major role in production by either operating their own informal enterprises or by supplying labour to other informal or corporate enterprises by providing their services to them (SNA 1993). Household enterprises, of course form an important part of the informal sector or informal enterprises owned by households (SNA 1993). The concern in this study is to identify the social category of people who are outside of a formalised and therefore more secured means of livelihood. This sector then, would comprise not only of people who are involved in unregistered enterprises, but also those who are involved in unregulated activities within the formal sectors. The members of this sector are owners and workers in household enterprises, both paid and unpaid, workers in informal activities like street-side hawkers, cobblers, rickshaw pullers, etc., as well as casual workers in formal sectors. Information on such workers can only be obtained from the household. The household is an important socio-economic decision making unit and has been recognised as such by many social scientists (see for example Wilk 1989; Wheelock 1992). Through a household approach one could examine the ways in which both formal and informal household and family strategies help in adapting to the impact of global changes at work (Wheelock and Oughton 1994).

The critical part of our research is classification of households as formal or informal, which depends on the composite household information, and therefore on the nature of income the household receives. In this classification if the major share of household income comes from activities that are informal then the household can be termed as informal; this will be discussed in some detail below. The identification of households as formal or informal is of importance as we are interested in scrutinising the behavioural difference of such households. It is felt that even in the same income or expenditure categories, the household behaviour is expected to be different as informality is related to future uncertainties. The informal nature of the members of informal households would possibly dictate different savings, and hence consumption propensities, and different access to credit compared to their formal counterparts. Informal households would be generally excluded from the welfare safety net. It is more useful to have income sources for classifying households than income sizes in an analytical Social Accounting Matrix (SAM). Information regarding the households such as location, possession of assets (e.g., agricultural land) and size and its composition are considered relevant in such classifications (SNA 1993).

In the present work therefore, a household is defined as belonging to the informal category, if most of its members are engaged in informal activities. Distinctions about household structure are also made on the basis of the region to which the household belongs. We will explain this in more detail in the following pages. As discussed earlier, the informal activities in which a household member is engaged, might be in both the formal or informal sectors. Such a dimension of the informal sector would be useful in analysing issues in a situation when the casual labour force even within a formal sector might be rising. The informal sector households might be characterised by the sense of uncertainty they have for the future, that might be reflected in their economic decisions. Duchin (1998) argues that household classification schemes should be such that they can serve as a starting point for distinguishing differences in lifestyles. She further adds that the different life styles in a society directly and indirectly effect the production structure of the economy. The household as a unit of analysis also provides opportunities for integrating socio-economic information of such households to the wider economy. The concept of gender also can be fitted into a household classification and such households can be analysed on the basis of their economic performance and member (female/male) balance.

The system of integrating households into Social Accounting Matrices (SAMs) reflects that households as a socio-economic entity, can be linked to the overall economy of a country. The primary economic functions of households as earners of income and as purchasers of final commodities can close the basic national accounting of an economy, by creating a circular flow of national income. However, the household classification system used in SAMs are more varied than classifying households only on the basis of income or any such single variable. The SAMs record the delivery of factor payments made by different sectors of the economy to institutions, such as households or companies and also expands the representation of different types of consumption of the economy. For example, it is possible to distinguish household consumption of domestically produced goods or imported goods or goods produced by the formal sector or informal sector, within a SAM framework.

CONSTRUCTION OF THE INDIAN SAM WITH INFORMAL SECTOR LINKAGES

The transaction matrix of SAM 1993–94 corresponds to the format given in Table 4.1. This transaction table provides the basis for the multiplier analysis undertaken in this study. We describe the various steps taken to construct this SAM in Figure 4.1.[1]

INPUT OUTPUT SECTORAL RECLASSIFICATION

The 115 sectors 1989–90 input-output table (CSO 1997) has been aggregated into 24 sectors. Appendix 4.1 explains the aggregation scheme with respect to the National Industrial Classification (NIC) and the 1989–90 Input Output table classification. The description of the 24 input-output sectors is given in Appendix 4.2. The

Table 4.1
The Social Accounting Matrix with the Informal Sector

	Prod-sectors	Factors of Prodn.	HH-formal	HH-informal	Capital	Government	Rest of world	Total
Prod-sectors	I/O flow		Cons. Expenditure from formal activities	Cons. Expenditure from informal activities	Investment (I/O)	Govt. Cons.	Exports	Gross Output
Factors of Prodn.	Allocation of VA to factors						Factor incomes received from abroad	Total income of factors
HH-formal		Allocation of formal earnings	Transfer	Transfer		Transfers to HHs	Remuneration from abroad	Total formal income
HH-informal		Allocation of informal earnings	Transfer	Transfer		–	–	Total informal income
Capital			Savings of organised	Savings of unorganised		Current account deficit	Foreign capital	Total savings
Government	Indirect taxes		Direct taxes		–	–	–	Total receipts
Rest of World	Imports	Factor payment abroad	–	–	Import of capital goods	–		Foreign exchange receipts
Total	Total costs of output	Total costs of output	Total expenditure of HH-formal	Total expenditure of HH-informal	Aggregate investt	Total govt. expd.	Foreign exchange expd.	

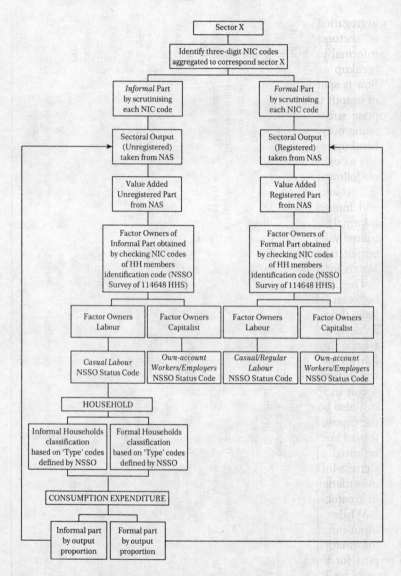

Figure 4.1: Flow Chart of the SAM with Informal Sector Classification

aggregation is done in the light of the formal-informal classification of sectors. To break up the intermediate flow into formal and informal parts, two aspects are to be considered. One is the output breakup and the other the input breakup. The production output flow is split into formal and informal parts by considering the share of output that is produced formally and informally, using the enterprise surveys, ASI and NAS. At present the inputs are broken up using output shares of formal and informal parts of a sector. Such breakups may not be very accurate as enterprise surveys are not usually as exhaustive. Nevertheless, under the present data constraint, we follow this procedure till we come up with any better information.

The sources used to break up the input-output sectors into formal and informal parts are presented in Appendix 4.3. The formal and informal breakup of these 24 sectors are based on registered and unregistered value of output and net value added data. The 1989–90 input-output table forms the basis for constructing the Social Accounting Matrix for 1993–94 with formal/informal breakup (see Table 4.2).

The 1989–90 Indian input-output table does not distinguish between formal and informal activities. It supplies the intermediate flow, the value added and the output information at the aggregate level. To make a distinction between formal and informal activities, we use the NAS and the Enterprise Surveys. The Enterprise Surveys provide us with information on the output of the unregistered sector, which from the production side can be identified with the informal sector in India. The share of output of the informal part to the total can also be obtained from the National Accounts Statistics. So from the input-output table, the gross outputs can be first broken up into formal and informal parts. The intermediate flows for the formal and informal sectors are determined using the formal-informal output shares. Information from the Annual Survey of Industries gives the information regarding output of the registered manufacturing sectors in greater details than available in NAS.

While constructing the 1993–94 SAM from the 1989–90 input-output table, the coefficients are updated using relative price information to arrive at 1993–94 values. The value added and outputs for the sectors are further adjusted into formal and informal parts for 1993–94, using GDP and NDP information available for the year from the National Accounts Statistics. Then the different factor earnings are distributed to the various households according to the ownership of factors of production of the household members to the households by types, i.e., formal or informal (construction of such households are described in the following sections). If most members

Table 4.2
Distribution of Formal-Informal Production by 24 Sectors, 1993–94

		Total Produce	
S. No.	Sector Names	Formal	Informal
1	Agriculture	3.72	96.28
2	Mining and quarrying	90.54	9.46
3	Food products	89.62	10.38
4	Sugar	66.66	33.34
5	Beverages	64.9	35.1
6	Textile	46.76	53.24
7	Wood	17.02	82.98
8	Household electricals	75.83	24.17
9	Other manufacturing	39.78	60.22
10	Watches and clocks	99.5	0.5
11	Leather	54.2	45.8
12	Rubber, plastic etc.	95.54	4.46
13	Basic chemicals	93.97	6.03
14	Non-metallic minerals	66.8	33.2
15	Iron and Steel	89.38	10.62
16	Miscellaneous metal products	36.85	63.15
17	Capital goods	87.74	12.26
18	Transport equipment	60.59	39.41
19	Electricity, gas and water supply	93.58	6.42
20	Construction	49.51	50.49
21	Combined services	35.67	64.33
22	Health and medical services	61.65	38.35
23	Other services	53.37	46.63
24	Public administration and defence	100.00	0.00

Source: National Account Statistics, 1997, Enterprise Surveys and ASI.

in a household own factors of production originating from the informal sector, then such households would predominantly receive the value added generated in such sectors and are informal households. Similarly, formal households would predominantly receive value added generated primarily from the formal sector.

FACTORS OF PRODUCTION

The distribution of workers by each of the 24 broad sectors into different types of factors of production is computed by using the manpower matrix obtained from the employment-unemployment survey of the National Sample Survey (Round 50). Once we map in the sectoral factors of production obtained from NSSO data analysis, we distribute the NAS value added for each sector according to the factor ownership. The National Account Statistics provide sectoral information with respect to a broad division of registered and unregistered part of value added. Labour and capital earnings of the formal sector from NAS is then distributed according to the NSSO share of each type of labour and capital ownership and wage and capital earning rates to get an estimate of the value added distributed to casual labour, regular labour, employers and own-account workers.

We then distinguish four factors of production casual labour, regular labour, employer (formal capitalist) and own-account worker (informal capitalist). The above chart shows that informal worker and own-account worker form a major share of most of the 23 sectors. Public administration and the defence sector is excluded as it is completely formal. There are seven sectors in which formal workers and employers are more than their informal counterparts. The distribution of workers by the 23 sectors is shown in Table 4.3. Within formal sectors, apart from agriculture, sectors like mining, manufacturing of food products, gur and khandsari, beverages, wood, non-metallic minerals and construction sectors are found to have a higher share of informal workers including own-account workers, compared to formal workers. It may be noted that the construction sector has a very large share of informal workers (Figure 4.2). We see that in agriculture the highest factor ownership is that of informal casual workers. Informal capital ownership (own-account worker) is primarily self-employed in this sector. Within formal sectors informal wage earnings (see Table 4.4) are high for sectors such as construction, mining, manufactured food products, gur and khandsari, beverages, wood products and leather. In case of capital, higher informal capital earnings are generated in sectors such as other services including transport, combined services such as trade, real estate etc., textiles, construction, and transport equipment. The sectors that have shown higher informal factors of production are mainly agro-based such as textiles, food products and service sectors. The construction sector hires the highest proportion of casual or informal labour force. Such sectors, which being mainly formal in terms of ownership, relate strongly to the informal sector through informal labour employment.

Table 4.3
Distribution of Factor Owners by 23 Industry Sectors

Sector Names		Wage Earners		Capital Owners		
		F	IF	F	IF	Total
Agriculture	F	21.00	61.95	4.32	12.73	2.23 (100)
	IF	0.00	31.27	8.69	60.04	64.01 (100)
Mining	F	25.90	46.56	9.84	17.70	0.63 (100)
	IF	0.00	8.00	7.44	84.56	0.12 (100)
Mfg. food products	F	41.07	49.13	4.47	5.34	0.87 (100)
	IF	0.00	33.85	2.71	63.44	0.21 (100)
Gur, khandsari	F	29.81	35.67	15.72	18.80	0.02 (100)
	IF	0.00	22.70	4.85	72.45	0.02 (100)
Beverages	F	13.43	33.49	15.19	37.89	0.68 (100)
	IF	0.00	17.10	0.16	82.75	0.68 (100)
Textiles	F	34.23	19.78	29.14	16.84	0.72 (100)
	IF	0.00	21.47	1.48	77.04	1.93 (100)
Wood	F	18.83	32.98	17.51	30.67	0.08 (100)
	IF	0.00	12.72	2.19	85.09	1.19 (100)
Batteries	F	44.90	6.88	41.82	6.41	0.05 (100)
	IF	0.00	14.74	26.17	59.09	0.07 (100)
Other manufacturing	F	29.52	20.76	29.19	20.53	0.53 (100)
	IF	0.00	37.52	6.26	56.22	0.80 (100)
Watches and clocks	F	26.31	2.70	64.37	6.61	0.01 (100)
	IF	0.00	39.71	0.00	60.29	0.00 (100)
Leather	F	31.87	24.78	24.39	18.97	0.08 (100)
	IF	0.00	20.59	0.00	79.41	0.17 (100)
Rubber, plastic	F	48.82	17.78	24.48	8.92	0.16 (100)
	IF	0.00	22.95	23.81	53.24	0.02 (100)
Basic chemicals	F	32.92	15.06	35.70	16.33	0.29 (100)
	IF	0.00	19.19	12.78	68.03	0.05 (100)
Non-metallic minerals	F	20.16	28.08	21.63	30.13	0.41 (100)
	IF	0.00	22.67	3.45	73.88	0.33 (100)
Iron and steel	F	40.85	20.74	25.47	12.93	0.20 (100)
	IF	0.00	36.82	16.94	46.24	0.04 (100)
Misc. metal products	F	39.84	18.56	28.38	13.22	0.09 (100)
	IF	0.00	21.60	10.49	67.91	0.41 (100)
Capital goods	F	40.40	10.53	38.92	10.15	0.30 (100)
	IF	0.00	13.12	4.99	81.89	0.19 (100)

Sector Names		Wage Earners		Capital Owners		
		F	IF	F	IF	Total
Transport equipments	F	52.15	3.53	41.51	2.81	0.07 (100)
	IF	0.00	26.06	4.53	69.41	0.12 (100)
Electricity, gas, etc.	F	54.78	6.78	34.21	4.23	0.32 (100)
	IF	0.00	0.00	2.27	97.73	0.07 (100)
Construction	F	4.89	77.10	1.07	16.93	1.51 (100)
	IF	0.00	79.73	1.14	19.13	1.80 (100)
Combined services	F	73.76	9.17	15.19	1.89	2.65 (100)
	IF	0.00	21.95	1.26	76.79	10.95 (100)
Health and medical services	F	86.68	4.55	8.34	0.44	0.28 (100)
	IF	0.00	92.12	0.81	7.07	0.42 (100)
Other services incl. trans., storage	F	33.01	15.93	34.44	16.62	1.71 (100)
	IF	0.00	49.08	0.90	50.02	2.46 (100)
All sectors		5.11	31.46	8.30	55.13	100.00

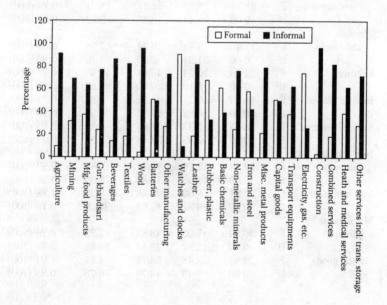

Figure 4.2: Factor Owners by 23 Sectors

Table 4.4
Distribution of Factor Income by 23 Industry Sectors

Sector Names		Wage Income		Capital Income		
		F	IF	F	IF	Total
Agriculture	F	26.62	41.14	16.65	15.60	0.92 (100)
	IF	0.00	16.24	26.22	57.53	33.67 (100)
Mining	F	35.22	25.75	24.84	14.18	1.22 (100)
	IF	0.00	4.86	20.63	74.51	0.21 (100)
Mfg. food products	F	56.66	27.56	11.44	4.34	0.70 (100)
	IF	0.00	24.50	8.96	66.54	0.13 (100)
Gur, khandsari	F	35.26	17.15	34.49	13.10	0.28 (100)
	IF	0.00	15.15	14.76	70.09	0.24 (100)
Beverages	F	17.31	17.55	36.35	28.79	0.30 (100)
	IF	0.00	12.41	0.51	87.07	0.22 (100)
Textiles	F	32.21	7.57	50.89	9.34	1.64 (100)
	IF	0.00	15.35	4.84	79.82	2.34 (100)
Wood	F	22.74	16.19	39.24	21.83	0.05 (100)
	IF	0.00	8.71	6.85	84.44	0.50 (100)
Batteries	F	34.78	2.17	60.13	2.92	0.51 (100)
	IF	0.00	6.71	54.33	38.96	0.52 (100)
Other manufacturing	F	28.32	8.10	51.97	11.61	0.78 (100)
	IF	0.00	25.43	19.35	55.22	0.68 (100)
Watches and clocks	F	17.45	0.73	79.24	2.58	0.14 (100)
	IF	0.00	31.24	0.00	68.76	0.00 (100)
Leather	F	32.39	10.24	46.01	11.36	0.15 (100)
	IF	0.00	15.18	0.00	84.82	0.17 (100)
Rubber, plastic	F	45.74	6.77	42.56	4.92	0.94 (100)
	IF	0.00	10.99	52.05	36.96	0.10 (100)
Basic chemicals	F	28.65	5.33	57.65	8.37	2.15 (100)
	IF	0.00	10.89	33.13	55.98	0.22 (100)
Non-metallic minerals	F	22.53	12.76	44.87	19.85	0.52 (100)
	IF	0.00	15.58	10.84	73.59	0.28 (100)
Iron and steel	F	39.21	8.09	45.38	7.32	1.28 (100)
	IF	0.00	20.32	42.68	37.00	0.19 (100)
Misc. metal products	F	36.94	7.00	48.83	7.23	0.29 (100)
	IF	0.00	12.87	28.52	58.62	0.79 (100)
Capital goods	F	32.87	3.48	58.78	4.87	1.04 (100)
	IF	0.00	8.49	14.74	76.78	0.33 (100)

Sector Names		Wage Income		Capital Income		
		F	IF	F	IF	Total
Transport						
equipments	F	39.42	1.08	58.24	1.25	0.73 (100)
	IF	0.00	17.69	14.03	68.28	0.55 (100)
Electricity, gas	F	44.35	2.23	51.40	2.02	2.07 (100)
	IF	0.00	0.00	6.82	93.18	0.22 (100)
Construction	F	10.15	65.02	4.14	20.69	2.98 (100)
	IF	0.00	70.77	4.62	24.61	3.38 (100)
Combined						
services	F	69.07	3.49	26.39	1.04	8.27 (100)
	IF	0.00	15.80	4.13	80.08	18.09 (100)
Health and						
medical	F	83.14	1.77	14.84	0.25	0.72 (100)
services	IF	0.00	86.84	3.50	9.66	0.45 (100)
Other services						
incl. trans.,						
storage	F	29.16	5.72	56.46	8.65	5.48 (100)
	IF	0.00	39.05	3.26	57.69	3.56 (100)
All sectors		13.77	17.811	23.81	44.62	100.00

As the information from the employment–unemployment (NSSO) survey allows us to map different types of workers in the formal and informal part of a sector, we get the worker composition of different sectors. Then by using wage rates from NSSO (Employment Report) for the different types of workers (Appendix 4.6), we can get the proportion in which each of the factor incomes can be divided by workers (which is divided by gender as well, and then aggregated to get the composite wage earning) in a sector. The wage rates are not at the sectoral level but at the overall level. For example we would only consider one casual wage rate for workers for all sectors. Here we assume that casual labour earnings are the informal labour incomes. Capital earnings are distinguished into formal and informal at present on the basis of information on capital ownership and aggregate earning rates obtained by a simple exercise (where capital earning rate implies operating surplus mixed income—registered and unregistered—by number of employers and own-account workers as given in NAS). Various sources can be scrutinised for getting wage rates for certain sectors. This could be done in the future for getting more accurate information about household income classification.

IDENTIFICATION OF
INFORMAL HOUSEHOLDS

The National Sample Survey Organisation (NSSO) survey assigns to each surveyed household a three-digit industry code based on the National Industrial Classification (NIC)[2] 1987 and a three-digit occupation code based on National Classification of Occupations (NCO) 1968. The survey also assigns a 'Type' code giving information on the characteristics of the surveyed households. This NIC and NCO listed as the principal industry-occupation code of a household and it depends on the industry-occupation of the member who earns the major share of income in that household. And if NIC of the members with the same principal occupation is different then, the maximum income fetching industry is used as the principal household industry. On the other hand, the 'Type' codes are constructed on the basis of composite income of all members accruing to a household. Household 'Type' code, which is identified differently for the rural and urban sectors, is based on the household's net total income from means of livelihood (NSSO Report 1993–94) during the last 365 days.

The NIC and NCO codes are classified as formal-informal separately for the rural and urban regions separately after scrutinising these activities and by using qualitative judgement (Appendices 4.4 and 4.5).

In the Table 4.4a the first column reports NSSO 'Type' codes, the last column reports how we have classified these 'Type' codes to identify the household as formal and informal.

In urban areas the 'Type' code of a household is assumed to determine whether the household can be classified as formal or informal. In rural areas, NIC and NCO codes are also used for classifying a household. Rural formal households are those where NIC, NCO and 'Type' codes are all formal (FFF) or if NIC is informal and the other two codes are formal (IFF). All the remaining rural households are classified as informal. The only exception being in rural agricultural households (households with NIC as agriculture), which are informal households.

The formal and informal households are further broken up into different household categories. These household classes are based on monthly per capita expenditure grouping. The scheme used to form rural and urban household classes is as shown in Table 4.4b.

For identification of the worker population, information about the working status of each household member (aged above five years) is

Table 4.4a
Description of Rural and Urban Household Classification

Rural

Type (NSSO)	Description	Household Classification
1	Self-employed in non-agriculture	
	Hires labour regularly	Formal
	Does not hire labour regularly	Informal
2	Agricultural labour	Informal
3	Other labour	
	Occupation formal	Formal
	Occupation informal	Informal
4	Self-employed in agriculture	Informal
5	If it is none of the above,	
	i.e., for other households	
	NCO formal	Formal
	NCO informal	Informal

Urban

Type (NSSO)	Description	Household Classification
1	Self-employed	
	Hires labour regularly	Formal
	Does not hire labour regularly	Informal
2	Regular wage/salary earner	Formal
3	Casual labour	Informal
4	Others	
	NCO formal	Formal
	NCO informal	Informal

Table 4.4b
Scheme for Rural and Urban Household Classes

Rural Class	Type	MPCE*
Poor agriculturist	Both@	L.E. Rs 350
Middle agriculturist	Both	Between Rs 351 and 650
Rich agriculturist	Both	Above Rs 651
Non-agriculturist	Informal	All groups

Urban Class	Type	MPCE*
Poor	Both@	L.E. Rs 450
Middle	Both	Between Rs 451 and 750
Rich	Both	Above Rs 751

Notes: *MPCE stands for monthly per capita expenditure.
@For both formal and informal households.

Table 4.5
Distribution of Formal-Informal Households
within 24 Sectors by Region (percentage)

S. No.	Sector Names	Rural		Urban	
		Formal	Informal	Formal	Informal
1	Agriculture	0.03	99.97	2.23	97.77
2	Mining and quarrying	28.44	71.46	86.01	13.99
3	Food products	23.76	76.24	49.63	50.37
4	Sugar	15.15	84.85	52.63	47.37
5	Beverages	15.92	84.08	33.63	66.37
6	Textile	21.75	78.25	62.73	37.27
7	Wood	8.18	91.82	27.12	72.88
8	Household electricals	81.25	18.75	89.07	10.93
9	Other manufacturing	29.21	70.79	58.77	41.23
10	Watches and clocks	80.25	19.75	82.35	17.65
11	Leather	12.07	87.93	42.78	57.22
12	Rubber, plastic etc.	56.41	43.59	76.72	23.28
13	Basic chemicals	59.30	40.70	89.15	10.85
14	Non-metallic minerals	9.76	90.24	59.27	40.73
15	Iron and Steel	29.69	70.31	85.71	14.29
16	Miscellaneous metal products	21.01	78.99	62.93	37.07
17	Capital goods	29.38	70.62	81.76	18.24
18	Transport equipment	42.86	57.14	94.35	5.65
19	Electricity, gas and water supply	65.75	34.25	91.41	8.59
20	Construction	11.42	88.58	21.27	78.73
21	Combined services	61.83	38.17	73.02	26.98
22	Health and medical services	60.60	39.40	78.55	21.45
23	Other services	22.59	77.41	44.18	55.82
24	Public administration and defence	83.76	16.24	97.75	2.25
	All India	3.89	96.11	47.00	53.00

taken into consideration in forming a worker group. Members who have stable employment such as drawing a regular salary/wage or hiring labour for one's own household enterprise are classified as formal workers. However, a rural household entrepreneur associated with the agriculture sector is marked as an informal worker. The rest of the working class, consisting of own-account workers and casual wage labourers, form part of the informal work force. It should be noted here that at present no time use information is available.

In this exercise, an issue of major importance is estimating the total number of workers and households that are differentiated in terms of 'informality'. As we have introduced the concept of informal household in this study, we need to make our own estimate of how many households exist in each category that we have defined and how many people live in each of such categories of households. To start the estimation of households the total number of workers as given by the CSO is broken down by each type of household on the basis of proportions obtained from the household survey data (NSSO, 1993–94) (see Table 4.5).

The member per worker information from the survey data normalised to the total all India population provides an estimate of total members belonging to each type of household. How total workers and population are distributed across households is shown in the Figure 4.3. Rural informal households contain the highest number of people, both workers and members. We then make crude estimates of household size by using NSSO's published report (NSSO, Report No. 402) and the analysed survey data. We estimate the total number of households as in Duchin (1998) by using the total number of members in each household category and the household size, as shown in the last column of Table 4.6.

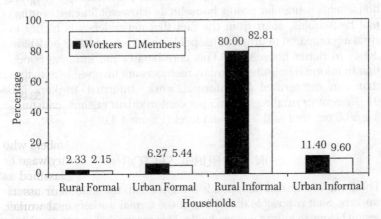

Figure 4.3: Distribution (%) of Member and Worker by Households

Table 4.6
Estimated Households by Categories for 1993–94

		Workers ('000)	Members ('000)	Member per Worker	Member per HH	HH Estimated ('000)
Rural poor	F	5,009	10,763	2.1	5.0	2,153
Rural middle	F	3,364	6,618	2.0	4.0	1,654
Rural rich	F	1,065	1,719	1.6	3.0	573
Urban poor	F	8,526	17,915	2.1	3.5	5,118
Urban middle	F	113,38	21,765	1.9	3.0	7,255
Urban rich	F	5,516	8,633	1.6	2.3	3,754
Rural poor: agri.	IF	21,8221	494,742	2.3	7.2	68,714
Rural middle: agri.	IF	34,116	95,202	2.8	7.0	13,600
Rural rich: agri.	IF	6,603	17,146	2.6	6.5	2,638
Rural non-agri.	IF	64,734	128,268	2.0	5.5	23,321
Urban poor	IF	27,387	48,177	1.8	5.0	9,635
Urban middle	IF	11,031	20,835	1.9	5.0	4,167
Urban rich	IF	7,687	16,217	2.1	3.7	4,383
All India		**404,597**	**888,000**	**2.2**	**6.0**	**146,966**

An interesting point that emerges from the Table 4.6, is that as expected, the dependency ratio (member per worker) in formal households is high for poorer households. However, in case of informal households, apart from the fact that dependency is higher in rural as compared to urban households, there is no decline of dependency in richer households. This corroborates the intuitive notion that in informal households, many members are involved in activities that can be termed as informal work. Informal workers are 91 per cent in rural regions, 65 per cent in urban regions, constituting 86.6 per cent at the all-India level (Figure 4.4).

IN THE RURAL SECTOR

The share of informal households is higher than the share of informal workers. So it is possible that many of the formal workers in the rural region belong to informal households. This means that the major share of household income in villages is from informal activities.

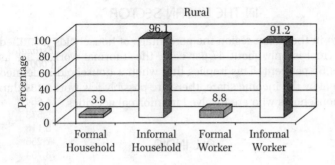

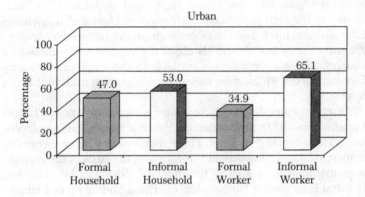

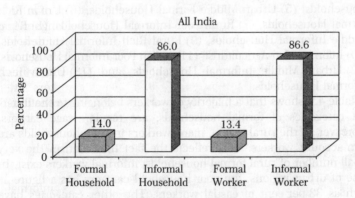

Figure 4.4: Distribution (%) of Households and Workers by Region

IN THE URBAN SECTOR

Though in the urban region the percentage of households identified as informal is only about 47 per cent, the informal workers are as high as 65 per cent. This implies that when a household is defined as formal by the income share, there are possibly few workers within such households who are involved in informal activities.

ALL INDIA

The very high share of informal workers and informal households in the rural region and the overall high rural population has contributed to the high percentage of informal workers and households at the all-India level. The classification from the household expenditure survey does not inform us about the number of workers in a household. This information is available in the employment/unemployment survey which gives information regarding each household member.

As mentioned earlier, we have distinguished four types of factors of production—(i) formal labour, (ii) informal labour, (iii) employers, and (iv) own-account workers. These four types of factor ownership are mapped into 13 household categories on the basis of the employment/unemployment survey information (NSSO, 1993–94), i.e., (1) Rural Poor Formal Households, (2) Rural Middle Formal Households, (3) Rural Rich Formal Households, (4) Urban Poor Formal Households, (5) Urban Middle Formal Households, (6) Urban Rich Formal Households, (7) Rural Poor Informal Households, (8) Rural Middle Informal Households, (9) Rural Rich Informal Households, (10) Informal Non-Agriculturist, (11) Urban Poor Informal Households, (12) Urban Middle Informal Households, and (13) Urban Rich Informal Households.

Table 4.6 shows that a majority of workers belonging to the different categories of formal households, are regular wage earners. Moreover, in the rural region, many workers in such households are own-account workers. This reflects the fact that even in the very small number of rural formal households, informal workers exist. In case of urban regions, the poor household category has a figure as high as 33 per cent of casual workers. The other categories have more prominent formal worker share.

In case of informal households, own-account worker shares are very high in rural agricultural households, which would imply small cultivators without any hired labour. The informal urban rich households have a high share of own-account workers.

The household worker structure together with average wage rates and earning rates for labour and capital separately for formal and informal types, determine the factor income accruing to a household. By using the survey information it is possible to map the four factors of production as mentioned above to the 13 household categories (see Table 4.7).

Table 4.8 shows the composition of different types of households in terms of their factor earnings. The structure shows that formal households earn mainly as regular wage earners. Informal households earn casual wages as well as earnings from own-account work. Factor ownership and factor earnings for households broadly distinguished as formal/informal within rural/urban regions are depicted in Figures 4.4a and 4.4b, respectively. The proportion of informal workers is higher in informal households, compared to formal workers in formal households. However, informal wage earnings are lower in informal households compared to formal earnings in the formal households. It should be noted that the earnings of own-account workers are mixed income, so informal capital income includes informal wage earnings to some extent.

Table 4.7
Worker Structure of Each Type of Household

Factor of Production		Regular Wage Labourer	Casual Wage Labourer	Employer	Own Account Worker	Total
Households type						
Rural poor	F	47.96	17.53	6.52	28.00	5,009 (1.24)
Rural middle	F	51.23	5.21	7.85	35.71	3,364 (0.83)
Rural rich	F	49.68	2.92	14.48	32.92	1,065 (0.26)
Urban poor	F	53.34	33.26	11.07	2.34	8,526 (2.11)
Urban middle	F	53.32	9.22	22.24	15.22	11,338 (2.80)
Urban rich	F	47.89	2.38	35.92	13.81	5,517 (1.36)
Rural poor: agri.	IF	1.97	38.06	5.59	54.38	218,225 (53.94)
Rural middle: agri.	IF	4.69	10.75	5.71	78.85	34,116 (8.43)
Rural rich: agri.	IF	4.92	6.20	8.79	80.08	6,603 (1.63)
Rural non-agri.	IF	5.07	30.00	5.88	59.05	64,736 (16.00)
Urban poor	IF	2.24	39.29	8.87	49.60	27,388 (6.77)
Urban middle	IF	2.96	20.90	22.62	53.52	11,031 (2.73)
Urban rich	IF	0.90	2.37	29.20	67.53	7,487 (1.90)

Table 4.8
Percentage Distribution of Factor Shares within Households

Factor of Production		Regular Wage Income	Casual Wage Income	Formal Capital	Informal Capital	Total
Households type						
Rural poor	F	61.42	7.47	14.06	17.06	100.00
Rural middle	F	61.59	2.08	15.90	20.42	100.00
Rural rich	F	54.77	1.07	26.90	17.26	100.00
Urban poor	F	63.38	13.15	22.16	1.32	100.00
Urban middle	F	52.74	3.03	37.06	7.16	100.00
Urban rich	F	41.37	0.68	52.28	5.68	100.00
Rural poor: agri.	IF	3.94	25.37	18.87	51.82	100.00
Rural middle: agri.	IF	8.47	6.46	17.37	67.71	100.00
Rural rich: agri.	IF	8.22	3.45	24.73	63.60	100.00
Rural non-agri.	IF	9.56	18.81	18.67	52.95	100.00
Urban poor	IF	4.15	24.27	27.76	43.82	100.00
Urban middle	IF	4.03	9.46	51.87	34.64	100.00
Urban rich	IF	1.08	0.95	59.27	38.70	100.00

Scrutinising the different broad categories of households in terms of formal and informal distinctions, depict the relative well-being of such households. Within formal households, 35.46 per cent are poor households (see Table 4.9). In case of informal households, as high as 61.96 per cent are poor households. This reflects the fact that poverty is more extensive in informal households.

We examine the distribution of population within different types of households. At the all-India level, it is observed that the nearly 39 per cent of the population live in poor households and 42 per cent and 27 per cent of the population reside in informal and formal poor households, respectively (see Figure 4.5). The rural–urban analysis reflects the fact that in the urban region nearly 37 per cent of the population are poor which is close to the 40 per cent of the rural population who are poor. Further if the poverty line is defined as household monthly per capita expenditure being Rs 207.93 (Nineth Five Year Plan) then, it is seen that the population belonging to informal households and living below the poverty line in rural, urban and all India are 40.17 per cent, 28.39 per cent and 39.31 per cent respectively. If we consider all households, 32.7 per cent of these lie below the below poverty line

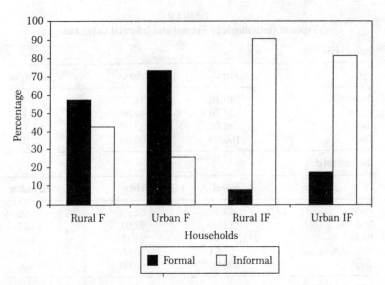

Figure 4.4a: Distribution of Factor Owners by Broad Household Categories

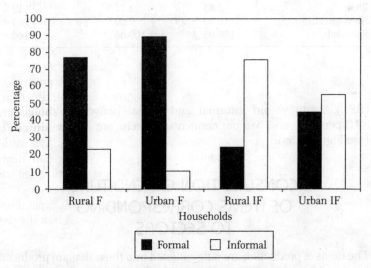

Figure 4.4b: Distribution of Factor Income by Broad Household Categories

Table 4.9
Types of Households by Formal and Informal Categories

Formal HH

	Rural	Urban	All India
Poor	49.16	31.74	35.46
Middle	37.76	44.99	43.44
Rich	13.08	23.28	21.10
Total	100.00	100.00	100.00

Informal HH

	Rural	Urban	All India
Poor	63.46	52.98	61.96
Middle	12.56	22.91	14.05
Rich	2.44	24.10	5.55
Non-agriculture	21.54	0.00	18.44
Total	100.00	100.00	100.00

All households

	Rural	Urban	All India
Poor	62.91	43.00	58.26
Middle	13.54	33.29	18.15
Rich	2.85	23.71	7.72
Non-agriculture	20.70	0.00	15.87
Sub total	100.00	100.00	100.00

(BPL). Again within informal and formal household categories, 39.3 per cent and 9.5 per cent respectively are below the BPL (see Figure 4.5a).

CONSUMPTION EXPENDITURE OF ITEMS CORRESPONDING TO SECTORS

The items of production are differentiated into those that are produced in the 24 input-output sectors with formal/informal distinctions

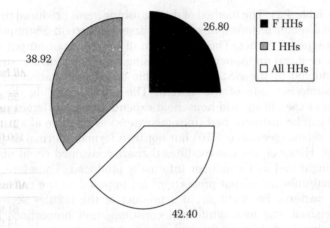

Figure 4.5: Population in Poor Households within Two Household Types (in percentage)

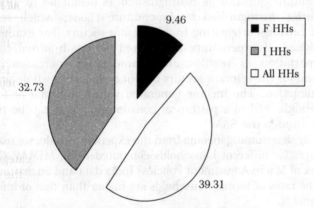

Figure 4.5a: Population in Below Poverty Line Households within Two Household Types (in percentage)

Notes: F HH = Formal Households, I HH = Informal Households. The pie does not add up to 100 per cent.

The numbers (%) reflect percentage of population within the specified household category.

(see Table 4.2). The method of distinguishing items produced by the formal sector or informal sectors is based on certain assumptions as discussed earlier. The description of the 24 input-output sectors is given in Appendix 4.2. Using the Expenditure survey conducted by the NSSO it is possible to get information on the consumption side of the system. The records provide the per capita expenditure and household expenditure on different items that can be distinguished (to some extent) as produce of a particular sector (see Table 4.10) but not with formal/informal distinctions. However, the commodities that are consumed could not be distinguished as formally or informally produced. Therefore, the formal/informal output proportions get imposed on the consumption pattern. For example, if a product of the textiles sector is purchased, the formal/informal consump- tion proportions gets translated as 47 per cent and 53 per cent respectively (output proportion).

To close the system by looping in the expenditure side of the model, the different items of expenditure are distinguished according to the production sectors. The households incurring the expenditure can also be distinguished as belonging to different categories distinguished by expenditure classes which receive factor earnings originating from different sectors. For example as mentioned, if expenditure is incurred on the informal part of transportation or textiles, this immediately increases direct demand for the relevant sectors output and starts a whole process of interaction. The income generated within informal or formal households lead to a pattern of consumption that can be traced again through the SAM.

While determining income from the expenditure side, we use saving rates for different households computed using MIMAP (Micro Impact of Macro Adjustment Policies) India data and an assumption that the rates of formal households are higher than that of informal households.

MULTIPLIER ANALYSIS

The SAM provides a fixed multiplier table. It can study impacts in a static framework. One of the limitations of the matrix multiplier is

Table 4.10
Sectoral Consumption Proportion by Formal and Informal Households

		Formal Households			Informal Households		
S. No.	Sector Names	Rural	Urban	Total	Rural	Urban	Total
1	Agriculture	4.33	1.26	2.37	37.97	25.95	36.37
2	Mining and quarrying	1.99	1.90	1.93	0.29	0.12	0.26
3	Food products	18.35	13.84	15.47	5.96	8.11	6.25
4	Sugar	1.70	4.73	3.63	2.10	1.20	1.98
5	Beverages	2.65	1.49	1.91	1.71	0.96	1.61
6	Textile	15.08	6.59	9.67	12.71	12.90	12.73
7	Wood	0.22	0.12	0.16	0.37	0.77	0.43
8	Household electricals	3.87	2.70	3.12	1.06	1.07	1.06
9	Other manufacturing	0.23	0.91	0.66	1.08	2.46	1.26
10	Watches and clocks	0.55	1.74	1.31	0.07	0.26	0.09
11	Leather	1.68	0.13	0.69	0.66	0.01	0.58
12	Rubber, plastic	4.25	0.64	1.95	0.68	0.02	0.59
13	Basic chemicals	0.33	3.34	2.25	0.76	0.84	0.77
14	Non-metallic mineral products	1.16	0.57	0.79	0.36	1.60	0.53
15	Iron and Steel	0.00	0.00	0.00	0.00	0.00	0.00
16	Miscellaneous metal products	1.55	2.61	2.22	2.20	2.17	2.20
17	Capital goods	0.03	0.00	0.01	0.00	0.01	0.00
18	Transport equipment	3.08	0.83	1.65	0.61	0.09	0.54
19	Electricity, gas and water supply	0.91	13.67	9.04	0.61	0.66	0.61
20	Construction	0.00	0.00	0.00	0.00	0.00	0.00
21	Combined Services	19.74	34.40	29.08	21.52	28.02	22.38
22	Health and medical services	8.91	2.96	5.12	1.52	3.68	1.81
23	Other services	9.40	5.57	6.96	7.79	9.09	7.96
24	Public administration and defence	0.00	0.00	0.00	0.00	0.00	0.00
	Total	100.00	100.00	100.00	100.00	100.00	100.00

that it implies unitary expenditure elasticities. Certain studies had developed more realistic alternatives by computing marginal expenditure propensities, corresponding to the observed income and expenditure elasticities of the different agents, under a fixed price assumption. The SAM multipliers can be used to estimate effects of exogenous changes on the endogenous variables as described. However, such analysis can be made subject to certain conditions, in particular the existence of excess capacity and surplus labour in the economy. As long as these conditions prevail, any exogenous change in demand can be satisfied through a corresponding change in output without having any impact on prices. In case of any injection anywhere in the SAM, for example a change in export demand from the textile industry or a subsidy or transfer accruing to a specific socio-economic household group, the effect will be transmitted through the interdependent SAM system. The total, direct and indirect effects of an exogenous shock to the endogenous accounts, i.e., the total outputs of various sectors of production, the total factor incomes and the total incomes of the various socio-economic household categories, can be estimated through the multiplier process.

In the present study the multiplier analysis is at an experimental stage. Unless case studies or more data on consumption differentiated by formal/informal types as well as savings data are made available by different type of households, the computation of income is difficult and so multiplier analysis would not be very accurate. Nevertheless, with the available data and various assumptions as mentioned earlier, we have formed a consistent SAM to undertake the simulation exercises.

The direct and indirect effects of any change in the exogenous variables of the SAM are reflected in the multipliers.[3] The impact of any change in the output of any of the 46 sectors on the factor incomes can be examined using multiplier analysis. **Findings of the multiplier analysis show that, when the relative value added generation is compared between formal and informal production, in most cases informal production generates higher value added.** On examining the composition of the value added, the informal value added generated seems to be higher when informal output is produced as compared to formal value added generation when the formal part of the output is produced.

As informal activities are more labour intensive it is easy to understand the higher labour income generation. Earnings generated by own-account work is higher in informal production processes. The very high labour intensity of informal sectors compared to their formal counterparts leads to the higher growth in the informal part of the value added and consequently has important implications for income distribution. Further, the higher direct and indirect output effects of the informal part of a sector, compared to the formal one within the same broad sectoral classification, is that there is the possibility of the existence of more excess capacity in the former compared to the latter (Khan and Thorbecke 1988). It should be emphasised again, that these results are subject to the limitations of this demand-oriented exercise and in particular the assumption of excess capacity and no supply constraints as mentioned earlier. The existence of supply constraints could alter some of the findings of the present study. As we are interested in the effects of major policy changes on the informal output and more particularly on informal households, we design simulations to study such impacts within the limitations of such an analysis.

SIMULATION ANALYSIS

Simulation exercises to examine the impact of policy options on household income are carried out using fixed price multiplier analysis. To examine the impact of higher exports on income distribution we have experimented with two labour intensive sectors, i.e., textiles and leather. The exports are increased alternatively for the formal and informal parts of the sectors. To study the implications of higher exports in the two sectors as mentioned, we have designed four simulation exercises. These simulations are:

Simulation 1. Exports of Textiles (formal) rise by 20 per cent.
Simulation 2. Exports of Textiles (informal) rise by 20 per cent.
Simulation 3. Exports of Leather (formal) rise by 64 per cent (equivalent to the level change in Simulation 1).
Simulation 4. Exports of Leather (informal) rise by 69 per cent (equivalent to the level change in Simulation 2).

In case of Simulation 1, when formally produced textile demand rises to fulfil 20 per cent rise in exports demand, the factor earnings of regular labour rises more than that of casual labour. The increase in formal capital earning is also higher than the informal capital earning. The highest rise in income is that of households belonging to the urban informal middle class category. Income rise is next highest for informal households belonging to rural poor agriculturists, non-agriculturists and poor urban categories. In case of Simulation 2, i.e., rise in exports of the informal textiles sector, both regular and casual labour income rise almost equally. However, in the case of capital earnings, the informal capital earnings seem to rise at a sharper rate than formal capital earnings. The urban informal poor and rural informal poor and rural informal non-agriculturists, are the household categories that have the highest rise in income due to the export rise in this sector. In general however, the rise in income is lower than in Simulation 1.

In Simulation 3, the exports of the formal leather sector are raised by 64 per cent. The higher increases are that of regular wages and formal capital. In comparison to the textiles sector, it may be noted that the impact of the leather sector on income generation is lower. The findings reflect the fact that households belonging to the urban informal middle class experience the highest rise in income.

In case exports of the informal leather sector (Simulation 4) rise by 69 per cent, the factor earnings of casual workers rise more compared to regular workers and the rise in capital earnings is more for own-account workers than their formal counterparts. In case of household incomes, this simulation shows that in general, as in the case of Textiles, the gain in income is lower in this case than that generated due to an increase in exports in the formal leather sector. The highest gain through this simulation accrues to the rural informal poor and non-agriculturist households.

The impact analysis using the multiplier matrix, shows that regular labour and informal capital have higher growth rates. The urban poor experience the highest income growth within formal households. In the case of informal households, the rural informal poor and non-agriculturist households have the highest growth rates, which are marginally higher than urban informal poor and middle income households. The analysis shows that in case there is an increase in demand of the informal part of a sector, this generates marginally higher income for the 'poor' category within the informal households, indicating that they are the ones who are larger in actual numbers and who are more interlinked with such production

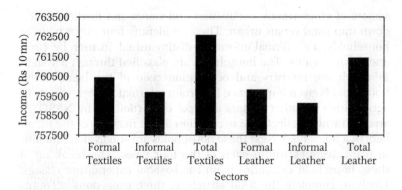

Figure 4.6: Impact on Total Household Income: Effect of Rise in Exports in Textiles and Leather Sectors

processes. A change in demand in the textiles sector has a higher impact than that of the leather sector on overall household income (see Figure 4.6).

CONCLUDING REMARKS

This study attempts to build up a macroeconomic framework incorporating the informal sector. The informal sector is primarily distinguished in terms of factors of production and households. Though we have also distinguished production into informal and formal parts, this does not take into account the distinctive production structure of the sectors. It should be noted, therefore, that the strength of this study lies in the classification of factors of production and households through the use of all India data and linking the workers and households to the overall macro set-up. Such an exercise enables impact analysis of macro policies on the factors and households, as distinguished in this study.

In building the SAM in this exercise, the production sectors are initially distinguished as formal and informal by using published data from the CSO. Factors of production are then broken down first into labour type (formal and informal) and capital type (formal and informal). At the next level labour is broken down according to

sectors of employment, occupation and status and further broken
down into rural versus urban. Then we identify four major types of
households, i.e., formal/informal—distinguished further by rural
and urban regions. The households are classified through a system
in which the industry and occupation code of the head of the
household is given importance in certain informal sectors, mainly in
agriculture. For other sectors a 'Type' code (defined by NSSO) is
analysed which reflects the occupation of the majority of the members in a household. Next these households are subdivided into four
to five categories within each of the four types. The break up of
these household categories is on the basis of expenditure classes.
Lastly to complete the SAM structure, three exogenous accounts
are defined, i.e., the government, the capital account and the rest of
the world.

The findings show that a large section of the Indian population is
involved in informal operations. There are certain sectors, which
have more of informal activities than others. Apart from the usual
agriculture and livestock related activities we find that activities in
textile production, wood and wood products, other manufacturing,
manufacture of miscellaneous metal products, construction and
combined services also have substantial informal share in production.
Informal worker shares in sectors like agriculture, construction,
mining, manufactured food products, gur and khandsari, beverages,
wood products and leather are higher than formal workers. Further,
the study shows that there are more poorer households within the
informal category.

An interesting finding that needs some further scrutiny is that the
informal households are more uniform in having higher a informal
worker share compared to formal workers in the formal households.
This is mainly true in case of rural formal households, which has a
substantial share of own-account workers.

The consumption behaviour of formal and informal sectors show
that on average informal households spend more on indigenously
produced items and vice versa. Of the total consumption of rural formal households, 56 per cent is spent on items produced by sectors
with a higher formal share in production and alternatively rural
informal households spend about 62 per cent of their total consumption on items produced by sectors with a higher informal share
in production. Similarly, in the urban region, formal households
spend a higher share of 69 per cent on items produced by sectors
with a higher formal share in production and informal households

spend slightly more than 50 per cent on items produced by sectors with a higher informal share in production.

We have used the findings as shown in this study and have built the SAM with a formal/informal distinction. The SAM analysis here consists of interpreting the coefficients and the multipliers. An extension of the study, are the simulation exercises carried out through hypothetical changes in exogenous variables resulting in different levels of factor and household level earnings. In the case of two types of production activities, i.e., formal and informal, the SAM multipliers can provide a comparison of the differential impact if exogenous demand for a particular type of product increases. For example, such an analysis would be able to trace which household would suffer in terms of lower value added distribution, if the government reduced certain types of expenditures. If the government increases investment in construction, households that earn as labourers from construction would have more income/ employment. The increased income going to the informal labourers can be estimated. At the same time, the impact on overall output and income and savings can also be quantified through the multiplier analysis of the SAM. If the government provides loans to cottage and small enterprises (within some broad sectors) their investment would increase which would again generate a whole series of interactions and the sectoral and overall impact can be measured. The simulation results from the multiplier analysis, confirm that expansion in informal sector production generates more income for the informal poor households as compared to an increase in formal sector production. The limitation of multiplier analysis is stated above.

The major strength of the study is to build up a database and identify the data limitations so that, in future, steps might be taken to improve such data sets. To provide a complete framework, in which the influence of policy changes or any exogenous change can be traced through different sectors and different socio-economic classes, it would be meaningful to use a general equilibrium model with endogenous determination of prices, in which we explicitly track informal transactions and 'agents'. Informality can be thought of along at least three axes. First, we can think of different technologies producing different 'versions' of similar goods. For example, we can imagine 'formal' and 'informal' goods or services competing in the same market (e.g., building services etc.). We can think of this as 'goods market informality'. Second, we can assume that each sector produces a single homogeneous good and that firms can substitute between formal and informal factors of production (formal and informal labour). Finally we can think of formal and informal households which are distinguished in terms of the sources of their income and their consumption pattern.

APPENDIX 4

APPENDIX 4.1

AGGREGATION SCHEME
FOR 24 INDUSTRY SECTORS

S. No.	Sector Names	NIC	IO89–90
1	Agriculture	000–069	000–022
2	Mining and quarrying	100–199	023–032, 058, 059
3	Food products	200–219 ([–]207)	035, 036, 038
4	Sugar	207	033–034
5	Beverages	220–229	037, 039, 040
6	Textile	230–269	041–049
7	Wood	270–279	050–051
8	Household electricals	363–369	086–088, 090
9	Other manufacturing	280–289, 380–389 ([–]382)	052, 053, 083, 098
10	Watches and clocks	382	097
11	Leather	290–299	054–055
12	Rubber, plastic etc.	310–319	056–057
13	Basic chemicals	300–309	060–068
14	Non-metallic minerals	320–329	069–071
15	Iron and Steel	330–339	072–075
16	Miscellaneous metal products	340–349	076–077
17	Capital goods	350–362, 390-399	078–082, 084, 085, 089
18	Transport equipment	370–379	091–096
19	Electricity, gas and water supply	400–439	100–102
20	Construction	500–519	099
21	Combined services	600–691, 750–759, 800–854, 920–922	106–112
22	Health and medical services	930–931	113
23	Other services	700–749, 830, 890–899, 940–990	103–105, 114
24	Public administration and defence	900–910	115

APPENDIX 4.2

DESCRIPTION OF THE 24 SECTORS

S. No.	Sector Names	Description
1	Agriculture	Agricultural crops, raising of livestock, forestry and logging and fishing.
2	Mining and quarrying	Mining and quarrying.
3	Food products	Manufacture of food products.
4	Sugar	Production of indigenous sugar, gur, etc.
5	Beverages	Manufacture of beverages, tobacco and related products.
6	Textiles	Manufacture of textile products.
7	Wood	Manufacture of wood and wood products; furniture and fixtures.
8	Household electricals	Manufacture of batteries, household electricals, etc.
9	Other manufacturing	Manufacture of machinemade and handmade pulp, paper and paper board including newsprint, containers and boxes of paper and paper board, miscellaneous pulp products, paper and paper board articles, printing and publishing of newspapers, periodicals, books, journals, atlases, maps, sheet music, directories, bank notes, currency notes, postage stamps, security passes, engraving, etching, block making, book binding, allied activities like envelope printing, picture post card printing, embossing, drills, coal cutting machines, earth moving, lifting and hoisting machinery, cranes, conveyors and road rollers and other heavy machinery and equipment used by construction and mining industries, prime movers, boilers and steam generating plants such as diesel engines, refrigerating, air conditioning plants for industrial use, domestic air conditioners and refridgerators, fire fighting equipment and appliances including fire engines, conveying equipment such as bucket elevators, derrick and size reduction equipment like crushers, ball mills etc., centrifugal machines, pumps, air and gas compressors and vacuum pumps, ball roller and tapered bearings, speed reduction units, sewing and knitting machines, washing machines, filteration and distillation

S. No.	Sector Names	Description
		equipment, arms and armaments and miscellaneous non electrical machinery and their repair services, manufacturing of surgical, medical laboratory scientific and mathematical instruments, water meters, steam meters and electricity meters, recording and regulatory devices for pressure, temperature weight level etc. photographic and optical goods (excluding photochemicals, sensitised paper and film), jewellery and related articles, minting coins, sports and athletic goods and play equipment, musical instruments, stationery articles like fountain pens, pencils, pens, pin cushions, tags, hair brushes, dusters, feather articles, signs and advertising displays, mechanical toys, other toys, bones, ivory, horns and similar products, wigs, costume and imitation jewelry novelties, lamp shades, presentation articles, badges and others, manufacture of aircrafts and parts and repair of enterprises not elsewhere classified.
10	Watches and clocks	Manufacture of watches and clocks.
11	Leather	Manufacture of leather and products of leather, fur and substitutes of leather.
12	Rubber, plastic	Manufacture of rubber, plastic, petroleum and coal products, processing of nuclear fuels.
13	Basic chemicals	Manufacture of basic chemicals and chemical products (except products of petroleum and coal).
14	Non-metallic minerals	Manufacture of non-metallic mineral products.
15	Iron and steel	Iron and Steel—ferro alloys, casting and forging and foundaries, non-ferrous basic metals (including alloys).
16	Miscellaneous metal products	Hand tools, bolts, nuts, locks, metal chains, agricultural hand tools and implements, general hardware, metal containers, steel trunks, safes, vaults, sanitary and plumbing fixtures and fitting of metal, stoves, hurricane lanterns, welded products, enamelling,

(Continued)

Appendix 4.2 *(Continued)*

S. No.	Sector Names	Description
		galvanising, plating and polishing of metal products, metal utensils, cutlery and kitchenware, metal furniture and fixtures, blades, springs, art metal ware, other metal products.
17	Capital goods	Capital goods and manufacture of office, computing and accounting machinery and parts.
18	Transport equipments	Manufacture of transport equipment and parts.
19	Electricity, gas and water supply	Electricity, gas and water supply.
20	Construction	Construction.
21	Combined services	Combined services including transport services, communication services, real estate, banking and insurance, education—scientific and research services.
22	Health and medical services	Health and medical services.
23	Other services	Other services including transport services, storage and warehousing, industrial. development and financial corporations etc.
24	Public administration and defence	Public administration and defence.

APPENDIX 4.3

AGGREGATION SCHEME
AND SOURCE OF INFORMATION

Sector	Commodity	ASI Sectors	Source*
1	Agriculture	NAS + 204	NAS
2	Mining		NAS
3	Mfg. food products	20 + 21–207–204	DME**
4	Sugar, gur	207	DME
5	Beverages	22	ASI
6	Textiles	23 to 26	ASI
7	Wood	27	ASI
8	Batteries	363 + 364	DME
9	Other manufacturing	28 + 38–382	ASI
10	Watches and clocks	382	DME
11	Leather	29	ASI
12	Rubber, plastic	31	DME
13	Basic chemicals	30	DME
14	Non-metallic minerals	32	ASI
15	Iron and steel	33	ASI
16	Misc. metal products	34	ASI
17	Capital goods	35 + 36–363–364	DME
18	Transport equipments	37	DME
19	Electricity, gas		NAS
20	Construction		NAS
21	Combined services		NAS
22	Health and medical services		NAS
23	Other services incl. trans, storage		NAS
24	Public admn. and defence		NAS

Notes: In case of reports other than NAS is in addition to NAS.

   *Source for distinguishing formal/informal share of each sector.
   Information about share in the net value added of registered and
   unregistered parts by broad sectors is as given in NAS.
   **DME includes OAME+NDME+DME.

APPENDIX 4.4

CLASSIFICATION OF HOUSEHOLDS BY NATIONAL INDUSTRIAL CLASSIFICATION (NIC) CODES

(A): Rural

NIC	Type	Description
0–069	Informal	Agriculture, hunting, forestry and fishing.
200	Informal	Slaughtering, preparation and preservation of meat.
201	Informal	Manufacture of dairy products.
203	Informal	Processing, canning, and preserving of fish, crustacea and similar foods.
207	Informal	Production of indigenous sugar, 'boora', 'khandsari', 'gur', etc. from sugar-cane; palm juice, etc.
220	Informal	Distilling, rectifying and blending of spirits; ethyl alcohol production from fermented materials.
223	Informal	Production of country liquor (arrack and toddy etc.).
225	Informal	Tobacco stemming, redrying and all other operations connected with preparing raw leaf tobacco.
234	Informal	Cotton ginning, cleaning and baling.
231	Informal	Cotton spinning other than in mills (charkha).
232	Informal	Weaving and finishing of cotton khadi.
233	Informal	Weaving and finishing of cotton textiles on handlooms.
236	Informal	Bleaching, dyeing and printing of cotton textiles (this group includes bleaching, dyeing and printing of not self-produced cotton textiles). No distinction is to be made between these activities carried out on fee or contract basis or by purchasing the material.
243	Informal	Bleaching and dyeing of woollen textiles.
246–248	Informal	Bleaching, dyeing and printing of silk textiles, spinning, weaving and processing of man-made textile fibres. Bleaching, dyeing and printing of artificial/synthetic textile fabrics by hand.
251	Informal	Preparatory operations (including carding and combing) on jute and mesta fibres.
261	Informal	Manufacture of all types of threads, cordage, ropes, twines and nets, etc.
262	Informal	Embroidery work, zari work and making of ornamental trimmings.
264	Informal	Manufacture of floor coverings of jute, mesta sann-hemp and other kindred fibres and of coir.

NIC	Type	Description
265	Informal	Manufacture of all types of textile garments and clothing accessories n.e.c. (except by purely tailoring establishments) from not self-produced material. (Note: in principle, the raw material is cut and sewn together in the establishments covered in this.)
267	Informal	Manufacture of made-up textile articles; except apparel.
270	Informal	Sawing and planing of wood (other than plywood).
272	Informal	Manufacture of structural woods (including treated timber) such as beams, posts, doors and windows (excluding hewing and rough shaping of poles, bolts and other wood material which is classified under logging).
273	Informal	Manufacture of wooden and cane boxes, crates, drums, barrels and other containers, baskets and other wares made entirely or mainly of cane, rattan, reed, bamboo, willow, fibres, leaves and grass.
274	Informal	Manufacture of wooden industrial goods n.e.c.
276	Informal	Manufacture of wooden furniture and fixtures.
277	Informal	Manufacture of bamboo, cane and reed furniture and fixtures.
279	Informal	Manufacture of products of wood, bamboo, cane, reed and grass (including articles made from coconut shells etc.) n.e.c.
290	Informal	Tanning, curing, finishing, embossing and japanning of leather.
293	Informal	Manufacture of consumer goods of leather and substitutes of leather; other than apparel and footwear. (Note: Manufacture of school bags and travelling accessories from water-proof textile fabrics is included in group 266.)
299	Informal	Manufacture of leather and fur products n.e.c.
320	Informal	Manufacture of refractory products and structural clay products.
322	Informal	Manufacture of earthen and plaster products.
390	Informal	Repair of agricultural machinery/equipment.
510	Informal	Plumbing and drainage.
513	Informal	Timber works (such as fixing of doors, windows, panels); structural steel works; R.C.C. work and binding of the bars and rood trusses.

(Continued)

Appendix 4.4 (*Continued*)

NIC	Type	Description
519	Informal	Other activities allied to construction not elsewhere classified.
651	Informal	Retail trade in vegetables and fruits.
652	Informal	Retail trade in meat, fish and poultry.
655	Informal	Retail trade in pan, bidi and cigarette.
690	Informal	Restaurants, cafes, other eating and drinking places.
691	Informal	Restaurants and hotels (excluding hotels, rooming houses, camps and other lodging places).
704	Informal	Passenger or freight transport via hackney-carriages bullock-carts, ekkas, tongas, etc.
705	Informal	Transport via animals like horses, elephants, mules, camels, etc.
706	Informal	Transport by man (including rickshaw pullers, handcart pullers, porters, coolies, etc.).
740	Informal	Warehousing of agricultural products without refrigeration.
834	Informal	Legal services such as those rendered by advocates, barristers, solicitors, pleaders, muktiars, etc.
850	Informal	Renting or transport equipment without operator n.e.c. (includes short-term rental as well as extended-term leasing with or without maintenance).
853	Informal	Renting of other industrial machinery and equipment. (This group includes the renting or leasing of all kind of machinery which is generally used as investment goods by industries.)
854	Informal	Renting or personal and household goods.
940	Informal	Religious services rendered by organisations or individuals.
953	Informal	Authors, music composers, singers, dancers, magicians, and other independent artistes not elsewhere classified.
960–964	Informal	Domestic services, laundry, cleaning and dyeing services, hair dressing such as those done by barbers, hair dressing saloons and beauty shops etc., portrait and commercial photographic studios, tailoring establishments.

NIC	Type	Description
969	Informal	Personal services not elsewhere classified.
970–975	Informal	Repair of footwear and other leather goods, repair of household electrical appliances, repair of TV, VCR, radio, transistor, tape-recorder, other electronic appliances, repair of watches, clocks and jewelry, repair of motor vehicles and motor cycles.
979	Informal	Repair enterprises not elsewhere classified.
990	Informal	Services not elsewhere classified.

(B): Urban

NIC	Type	Description
0–069	Informal	Agriculture, hunting, forestry and fishing.
207	Informal	Production of indigenous sugar, 'boora', 'khandsari', 'gur', etc. from sugar-cane; palm juice, etc.
223	Informal	Production of country liquor (arrack and toddy etc.).
231	Informal	Cotton spinning other than in mills (charkha).
232	Informal	Weaving and finishing of cotton khadi.
233	Informal	Weaving and finishing of cotton textiles on handlooms.
273	Informal	Manufacture of wooden and cane boxes, creates, drums, barrels and other containers, baskets and other wares made entirely or mainly of cane, rattan, reed, bamboo, willow, fibres, leaves and grass.
277	Informal	Manufacture of bamboo, cane and reed furniture and fixtures.
279	Informal	Manufacture of products of wood, bamboo, cane, reed and grass (including articles made from coconut shells etc.) n.e.c.
320	Informal	Manufacture of refractory products and structural clay products.
322	Informal	Manufacture of earthen and plaster products.
510	Informal	Plumbing and drainage.
651	Informal	Retail trade in vegetables and furits.
652	Informal	Retail trade in meat, fish and poultry.
655	Informal	Retail trade in pan, bidi and cigarette.
704	Informal	Passenger or freight transport via hackney-carriages bullock-carts, ekkas, tongas etc.

(Continued)

Appendix 4.4 (*Continued*)

NIC	Type	Description
705	Informal	Transport via animals like horses, elephants, mules, camels, etc.
706	Informal	Transport by man (including rickshaw pullers, handcart pullers, porters, coolies, etc.).
740	Informal	Warehousing of agricultural products without refrigeration.
834	Informal	Legal services such as those rendered by advocates, barristers, solicitors, pleaders, muktiars, etc.
854	Informal	Renting or personal and household goods.
953	Informal	Authors, music composers, singers, dancers, magicians, and other independent artistes not elsewhere classified.
960	Informal	Domestic services, laundry, cleaning and dyeing services, hair dressing such as those done by barbers, hair dressing saloons.
975	Informal	Repair of other electronic appliances, repair of watches, clocks and jewelry, repair of motoor vehicles and motor cycles.

APPENDIX 4.5

SECTORS CLASSIFIED THROUGH THE NATIONAL CLASSIFICATION OF OCCUPATION (NCO) CODES

(I) Urban Occupation Codes

NOC	Type	Description
070–073	Follows NIC	Physicians and surgeons: allopathic, ayurvedic, homeopathic and unani.
085–089	Follows NIC	Midwives and health visitors, X-ray technicians, etc.
099	Follows NIC	Scientific, medical and technical persons, other.
140–199	Follows NIC	Professional workers: jurists, teachers, journalists, etc.
220–229	Follows NIC	Working proprietors, directors and managers, wholesale and retail traders.
340–434	Follows NIC	Clerical and related workers, manufacturers and agents, salesmen, shop assistants and demonstrators, etc.
431	Informal	Street vendors, canvassers and news vendors.
439	Informal	Salesmen, shop assistants and related workers, n.e.c.
440–534	Follows NIC	Insurance, real estate, securities and business service, ayahs, nurse, maids, hotel and restaurant keepers, etc.
531	Informal	Domestic servants.
539	Informal	Maids, and related house keeping service workers, n.e.c.
540	Follows NIC	Building caretakers.
541	Follows NIC	Sweepers, cleaners and related workers.
542	Informal	Waterman.
549	Follows NIC	Building caretakers, sweepers, cleaners and related workers, n.e.c.
550	Informal	Laundrymen, washermen and dhobis.
551	Follows NIC	Dry-cleaners and pressers.
559	Follows NIC	Laundrymen, Dry-cleaners and pressers, n.e.c
560	Follows NIC	Hair dressers, barbers, beauticians and related worker.
574	Informal	Watchmen, chowkidars and gate keepers
579	Follows NIC	Protective service workers, n.e.c.
590–689	Follows NIC	Service workers, n.e.c., farmers, fishermen, hunters, loggers and related workers.

(Continued)

Appendix 4.5 (*Continued*)

NOC	Type	Description
710–759	Follows NIC	Miners, quarrymen, well drillers, spinners, weavers, paper makers and their related workers.
772–819	Follows NIC	Crushers and pressers, oil seeds, khandsari, sugar and gur makers, shoemakers, carpenters and related workers.
820–839	Formal if IEM=1	Stone cutters and carvers, blacksmiths, tool makers and machine tool cperators.
880–889	Follows NIC	Jewelry and precious metal workers and metal engravers (except printing).
892	Informal	Potters and related clay and abrasive formers.
899	Follows NIC	Glass formers, potters and related workers, n.e.c.
934–939	Follows NIC	Painters.
942	Informal	Basketry weavers and brush makers.
950–957	Follows NIC	Bricklayers and other construction workers (excluding hut builders and thatchers, these workers, n.e.c.).
958	Informal	Hut builders and thatchers.
959	Informal	Well diggers and construction workers, n.e.c.
987	Informal	Drivers, animal and animal drawn vehicle.
988	Informal	Cycle rickshaw drivers and rickshaw pullers.
989	Follows NIC	Transport equipment operators and drivers, n.e.c.
999	Informal	Labourers, n.e.c.

(II) Rural Occupation Codes

NOC	Type	Description
070–073	Follows NIC	Physicians and surgeons: allopathic, ayurvedic, homeopathic and unani.
085–089	Follows NIC	Midwives and health visitors, X-Ray technicians, etc.
140–199	Follows NIC	Professional workers: jurists, teachers, journalists, etc.
220–229	Follows NIC	Working proprietors, directors and managers, wholesale and retail trade.

NOC	Type	Description
340–399	Follows NIC	Clerical and related workers.
440–534	Follows NIC	Insurance, real estate, securities and business service, ayaha, nurse, maids, hotel and restaurant keepers, etc.
531	Informal	Domestic servants.
539	Informal	Maids and related house keeping service workers, n.e.c.
540	Follows NIC	Building caretakers.
541	Follows NIC	Sweepers, cleaners and related workers.
542	Informal	Waterman.
549	Follows NIC	Building caretakers, sweepers, cleaners and related workers, n.e.c.
550	Informal	Laundrymen, washermen and dhobis.
551	Informal	Dry-cleaners and pressers.
559	Informal	Laundrymen, dry-cleaners and pressers, n.e.c.
560	Informal	Hair dressers, barbers, beauticians and related worker.
574	Informal	Watchmen, chowkidars and gate keepers.
579	Follows NIC	Protective service workers, n.e.c.
590–599	Follows NIC	Service workers, n.e.c.
600–689	Informal if NIC = (900,903)	Farmers, fishermen, hunters, loggers. and related workers.
710–749	Informal	Miners, quarrymen, well drillers, paper. makers, chemical processors and their related workers.
750–759	Informal	Spinners, weavers, knitters, dyers and related workers.
772–779	Informal	Food and beverage processors excluding supervisors and foremen, grain millers and related workers.
780–789	Follows NIC	Tobacco preparers and tobacco product makers.
790–799	Informal	Tailors, dress makers, sewers, upholsterers and related workers.
800–836	Informal	Shoemakers and leather good makers, carpenters, stone cutters, blacksmiths and related workers.
839	Informal	Blacksmiths, tool makers and machine tool operations, n.e.c.
880–889	Informal	Jewelry and precious metal workers and metal engravers (except printing).

(Continued)

Appendix 4.5 (*Continued*)

NOC	Type	Description
892	Informal	Potters and related clay and abrasive formers.
899	Follows NIC	Glass formers, potters and related workers, n.e.c.
934–939	Follows NIC	Painters.
942	Informal	Basketry weavers and brush makers.
958	Informal	Hut builders and thatchers.
959	Informal	Well diggers and construction workers, n.e.c.
987, 988	Informal	Drivers, animal and animal drawn vehicle, cycle rickshaw drivers and other transport equipment operators and drivers.
989	Follows NIC	Transport equipment operators and drivers, n.e.c.
999	Informal	Labourers, n.e.c.

APPENDIX 4.6

PER DAY WAGE RATE FOR LABOURERS BY REGION AND GENDER

Sector	Casual Labour: Agriculture		Regular Labour: Agriculture		Casual Labour: Others		Regular Labour: Others	
	Female	Male	Female	Male	Female	Male	Female	Male
Rural	14.96	21.30	22.83	27.47	17.08	29.66	36.23	61.93
Urban	16.28	25.19	46.66	51.40	18.98	33.20	64.05	81.09
All-India	15.62	23.25	34.75	39.44	18.03	31.43	50.14	71.51

Source: 'Employment and Unemployment in India', 1993–94, Fifth Quinquennial Survey, The National Sample Survey 50th Round, Report No. 409, New Delhi.

NOTES

1. For the full SAM, see Sinha et al. (2003).
2. The NIC classification is based on the nature of economic activity carried out in an establishment and the codes for these activities are grouped at one-digit, two-digit, three- and four-digit levels
3. The multiplier matrix is available in Sinha et al. (1999).

REFERENCES AND
SELECT BIBLIOGRAPHY

Adelman, Irma and Sherman Robinson (1989), 'Income Distribution and Development', in H. Chenery and T.N. Srinivasan (eds), *Handbook of Development Economics*, vol. II, Amsterdam: Elsevier Science Publishers B.V.

Bakkar, I. (1994), *The Strategic Silence, Gender and Economic Policy*, London: Zed Books.

Ballantine, J. and R. Soligo (1978), 'Consumption and Earnings Pattern and Income Distribution', *Economic Development and Cultural Change*, vol. 26.

Beneria, L. (1992), 'Accounting for Women's Work: The Progress of Two Decades', *World Development*, vol. 20, no. 11.

——— (1995), 'Toward a Greater Integration of Gender in Economics', *World Development*, vol. 23, no. 11.

Cagatay, N., D. Elson and C. Grown (1995), 'Introduction' to 'Gender, Adjustment and Macroeconomics', *World Development*, vol. 23, no. 11.

Central Statistical Organisation (1989), *National Accounts Statistics*, Government of India, New Delhi.

——— (1997), *Input-Output Transactions Table, 1989–90*, Government of India, New Delhi.

Charmes, J. (1990), 'A Critical Review of Concepts, Definitions and Studies in the Informal Sector', in Davis Turnham, Bernard Salome and Antoine Schwartz (eds), *The Informal Sector Revisited*, OECD, Paris.

Decaluwe, B., A. Patry, L. Savard and E. Thorbecke (1999), 'Poverty Analysis within a General Equilibrium Framework', Working Paper 9909, CREFA 99–06, Quebec: University of Laval.

Duchin, Faye (1998), *Structural Economics: Measuring Changes in Technology, Lifestyle, and the Environment*, California: Island Press.

Duchin, Faye and Anushree Sinha (1999), 'Structural economics and the Quality of Life', *Feminist Economics*, vol. 5, no. 2.

Duchin, Faye and K. Nauphal (1996), *Incorporation of the Institutional Accounts for the Dominican Republic into the Input-Output Framework*, Report to the Central Bank of the Dominican Republic.

Earth Summit (1992), United Nation Conference on Environment and Development.

Elson, D. (1995), 'Gender Awareness in Modeling Structural Adjustment', *World Development*, vol. 23, no. 11.

Erturk, K. and N. Cagatay (1995), 'Macroeconomic Consequences of Cyclical and Secular Changes in Feminization: An Experiment at Gendered Macromodeling', *World Development*, vol. 23, no. 11.

Ghosh, A., A. Sinha, D. Chakraborty and S. Bhattacharya (1991), *Measurement of the Impact of Agricultural output on the Market for Manufactures*, New Delhi: Himalaya Publishing House.

Hart, K. (1971), 'Informal Urban Opportunitues and Urban Employment in Ghana', *Journal of Modern African Studies*, vol. 2.

Himmelwait, S. and S. Mohun (1977), 'Domestic Labor and Capital', *Cambridge Journal of Economics*, vol. 1, March.

Hussmanns, Ralf (1996), 'ILO's Recommendations on Methodologies Concerning Informal Sector Data Collection', in Herman Bohuslav and Wim Stoffers (eds), *Unveiling the Informal Sector: More than Counting Heads*, Aldershot: Avebury.

Hugon, P. (1990), 'The Informal Sector Revisited (in Africa)', in Davis Turnham, Bernard Salome and Antoine Schwartz (eds), *The Informal Sector Revisited*, OECD, Paris.

Inter-Secretarial Working Group on National Accounts (1993), 'System of National Accounts 1993', Commission of European Communities, Brussels.

Keuning, J.S. and W.A. De Ruijter (1988), 'Guidelines to the Construction of a Social Accounting Matrix', *Review of Income and Wealth*, 34.

Khan, Haider A. and E. Thorbecke (1988), 'Macroeconomic Effects and Diffusion of Alternative Technologies Within a Social Accounting Matrix Framework', Aldershot: Gower Publishing.

Lubell, Harold (1991), 'The Informal Sector in the 1980s and 1990s', OECD, Paris.

Meagher, Kate and Mohammed-Bello Yunusa (1996), 'Passing the Buck: Structural Adjustment and the Nigerian Urban Informal Sector', United Nations Research Institute for Social Development, Geneva.

Mohammed, S. (1981), 'Trade, Growth and Income Distribution: A case study of India', *Journal of Development Economics*.

National Industrial Classification [All Economic Activities] (1998), Central Statistical Organisation, Department of Statistics, Ministry of Planning and Programme Implementation, Government of India, New Delhi.

Ninth Five Year Plan (1997–2002), vol. 5, Planning Commission, Government of India, New Delhi.

Paukert, F. and J. Skolka (1972), 'Redistribution of Income, Patterns of Consumption and Employment: A Framework Analysis', Mimeo (ILO, Geneva.

Planning Commission of India (1973), 'A Technical Note on the Approach to the Fifth Plan of India', Government of India, New Delhi.

Pyatt, Graham (1988), 'A SAM Approach to Modeling', *Journal of Policy Modeling*, 10.

Pyatt, Graham and E. Thorbecke (1976), *Planning Techniques for a better Future*, International Labour Office, Geneva.

Pyatt, Graham and Jeffere I. Round (eds) (1985), *Social Accounting Matrices: A Basis for Planning*, The World Bank, Washington, D.C.

Ranais, Gustav and Frances Stewart (1997), 'The Urban Informal Sector Within a Global Economy', in U. Kirdar (ed.), *Cities Fit for People*, United Nations, Geneva.

Sadoulet, Elisabeth and Alain de Janvry (1995), 'Quantitative Development Policy Analysis', Baltimore: John Hopkins University Press.

Sethuraman, S.V. (1981), 'The Urban Informal Sector in Developing Countries: Employment, Poverty and Environment', International Labour Office, Geneva.

Sinha, Anushree (1998), 'Macroeconomic Analysis of the Indian Informal Sector within a Social Accounting Matrix Framework', Paper presented at the 12th International Input Output Conference at New York University.

Sinha, Anushree, K.A. Siddiqui and N. Sangeeta (2003), 'The Impact of Alternative Economic Policies on the Informal Sector: A Multi-sectoral Study', New Delhi: NCAER.

Sinha, R., P. Pearson et al. (1979), *Income Distribution, Growth and Basic Needs in India*, Delhi: Vikas.

SNA (1993), *System of National Accounts, 1993*, Commission of the European Communities, World Bank, Washington, D.C.

Soto, Hernando de (1989), *The Other Path: The Invisible Revolution of the Third World*, London: I.B. Tauris.

Stone, R. (1970), 'Demographic Input-Output: An Extension of Social Accounting', in A.P. Carter and A. Brody (eds), *Contribution to Input–Output Analysis*, vol. 1, Amsterdam: North Holland Publishing.

——— (1971), 'Demographic Accounting and Model Building', Organisation for Economic Co-Operation and Development (OECD), Paris.

Stone, R. (1981), 'Aspects of Economic and Social Modelling', Librairie Droz, Geneva.

_____ (1985), 'The Dissaggregation of the Household Sector in the National Accounts', in G. Pyatt and J.I. Round (eds), *Social Accounting Matrices: A Basis for Planning*, World Bank, Washington.

_____ (1986), 'Social Accounting: The State of Play', in *Scandinavian Journal of Economics*.

The National Sample Survey 50th Round (1993–94), 'Schedule 1.0 on Consumer Expenditure and Schedule 10.0 on Employment and Unemployment', Data processed at NCAER.

_____ (1997), 'Employment and Unemployment in India, 1993–94— Fifth-Quinquennial Survey, NSS Fiftieth Round. Report No. 409', New Delhi.

Thorbecke, E. and H.S. Jung (1996), 'A Multiplier Decomposition Method to Analyze Poverty Alleviation', *Journal of Development Economics*, 48.

Turnham Davis, Bernard Salome and Antoine Schwartz (eds) (1990), *The Informal Sector Revisited*, OECD, Paris.

Weisskoff, R. (1973), 'A Multi-Sector simulation Model of Employment, Growth and Income Distribution in Puerto Rico; A Re-Evaluation of "Successful" Development Strategy' (Mimeo), Economic Growth Centre: Yale University.

Weisskoff, R. and E. Wolff (1977), 'Linkages and Leakages: Industrial Tracking in an Enclave Economy', *Economic Development*, vol. 25.

Wheelock, J. (1992), 'The Flexibility of Small Business Family Work Strategies', in K. Caley, F. Chittenden, E. Chell and C. Mason (eds), *Small Enterprise Development: Policy and Practice in Action*, London: Paul Chapman.

Wheelock, J. and E. Oughton (1994), *The Household as a Focus for Comparative Research*, Centre for Rural Economy, Department of Agricultural Economics and Food Marketing, University of Newcastle upon Tyne.

Wilk, R.R. (1989), 'Decision Making and Resource Flows within the Household: Beyond the Black Box', in R.R. Wilk (ed.), *The Household Economy: Reconsidering the Domestic Mode of Production*, Boulder: Westview.

World Bank (1994), 'Enhancing Women's Participation in Economic Development', World Bank, Washington, D.C.

5

Unorganised Manufacturing and the Gross Domestic Product

N. Lalitha

INTRODUCTION

The unorganised or informal sector[1] plays an important role in employment and income creation and thereby in poverty reduction, particularly in developing countries. Factors like the growing labour force but limited labour absorbing capacity of the organised sector and the seasonal nature of the farm sector, where underemployment is widely prevalent, have contributed to the growth of employment in the unorganised sector. Structural adjustment policies leading to restructuring of enterprises, have also contributed to the growing importance of the informal sector. However, income from this sector does not grow at the same rate at which employment grows. This is because much of the employment in the informal sector is poverty induced and a strategy of survival, and is not exactly pursued as a business of making profits. Despite this, the growing employment in this sector has encouraged policy-makers to examine the contribution made by this sector to the national income, and has stimulated research on ways to improve the income contribution made by this sector.

India is one of the few countries in the world where systematic efforts are made to collect information on the informal sector. Thus an estimate of the workforce in the informal sector can be obtained from the (*a*) population census, (*b*) economic census, and (*c*) the follow-up surveys on the economic census. While the Central Statistical Organisation (CSO) of the Government of India conducts the economic census, the National Sample Survey Organisation (NSSO) of the Government of India, is engaged in the task of compiling information on the informal sector through the follow-up surveys on the Economic Census. However, the differences in the definitions adopted, to define the unorganised sector in each source, make them non-comparable. For instance, the follow-up surveys define a household (HH) industry as an enterprise run by one or more members of a HH, irrespective of whether or not the enterprise is located in the same premises of the HH; the 1991 Census defines HH industry as an activity conducted by the head of the HH and/or by the members of the HH at home or within the village in rural areas and only within the precincts of the house where the HH lives in urban areas. Second, in the follow-up surveys, an enterprise run by two or more HHs on a partnership basis is also treated as a HH enterprise whereas the population census is silent on this aspect.

However, the follow-up surveys provide valuable information that range from registration of the unit to value added by the unit. These value added figures are used in the estimation of the unorganised sector's contribution to national income. Various sectors like the primary, secondary and tertiary sectors contribute to the national income estimations. The procedures adopted to measure the contribution vary depending on the type of sector we are looking at. Thus the gross value added approach, or the production approach, is used in estimating the contribution of agriculture, fishing, mining and manufacturing. In the production approach the contribution is assessed by considering the sectors output and subtracting the value of material input. In the income approach that is adopted in the service sectors, the factor income that accrue to the different components of production, such as land, labour, capital and organisation, is considered along with the consumption of fixed capital.

The focus of this paper is on estimating the income contribution of the unorganised manufacturing sector where the organisation of the paper is as follows. The section, following this introduction, presents a brief review of available evidence on the aspect of measuring the unorganised sector's contribution to national income, particularly in the context of India. This is followed by the growth characteristics of the unorganised manufacturing sector over a period of time as evident from the follow-up surveys presented in the section on the unorganised manufacturing sector. The section on income contribution by the unorganised manufacturing sector discusses the method adopted by the CSO in estimating the income contribution. The section following this highlights the issues concerning the methodology in estimating the income and the last section concludes with a few suggestions.

SELECTIVE REVIEW OF LITERATURE

Considerable amount of research, in the form of case studies, has been carried out in India as well as in other countries to understand the dynamics of the informal sector. While a few studies have attempted a discussion on the measurement of income contribution by this sector, yet another set has discussed the gender composition of the informal sector and its contribution to the GDP. These are mentioned in the following paragraphs.

Kulshreshtha and Singh (1996) point out that in sectors where the income approach has been followed in the estimation of GDP, GDP by gender can be arrived at, provided information on the workforce and wages are available by gender. However such data in India are scanty. They observe that even in the framework of the System of National Accounts of 1993, valuation of services of housewives can be measured using the income approach but with very many assumptions.

Unni (1998) also observes that while estimates on labour force by gender can be collected and are being collected in India and other countries too, no country produces gender disaggregated GDP estimates because of difficulties in meaningfully estimating the contribution to GDP by gender. One simplest way that has been adopted in a few studies (Mukherjee 1985, Kulshreshtha and Singh 1996; Lalitha 1999) is to allocate the aggregate contribution to GDP by various categories by gender, in proportion to their share in the workforce. This method however reflects only the percentage share of women in the workforce.

A few countries where the unorganised sector already accounts for a sizeable share in employment, have started collecting information systematically visualising further growth of this sector. A precise compilation of this effort is presented in Brigette Du Jeu (1998), which highlights the importance of the informal sector in terms of non-agricultural employment and gross domestic product (GDP) particularly in some of the Asian and African countries (see Table 5.1). According to this estimate, the share of the informal sector in non-agricultural GDP and total GDP accounts for 47 and 63 per cent respectively. However, the employment figures and the GDP estimates

Table 5.1
Share of the Informal Sector in Non-agricultural,
Total Employment and GDP

	Non-agricultural		Total	
	Share of the Informal Sector in Non-agricultural Employment	Share of the Informal Sector in Non-agricultural GDP	Share of the Informal Sector in Total Employment	Share of the Informal Sector in Total GDP
Benin 1993	93	57	41	37
Burkina Faso 1992	77	40	9	25
Chad 1993	74	45	12	31
Colombia 1992 (10 metropolitan areas)	–	–	55	18
Fiji 1990	–	–	43	2
India 1993–94	–	47	–	63
Madagascar (Antananarivo) 1995	–	26	–	17
Mali 1989	79	42	13	23
Mauritania 1989	75	14	–	10
Mauritius 1992	–	–	24	19
Niger 1987	–	–	–	30
Philippines 1988	–	–	26	12
Senegal 1991	76	41	–	–
Tanzania 1991	–	–	22	32
Tanzania 1995 (Dar es Salaam)	–	–	30	65
Thailand 1995	–	–	6	1
Tunisia 1995	49	23	38	20

Source: Brigette Du Jeu 1998.

between different countries are non-comparable due to the following
factors: (a) surveys in many countries cover only the urban cities or
only the capital city and hence are not uniform in their area of coverage; (b) inclusion or exclusion of the agricultural sector in the informal sector; (c) inclusion or exclusion of paid domestic workers; and
(d) the criterion that is adopted to define the informal enterprise.
Though the methods adopted to estimate the income from this sector

are not clear from this work, yet it gives an idea of the coverage and information collected through surveys in different countries.

Kulshreshtha and Singh (1999) have analysed the GDP from the unorganised manufacturing and trade segment after the introduction of the 1993–94 series. They observe that the decline in the share of the unorganised segment in the GDP could be attributed to the reduction in the market response to these activities resulting in a fall in the productivity of labour and their wages and agree that the value added per worker particularly in the unorganised service sector are gross underestimates. On the new methodology concerning the unorganised manufacturing sector they suggest that more recent data regarding the small-scale industry segment needs to be included.

Lalitha (2000) discusses the salient features of the new series with the base 1993–94 concerning the unorganised manufacturing sector at the macro as well as at the state level. She finds that the state governments have considerable freedom in that they can either follow the methodology adopted by the CSO, or their own, in the income estimation of different sectors. Thus prior to the 1993–94 series, in Gujarat, the contribution to the unorganised manufacturing sector was arrived at, as a product of value added per enterprise and the number of enterprises. This figure worked out for a base year was moved forward using certain indicators. Sivasubramonian (2000) presents a very detailed analysis of estimation procedures that were adopted for different sectors both prior and after independence. His analysis prior to 1946–47 informs the reader that the residual method of arriving at the workforce with the unorganised sector was adopted earlier too. In those days, the contribution of the unorganised sector was estimated by multiplying the average annual earnings of workers by the number of workers. The number of workers was arrived at by using the factory sector data and the Census estimates. Statistics of employment in the formal sector, were obtained from all those units which were regulated by the Factories Act of 1881 (those that employed more than 50 persons and the subsequent revisions made to this act). By interpolating the census year estimates of the total working force under the head industry, the annual workforce with the industry was worked out. Subtracting the formal sector employment from this figure gives the rough estimate of the number of workers in the small-scale sector and cottage industry. The number of workers using this method was estimated at 13,314,000 in 1900–1901. It declined to 12,265,000 in 1946–47 due to the decline in the workforce in certain industries.

Sivasubramonian details the data deficiencies encountered in building up the wage series for this sector. In the pre-Independence days, no distinction was made between the wages in urban and rural areas and in certain informal activities wages were paid in kind. Also the wages data were available for a few provinces only and assumptions had to be made for different skills and artisan workers. The number of days of employment also varied in different professions. After making provisions for all these, the annual wage thus arrived at was taken to be equal to the net value added per worker. However, the problem in this method was it did not account for the share of other factor payments. The net value added by the unorganised manufacturing sector in current prices using this method was estimated at Rs 1,165 million in 1900–1901 and Rs 4,942 million in 1946–47.

THE UNORGANISED-MANUFACTURING SECTOR OF INDIA

Before we actually look at the contribution made by this sector, it is essential to understand the growth characteristics of this sector in India. In the Indian National Accounts Statistics (NAS) the unorganised manufacturing sector refers to those units, which are not registered under Sections 2m(i) and (ii) of the Indian Factories Act 1948. In other words, manufacturing enterprises using power and employing less than 10 workers and those not using power and employing less than 20 workers constituted the unorganised manufacturing sector. Table 5.2 presents some of the important features of the unorganised manufacturing sector in India.

It is evident from Table 5.2 that during the entire period of study (1978–95), employment and value addition of the unorganised manufacturing sector increased by about 82 per cent while the number of enterprises grew at the rate of 70.59 per cent. However the kind of growth witnessed in 1984–85 in all the three indicators is not observed in the following years. Two explanations can be given for this. One, as a result of partial liberalisation measures, such as broad banding and expansion of capacity, particularly in the engineering and automobile industries, the unorganised manufacturing activities also got a fillip. Second, while the 1978–79 follow-up survey was based on the 1977 Economic Census, 1984–85 was based on the 1980 Economic Census. The 1989–90 follow-up survey was also based on the 1980 Economic Census, the difference being that the

Table 5.2
Unorganised Manufacturing Sector in India

Year	Number of Enterprises	Number of Workers	Total Value Added (Rs)	Value Added per Worker (Rs)
1978–79	8.50	18.21	61,512	3,377.90
1984–85	19.72	36.95	101,992	2,760.20
	(133.0)	(103.0)	(65.88)	(–18.28)
1989–90	16.29	35.47	109,897	3,096.61
	(–17.39)	(–4.00)	(7.69)	(12.18)
1994–95	14.50	33.20	111,978	3,372.80
	(–11.0)	(–6.4)	(1.95)	(8.91)
1978–95	70.59	82.31	82.00	(–0.15)

Source: Follow-up surveys on the unorganised manufacturing sector: 1978–79,
1984–85, 1989–90 and 1994–95.

Notes: 1. All figures other than the value added per worker are in millions.
2. Figures in parentheses and the last row indicate the percentage change over the previous period.
3. Value added figures are in constant prices deflated using the implicit deflators.

1977 Economic Census defined the establishments as those, which had at least one hired worker and thus did not cover the own-account enterprises utilising family labour. The 1980 census, however, covered both establishments and enterprises (Saluja 1988). The impact of this on the follow-up survey could be that the own-account manufacturing establishments (OAMEs) would have been underestimated in the 1978–79 survey. On the other hand, dropping off of the output condition in 1984–85 in the case of non-directory manufacturing establishments (NDMEs) would have had only marginal impact in increasing the number of NDMEs. This is because the number of units producing goods of over Rs 100,000 per year that was excluded in 1978–79 is unlikely to be very large.

It may be noted that while the units and employment have doubled in 1984–85, the value addition has increased by 65 per cent only. In other words, the value added per worker declined from Rs 3,377 to 2,760 in 1984–85. Implicitly, the value addition in the informal sector does not increase at the same rate as the employment and not all the employment in this sector adds positively to the value addition. This is obvious from the fact that, despite a decline in employment by 1.48 million the total value added in 1989–90, has increased by 7,845 million in real terms and the value added per worker has also increased to Rs 3,096 from 2,760. A similar scenario emerges in 1994–95, where the total value added as well as the value added per worker has improved from the previous levels despite a decline in employment by 2.27 million. Interestingly, in 1994–95, the value added per worker is the same as what it was in 1978–79 indicating that productivity per worker actually declined over the years with an increase in employment.

This leads to the argument whether the lower labour productivity indicates that employment in the informal sector has reached saturation level. But in a country like India where the labour absorption capacity of organised manufacturing is determined by the technology and financial resources and the agricultural sector is already burdened with low productivity and underemployment, the informal sector will continue to attract a labour force who are willing to work at the subsistence level of wages rather than remain unemployed. The value addition contributed by these labourers or the productivity per worker is low. But it should be recognised that productivity per worker or the value added per worker in the unorganised sector depends on factors such as the demand for labour, use of technology, remuneration paid, availability of skilled labour and timely availability of credit. Implicitly, the aggregate demand for labour is low while supply is high, which leads to some sectors acting as a sponge or providers of soft employment where labourers are underemployed and earning low wages. Basically employment in this sector increases because of (a) the absence of entry or exit barriers and (b) small-scale operations mainly using indigenous resources and labour intensive technology. However, the growing employment in this sector has made many governments examine the income earning capacity of this sector and look for ways to improve the income generated from this sector. While this has prompted some of the developing countries to launch surveys to get a realistic picture of this sector, in India—where systematic data collection is already in place—the methodology of estimating the income contribution was revised recently, which is discussed in the following paragraphs.

INCOME CONTRIBUTION BY THE UNORGANISED MANUFACTURING SECTOR

In India, the income contributed by the various sectors is presented in the National Accounts Statistics Series, which is published by the CSO. The National Accounts Statistics Series, which give the income estimates of the different sectors of the economy, have so far been revised four times. First from 1948–49 to 1960–61 in August 1967. (The methodology adopted prior to this was discussed in the section on the selective review of literature.)

With gradual improvement of data and refinement of methodology proposals for the revision of the series were made through the publication in 1961 by the CSO. After wide ranging discussions, the revised series of national income with 1960–61 as the base year was published in 1967. The scope of the National Accounts Statistics Series also widened to include the private consumption expenditure, saving, capital formation and public sector accounts etc (Sivasubramonian 2000).

With availability of new data from the population census, livestock census, cost of cultivation surveys and non-agricultural enterprise surveys, the series was revised from 1960–61 to 1970–71 in January 1978. In the 1970–71 series, the production approach was followed in estimating the income from the unorganised manufacturing sector. Here the estimates of value added by industry were first built up for the base year 1970–71 on the basis of value added per worker (VAW) in each industry group and the estimated working force. The VAW were based on the results of the 29th Round (1974–75) survey of NSSO on household non-agricultural enterprises and the results available from the centrally sponsored scheme on survey on Small-Scale Industries (1970–71) and Census of Small-Scale Industries (1972) undertaken by the office of the Development Commissioner, small-scale industries. The estimates of the working force were built on the basis of population census results duly adjusted for the number of workers in the registered sector obtained from the Annual Survey of Industries (ASI). The estimates for other years at 1970–71 prices were first worked out by carrying forward the base year estimates with the help of indicators of physical output-input and appropriate indices of industrial production (CSO 1989: 94).

The 1970–71 series was changed to the base year 1980–81 in February 1988. In this series, using the production approach, the value added for the sector was arrived at, as a product of the value added per worker and the workforce in this sector. Here the value added per worker was obtained from the follow-up surveys on the unorganised manufacturing sector and the estimates of the workforce were obtained from the census.[2] These data from two different sources are used because of the fact that 'the sample survey based results are good for estimating ratios rather than the population totals' (Kulshreshtha and Singh 1999). Like the earlier series, the income estimates were first worked out for the base year and then carried forward to subsequent years on the basis of indicators representing physical volume of activity, which were drawn from several sources (for details see CSO 1989).[3] At the time of preparing the 1981 series, though the NSSO's 33rd (1978–79) round results on the follow-up surveys on the unorganised manufacturing sector were available, they were however not used. This is because

at the aggregate level, the estimates of value added published in the NAS and the total value added obtained as a product of the value added per worker obtained from the combined results of the Non-Directory Manufacturing Establishments (NDMEs), Own-Account Manufacturing Enterprises (OAMEs), and Directory Manufacturing Establishments (DMEs) and the revised estimates of the workforce were quite comparable. Since the NAS estimates are published at the disaggregated level and the use of combined results of NDME, OAME, and DME would have brought about violent fluctuations at the industry level, *it was not considered desirable to utilise these results* (emphasis added by us) for purposes of working out industry-wise estimates of GVA for the year 1980–81 (CSO 1989).

The 1984–85 (40th round) results of the unorganised manufacturing sector were however found suitable to be used in the national income estimates. Thus the base year estimates using the 1984–85 survey were prepared for 1984–85, and physical indicators were used for carrying forward these estimates to other years.[4] It may be mentioned that for the industrial groups tobacco and textiles, the results of the 40th round were found comparable with the data from the Directorate of Tobacco Development and Development Commissioner of Textiles. Therefore, the follow-up survey results were used for these sectors also and the use of physical indicators to carry forward the benchmark estimates continued till the recent revision in March 1999.

THE 1993–94 SERIES

In March 1999, the CSO released a new series of National Accounts Statistics with 1993–94 as the base year in place of the 1980–81 series. In this revision exercise the CSO has taken the effort to revise the base year to a more recent year for a meaningful analysis of the structural changes in the economy. Further, the existing data base and methodology employed in the estimation of various macro economic aggregates including the choice of the alternative data bases on individual subjects were reviewed and efforts were also taken to the extent feasible, to implement the recommendations of the 1993 system of National Accounts.

Though the recommendations of the 1993 system of National Accounts are more relevant for the informal service sectors rather than the manufacturing sector, the CSO however introduced new data wherever available. As far as the unorganised manufacturing sector was concerned, the new data introduced pertain to the: (1) workforce participation rates (WPRs) from the employment and unemployment survey results of the NSS 50th round (1993–94), which were used in place of the WPR from the population Census which underestimated the female workers; (2) GVA per worker from the unorganised SSI obtained from 1987–88 SSI census and moved forward to 1993–94 (earlier the results of the first all-India Census on SSI in 1972, were used in the 1970–71 series); (3) GVA per worker ratio from the latest NSS 51st (1994–95) round of follow-up survey on the unorganised manufacturing sector; and (4) the revised estimates of the Index of Industrial Production 1993–94 in the place of physical indicators that were used in the 1980–81 series.

Before we discuss the methodology to estimate the contribution of the unorganised manufacturing sector, some information about the 1994–95 unorganised manufacturing sector results and the SSI data used in the 1993–94 series would be in order. First, compared to the 40th round (1984–85), employment in the 51st round (1993–94), recorded a decline to the tune of 3.75 million workers. Second, the growth rate of employment, GVA and GVA per worker calculated for different sectors between 1984–85 and 1994–95 show that (see Table 5.3) employment and GVA have declined in the manufacture of food products, cotton textiles, textile products, leather products, chemical products, basic metal products, non-electrical machinery and repair of capital goods. Also, GVA per worker has declined in a few sectors like manufacture of beverages, textile products, wood products, paper products, and metal products and transport products. Third, as per the SSI census results, of the total units that were covered, those registered under the Factories Act accounted for 7.53 per cent only, while the remaining 92.47 per cent were not registered under the Factories Act (hereafter referred to as registered and unregistered SSI respectively). Further, the registered SSI and the unregistered

Table 5.3
All-India Growth Rate of Employment and GVA
per Worker in the Unorganised Sector, 1984–95
(constant prices)

Industry	Unorganised Manufacturing Sector		
	TE	GVA	VAW
Food products	-1.54	-0.58	0.96
Beverages	0.91	-0.52	-1.43
Cotton	-10.57	-5.43	5.14
Wool, silk	3.46	9.20	5.74
Jute	5.74	10.44	4.69
Textiles	-6.07	-6.87	-0.81
Wood products	0.86	-1.97	-2.83
Paper products	3.39	1.84	-1.54
Leather products	-4.11	-3.52	0.58
Chemical products	-0.36	-0.20	0.16
Rubber products	5.35	9.42	4.07
Non-metallic	-0.06	3.97	4.03
Basic metals	-1.43	-0.31	1.12
Metal products	0.98	0.08	-0.90
Non-electrical	-0.16	-0.73	-0.57
Electrical	3.26	4.05	0.79
Transport equipment	1.26	-12.51	-13.77
Other manufacturing	7.12	12.61	5.48
Repair of capital goods	-12.36	-5.62	6.74
Repair services	–	–	–
All industries	-1.07	1.03	2.09

Source: 40th (1984–85) and 51st (1994–95) rounds of NSSO on the unorganised manufacturing sector.

SSI units accounted for 30, 43 and 70, 57 per cent of the employment and gross value added respectively.

The revised methodology concerning the unorganised manufacturing sector in the 1993–94 series states that

in the new series, estimates of gross value added (GVA) from the units in the small scale industries (SSIs) and others have been compiled separately. For estimating the GVA from the unregistered units belonging to SSI group (unregistered SSI), the GVA and employment relating to small scale units covered under Annual Survey of Industries (ASI) have been subtracted from those obtained from the results of Second All-India Census on

Small Scale Industrial Units, 1987–88 published by Development Commissioner, SSI. Estimates of GVA per worker relating to unregistered SSI, thus obtained for 1987–88, have been adjusted to 1993–94 prices using the wholesale price index (WPI) and the working force has been extrapolated to 1993–94 using the inter-survey growth rate observed between 1987–88 (43rd round) and 1993–94 (50th round) of the NSSO employment and unemployment survey. Based on estimates of working force and value added per worker, GVA from the unregistered SSI has been estimated.

The estimates of working force for 1993–94 pertaining to 'other unregistered' manufacturing units, i.e., units other than those belonging to unregistered SSI mentioned above have been obtained by subtracting units belonging to ASI and unregistered SSI from the total manufacturing working force. This working force has then been distributed between the own account manufacturing enterprises, non-directory manufacturing and directory manufacturing establishments (OAME, NDME, DME) by location (rural/urban) based on the corresponding ratios obtained from results of NSSO 51st round (1994–95) survey on unorganised manufacturing sector (Kulshreshtha and Singh 1999).

Respective estimates of value added per worker as obtained from the results of the 51st round that have been duly adjusted for the 1993–94 price are multiplied with the workforce to arrive at the total GVA.

As per the new methodology, the workforce in the unorganised manufacturing sector in 1993–94 is estimated to be 37.73 million. The income from this sector as per the new series stands at Rs 43,6200 million (ibid.: 223, 227). This base year estimate will be moved forward using the Index of Industrial Production, which has also been revised in 1993–94. Table 5.4 gives the GVA of the unorganised manufacturing sector using the 1993–94 series and 1981 series. At current prices, while the GDP contribution of the total manufacturing sector has increased at the rate of 13.66 per cent per annum, that of the unorganised manufacturing sector has increased at the rate of 13.38 per cent per annum. The income contribution of the unorganised sector in the new series is less by Rs 27,970 million compared to the 1980–81 series.

To summarise this section, efforts to include the unorganised manufacturing sector in the national income estimates were undertaken even prior to Independence and estimation of the

Table 5.4
Comparison of GDP at Current Prices, New and
Old Estimates (in Million Rs)

Year	Total Manufacturing		Registered		Unregistered	
	New	Old	New	Old	New	Old
1993–94	1,266,970	1,276,460	830,770	812,290	436,200	464,170
1994–95	1,550,160	1,597,130	1,035,750	1,017,400	514,410	579,730
1995–96	1,920,700	1,983,480	1,281,750	1,260,840	638,950	722,640
1996–97	2,152,930	2,226,090	1,443,330	1,434,590	709,600	791,500
1997–98	2,301,520	NA	1,518,840	NA	782,680	NA
1998–99	2,509,050	NA	1,657,250	NA	851,800	NA
Growth rate	13.66		13.81		13.38	

Sources: Figures for 1993–94 to 1996–97 from Sivasubramonian (2000), the rest are from National Accounts Statistics 2000.

Notes: New and old refer to the 1993–94 and 1980–81 series respectively.
NA=Not available.

workforce as the residual of the organised manufacturing has been followed from pre-Independence times till today. The production approach is followed to estimate the contribution from this sector. In each revision, the CSO has included new sets of data wherever available.

ISSUES CONCERNING
THE NEW METHODOLOGY

1. Based on the structural adjustment experience of the Latin American countries, in India too, academicians expected that as a result of liberalisation measures, which favour capital-intensive technology, displacement of labour would take place from the organised to the unorganised sectors (Ghose 1992; Bhalla 1994). Besides this direct displacement, the restructuring of the manufacturing establishments in the 1990s was expected to increase the contracting out of labour intensive jobs to ancillary and small establishments thus increasing the number of self-employed workers. However, the follow-up survey data of the year 1994–95 points out a substantial decline in the workforce with the own-account manufacturing enterprises or the self-employed category (Lalitha 2000). Further, a comparison of the 51st round estimates with the earlier rounds

reveal that the total employment has actually declined from 36.95 to 33.20 million (see Table 5.2). This decline could be attributed to both underestimation as well as inadequate coverage of the self-employed and the contractual workers in the follow-up surveys.

Hence, it was expected that the use of worker participation rates from the NSS employment survey would give a more realistic estimate of the workforce in the unorganised manufacturing sector. The estimate of workforce in the unorganised manufacturing sector as per the new methodology however stands at 37.7 millions. Availability of the workforce estimate based on the methodology adopted in the 1980–81 series, would have enabled a meaningful comparison with the new estimate. Nevertheless, the comparison of the workforce, as per the 1993–94 revision and the follow-up survey estimate, reveals that the new methodology has led to an increase in the workforce in the unorganised manufacturing sector by only 4.5 million.

2. The GVA of the unorganised manufacturing sector estimated by the new methodology stands at Rs 43,6200 million in 1993–94 as against Rs 46,4170 million estimated in the 1980–81 series. This decline in the GVA as per the new series could be attributed to several reasons, which range from the reality of the operation of the industrial sectors, the declining labour productivity and the recession during the 1990s, to the trade liberalisation measures, which largely benefited the organised sector. Perhaps, the restructuring of the financial institutions and the decline in the household savings in the early 1990s largely restricted the availability of the funds to the self-employed, which resulted in the decline of the OAMEs and NDMEs (Lalitha 2000). While the prevailing economic scenario explains one side of the story, the other side could be attributed to the vagaries of the data. In the absence of proper maintenance of books of accounts by the enterprises, the value added figures are just obtained by memory recall and there could be gross underestimation of the value added figures for the fear of paying tax or to avoid compliance with any of the government procedures. Perhaps due to this reason we observe a decline in value added despite the positive growth in employment in wood, paper products and transport equipment (see Table 5.3). Besides, there could be some human errors too in classifying the inputs and outputs in relevant categories leading to errors in estimating the value addition.

3. It has been mentioned in the draft brochure (CSO 1999), that the new series will be moved forward with the help of the Index of Industrial Production 1993–94, where weight is assigned to the unorganised manufacturing sector for the first time.

The weightage has been arrived at by using the data on the DME, NDME and the OAME from the surveys of 1989–90 and 1994–95 (it may be mentioned here that though the 1989–90 data were available prior to the 1994–95 survey, those estimates were not considered for national income estimates). However in the absence of availability of regular monthly production data from the unorganised manufacturing sector, the item basket has been identified on the basis of data from the registered sector only. Further, the source agency responsible for the small-scale sector could not line up the production data for the items of the revised series. As such, the revised IIP has taken into account only the data of 18 items of SSI sector included in the existing series. The new series of IIP would be revised on availability of data on additional items of the small-scale sector. Till such time, the contribution of the unregistered sector, which is growing significantly as compared to the registered sector will not be reflected in the compilation of the revised IIP for want of data from this sector (CSO 1998).

There has been no SSI census conducted after 1987–88, though the follow-up surveys are regularly conducted at an interval of five years. Hence in future also, the reliance will be only on the ASI. Implicitly, in the absence of regular flow of data on the unorganised manufacturing sector, the GVA of the unorganised sector will entirely reflect the trends in the organised sector. This is also evident from Table 5.4, where while the growth of the registered sector from 1993–94 to 1997–98 has been 13.81 per cent per annum that of the unregistered sector has been at the rate of 13.38 per cent per annum. With the declining rate of productivity per worker in the unorganised manufacturing sector (see Tables 5.2 and 5.3), a growth rate that is close to the growth rate of the organised sector suggests the role of the IIP.

The data from ASI also suffer from the problem of non-reporting, which is most likely to have gone up after the liberalisation. Since with a steady decline and deregulation of output and investment controls, there is no incentive for the enterprises to report the details of their functioning to any agency (Nagraj 1999). The press release of the CSO itself reports that

for the registered sector also, the quality of production data suffer from substantial non-response on the part of manufacturing units and consequential estimation resorted to by the agencies … The industrial growth based on the revised IIP do not seem to reflect the perceived ground realities. The quality aspect may have to be improved (CSO 1998: 5).

Nagraj's (1999) correlation coefficients estimated between the growth rates of the IIP and the registered and total manufacturing also bring out the deficiency of the IIP. His correlation analysis done for two overlapping time series data viz., 1970–71 to 1984–85 and 1980–81 to 1995–96 show that while the coefficients are statistically significant in the former period, in the latter period they are not significant, indicating that the IIP has become unrepresentative of the underlying output trends as reflected in the ASI data.

4. Similar to the 1970–71 series where the results of the first Census on Small-Scale industrial units of 1972 were used, in the 1993–94 series too, an attempt has been made to include the results of the SSI Census. However, now the time lag is huge and not only that, in the present economic conditions, the small-scale sector is more dynamic and the turnover rate is also high. Hence, extrapolating the workforce growth at a certain compound rate of growth will not reveal the reality. Further, with the SSI unregistered sector constituting about 92 per cent of the total units in the SSI Census, it is highly possible that this sector overlaps with the Directory Manufacturing Establishments (DMEs) of the unorganised manufacturing sector covered by the follow-up surveys. Keeping in mind the investment criteria used to define the SSI, these unregistered SSI are likely to match with the investments particularly in the DME segment of the unorganised manufacturing sector. Therefore, the GVA per worker of the unregistered SSI sector will naturally have the element of GVA per worker of the unorganised manufacturing sector. On this count we argue that the follow up surveys with the well defined data by type of enterprises viz., OAME, NDME and DME actually offsets the need to use the GVA per worker from the SSI unregistered sector. Nevertheless, inclusion of the unregistered SSI data has increased the total GVA of the unorganised sector as shown in Table 5.5.

Table 5.5
All-India Estimate of the Gross Value Added by the
Unorganised Manufacturing Sector, 1993–94

	Workforce (million)	Total GVA (Rs in million)
Unregistered SSI	2.56	123,476
OAME + NDME + DME	32.67	304,312
		427,788

Source: Calculations based on Tables 5.3 and 5.4 of Kulshreshtha and Singh (1999).

Table 5.6
Share of the Unorganised Manufacturing Sector and the
Unregistered SSI Sector in GVA, 1993–94

Group	GVA of Unorganised Manufacturing Sector		GVA of Unregistered SSI		
	Value in Rs	% Share to total	Value in Rs	% Share to total	Total GVA
Food products	308,006	68.58	141,115	31.42	449,121
Beverages	235,193	91.83	20,934	8.17	256,128
Cotton	465,649	98.85	5,436	1.15	471,086
Silk, wool	62,855	85.36	10,780	14.64	73,635
Jute	30,136	96.33	1,149	3.67	31,285
Textile	169,105	75.95	53,558	24.05	222,663
Wood products	370,897	77.70	106,425	22.30	477,322
Paper products	99,610	57.78	72,785	42.22	172,395
Leather products	94,668	70.41	39,793	29.59	134,461
Chemical products	62,709	26.45	174,369	73.55	237,077
Rubber products	59,921	48.67	63,200	51.33	123,121
Non-metallic	143,263	68.13	67,003	31.87	210,266
Basic metals	58,717	36.40	102,595	63.60	161,312
Metal products	199,482	55.69	158,738	44.31	358,220
Non-electrical	64,862	43.16	85,413	56.84	150,275
Electrical machinery	94,444	56.53	72,620	43.47	167,064
Transport equipment	52,580	63.25	30,555	36.75	83,135
Other manufacturing	391,412	93.26	28,291	6.74	419,703
Repair of capital goods	79,614	100.00	0	0.00	79,614
Total	3,043,127	71.14	1,234,758	28.86	4,277,885

Note: Calculations based on Tables 5.3 and 5.4 of Kulshreshtha and Singh
(1999).

As shown in the panel, the contribution of the unorganised manufacturing sector in 1993–94 (computed using the data given
in Tables 5.3 and 5.4 of Kulshreshtha and Singh 1999) stands at
Rs 427,788 million. Of this, the unregistered SSI accounts for
Rs 123,476 million or 28.86 per cent of the total GVA. Further, in
chemicals, rubber, basic metals and non-electrical, the share of unregistered SSI in total GVA of that sector accounts for 73.6, 51.3, 63.6 and
56.8 per cent respectively and in other sectors also the unregistered
SSIs contribution is sizeable as shown in Table 5.6. Suppose, this GVA

of the unregistered SSI is excluded then the GVA of the unorganised manufacturing sector stands at Rs 304,312 million.

5. Further, the present methodology, which moves forward (1) the GVA per worker of the (SSI unregistered sector part) base year 1987–88 to 1993–94, using the whole sale price index and (2) the workforce in SSI unregistered sector by using the inter-survey growth rates of the unorganised sector bypasses the important changes that would have occurred due to the introduction of structural adjustment programme both in GVA as well as in employment. Further, while the population may grow at an exponential rate, the workforce may not show a compound increase. Given the fact that these data are a decade old and the SSI sector particularly the unregistered SSIs are susceptible to the changing economic situations, use of these data needs to be reconsidered.

6. In the earlier series data from two sources (follow-up surveys and censuses) were used, besides the physical indicators in building up the value added series of the unorganised sector. In contrast in the 1993–94 series, data from different sources, such as the Population Census, the NSS employment survey, the Census of SSI units, the follow-up survey on the unorganised manufacturing sector and the Index of Industrial Production were used, the pros and cons of which are bound to influence the final outcome.

These are some of the issues that need to be addressed when the CSO revises the National Accounts Statistics series in future.

CONCLUSION

Given the growing percentage of the workforce in the unorganised sector, the government is keen to estimate the contribution of this sector to the national income. India is one of the few countries in the world where systematic efforts are made to record the growth of the informal sector. However the range of data collection needs to be improved, to cover all types of informal workers, which will reduce the need to use different sources of data to obtain an estimate of the workforce in this sector. One approach

could be to determine the employment in the informal sector directly through sample survey of the HHs—first identify the workers in the HH through a sample and then determine if they are themselves the own account enterprise or they work in an enterprise that is informal and thereafter by reaching the informal enterprise, estimate the size of the informal sector (Kulshreshtha and Singh 1999: 220).

This method, already tried in the CSO surveys, has yielded better results. The other issue is regarding the underestimation of the value added by the unit. In this context, the suggestion is to collect information on consumer expenditure from the entrepreneur's household.

The estimate of consumer expenditure collected from the respective entrepreneur's household through an abridged schedule should yield a rough estimate of GVA from the enterprises, when allowances have been made for possible underestimation of consumer expenditure through abridged schedules and for the difference between income and expenditure. Data on fixed capital and on remuneration paid to hired employees if any would also throw light on the quality of GVA data (Country Paper 2000).

Apart from the quality of the data on value added per worker, there are some sectors where the productivity is genuinely low but there are certain dynamic sectors within the informal sector whose contribution to national income is sizeable. Therefore government efforts such as credit, subsidy and training programmes should be targeted at these sectors to improve labour productivity.

In the case of the organised sector, while the workforce estimate can be obtained from the ASI and the value added from the National Accounts Statistics, in the case of the unorganised manufacturing sector we can get only the value addition from the NAS. It is suggested that along with the gross value added of the unorganised manufacturing sector, the corresponding official estimate of the workforce should also be published which will be useful for researchers. The use of the SSI Census data and the Index of Industrial Production 1993–94 in estimating the GVA and extrapolating the base year estimate need to be reviewed.

Compared to other countries where the informal sector surveys are limited to the urban areas or capital cities, in India, the unorganised sector surveys cover the whole of India, which itself is a mammoth task. Besides coinciding with the population census, attempts have also been made to revise the series, which is much appreciated. But given the fact that manufacturing within the unorganised sector is an important activity because of its value addition, if some of the concerns that have been raised are taken care of, over a period of time, a realistic picture of this sector will surely emerge.

NOTES

1. In India, in the National Accounts Statistics, the informal sector is approximated by the 'unorganised sector'.
2. Intercensal projections were used for preparing annual estimates of work force till recently.
3. For instance, the index of value of output of paddy and net availability of wheat, sugarcane, oilseeds and pulses at 1980–81 prices with value of output for 1980–81 as weights was used for the food products; value of output of cattle and buffalo hides and goat and sheep skins at 1980–81 prices was used for the leather and leather and fur products; and for electrical machinery, the index of industrial production of the relevant group was used as the indicator.
4. Gross value added estimates based on the survey results of 1984–85, are available in the various volumes of National Accounts Statistics beginning from 1990–91 to 1997–98.

REFERENCES

Bhalla, Sheila (1994), 'Workforce Restructuring Wages and Want: Recent Events, Interpretations and Analysis', *The Indian Journal of Labour Economics*, vol. 39, no.1.

Brigette Du Jeu (1998), 'Contribution of Informal Sector to Employment and Value Added in Selected Countries', Paper presented at the second meeting of the expert group on informal sector statistics, Ankara, 28–30 April 1998.

Central Statistical Organisation (1989), 'Sources and Methods', Government of India, New Delhi, 94.

――― (1998), Press Release on Shifting the Base Year of Index of Industrial Production (IIP) from 1980–81 to 1993–94.

――― (1999), 'Draft Brochure on New Series on National Accounts Statistics (Base year 1993–94),' Government of India, New Delhi.

Country Paper (2000), Measure of Informal Sector: The Indian Experience, India, Fourth Meeting of Expert Group on Informal Sector Statistics, CSO, New Delhi.

Ghose, Ajit K. (1992), 'Economic Restructuring, Employment and Safety Nets: A Note in Social Dimensions of Structural Adjustment in India', Papers and Proceeding of Tripartite Workshop, New Delhi, 10–11 December 1991, ILO, Asian Regional Team for Employment Promotion (ARTEP).

Kulshreshtha, A.C. and Gulab Singh (1996), 'Domestic Product by Gender in the Framework of 1993 SNA', *Economic and Political Weekly*, vol. 31, no. 51.

178 ◆ N. Lalitha

Kulshreshtha, A.C. and Gulab Singh (1999), 'Gross Domestic Product and Employment in the Informal Sector of the Indian Economy', *The Indian Journal of Labour Economics*, vol. 42, no. 2: 223, 227.

Lalitha, N. (1999), 'Women in the Unorganised Manufacturing Sector in India: A Sectoral Analysis', *The Indian Journal of Labour Economics*, vol. 42, no. 4.

——— (2000), 'Unorganised Manufacturing Sector in the National Economy and Gujarat State: An Analysis of its Growth Dynamics and Contribution to National Income', Report No. 6 on Contribution of the Informal Sector to the Economy, National Council of Applied Economic Research.

Mukherjee, M. (1985), 'Contributions to and the Use of Social Product by Women', in Devaki Jain and Nirmala Banerjee (eds), *Tyranny of the Household*, New Delhi: Shakti Books.

Nagraj, R. (1999), 'How Good are India's Industrial Statistics? An Exploratory Note', *Economic and Political Weekly*, vol. 34, no. 6.

Saluja, M.R. (1988), 'Database of the Unorganised Manufacturing Industry: An Appraisal', in K.B. Suri (ed.), *Small Scale Enterprises in Industrial Development: The Indian Experience*, New Delhi: Sage.

Sivasubramonian, S. (2000), 'The National Income of India in the Twentienth Century', New Delhi: Oxford University Press: 287.

Unni, Jeemol (1998), 'Women in the Informal Sector: Size and Contribution to Gross Domestic Product', Working Paper No. 101, Gujarat Institute of Development Research, Ahmedabad.

Savings from Informal Households

BASANTA K. PRADHAN, P.K. ROY AND M.R. SALUJA

INTRODUCTION

In a country such as India, where a major segment of the population draws its livelihood from the informal sector, a study of this sector's important indicators is of great significance. These indicators include the income, savings and investment habits of households, classified by type of activity. Once the indicators are known, it may be possible to introduce specific policy measures to reduce vulnerability in the household informal sector. This study of the saving behaviour of households belonging to the informal sector is an effort to that end. The present paper discusses the empirical findings regarding different facets of savings and investment.

The broad objectives of the study are:

(i) To obtain a profile of the households in the informal sector by type of economic activity and to analyse their pattern of income, savings and investment.
(ii) To study the relation between savings and its determinants.
(iii) To analyse the income and savings pattern of female-headed households.
(iv) To find out the proportion of dissavers and pattern of dissaving.

The household sector occupies a strategic place among various economic units in the country as it contributes substantially to the savings efforts. The earnings of two types of households dominate in the informal/unorganised sector viz., those engaged in self-employment in agricultural/farm and non-farm activities and those engaged in wage earning in the informal sector. Several factors influence the behaviour of savings in the household sector. Some of these are:

- Economic factors like income and its distribution.
- Demographic factors like household size, age structure and marital status of the head, etc.
- Sociological factors like occupation, education level, etc.

All these factors influence the level of savings, as well as its destination. From the policy perspective, it is necessary to know the level and pattern of savings and the degree of substitutability between different forms of savings in order to devise appropriate instruments to influence both the behaviour and rate of savings.

DATABASE AND METHODOLOGY

The estimates of domestic savings in India are compiled and published by the Central Statistical Organisation (CSO). For this purpose the economy is divided into three broad institutional sectors, viz., (i) public sector, (ii) private corporate sector, and (iii) household sector. The savings of the public sector are estimated from budget documents in the case of administration and departmental enterprises and the results of annual accounts of companies and corporations in the case of non-departmental enterprises. Estimates of the savings of the private corporate sector are based on the results of the analysis of Reserve Bank of India (RBI) studies on company finances and other data collected by the RBI. Estimates are prepared separately for non-financial companies and financial institutions.

The household sector comprises, apart from individuals, all non-government, non-corporate enterprises like sole proprietorships and partnerships owned and/or controlled by individuals and non-profit institutions which furnish educational, health, cultural, recreational and other social and community services to households. The savings of the household sector are taken as the sum of this sector's investments in various instruments of financial saving and in the form of physical assets. The savings of households in the form of physical assets, currency and a number of other instruments of financial saving are taken as residuals, i.e., by subtracting the estimates of the public and the private corporate sectors from the corresponding estimates of the entire economy. According to the CSO itself, the estimates of household savings are not satisfactory. The CSO has suggested conducting household surveys to collect direct data on annual investments made by individuals and non-corporate institutions in different categories of financial and physical assets.

The National Council of Applied Economic Research (NCAER), under the Micro Impact of Macro and Adjustment Policies (MIMAP–India) project, conducted a detailed household survey in 1996 with July 1994–June 1995 as the reference year, to obtain the distribution of income and expenditure of households. Data were also collected regarding financial and physical investments of households. This survey collected information from 3,364 rural and 1,492 urban households. A brief description of the sample design and concepts and definitions is given in the appendix. This is perhaps the only all-India household survey on income and expenditure conducted in recent times. The earlier survey on *Household Income and its Disposition* was also conducted by the NCAER in 1975–76. The MIMAP survey is designed to estimate the income and expenditure of households by occupational categories. This survey also collected data on the composition of physical and financial investment by different occupational categories of households, separately for rural and urban areas.

METHODOLOGY OF DATA COLLECTION

It is well known that in any income–expenditure survey there is an inherent under reporting of income. Respondents tend to suppress their income particularly when questions relating to its disposition are not asked. For this purpose, a cash flow statement at the household level (in the MIMAP survey) is prepared to check whether cash inflows during the year match with cash outflows. Similarly, details of all sources of funds and all uses of funds were prepared at the household level to check inconsistencies in the data in the field itself. It was decided to allow ±5 per cent differences in sources and uses of funds due to memory lapses of the respondent. The questionnaire was re-canvassed where the difference exceeded this limit. However, in spite of repeated visits and canvassing, some of the respondents were unable to give the details of the match of sources of funds with the use of funds. For a variety of reasons, this occurred more where the respondents were illiterate, as also at the highest level of income. Such questionnaires were not accepted for analysis. Thus the survey differs from others as it tried to cross-check the gap between sources and uses of funds at the household level. The data collected for the MIMAP survey pertains to the agricultural year 1994–95.

DEFINITION OF INFORMAL SECTOR

According to the System of National Accounts (SNA)—1993, the informal sector consists of units engaged in the production of goods and services, with a low level of organisation, with little or no division between labour and capital, and labour relations based on casual employment and/or social relationships as opposed to formal contracts. These units belong to the household sector, and the owners of these units are personally responsible for all financial and non-financial obligations in the process of production. As per the resolution of the Fifteenth International Conference of Labour Statisticians, January 1993, duly endorsed by the SNA for statistical purposes, the informal sector is regarded as a group of production units which form part of the household sector as household enterprises. Within the household sector the informal sector comprises own-account enterprises and enterprises of informal employees.

According to the concept paper presented by the CSO at the first meeting of the 'Expert Group on Informal Sector Statistics', the SNA 1993 does not provide a clear-cut and precise definition of the term 'informal sector'. Some steps are being taken in the direction of defining this term.

In India, the term 'informal sector' has not, so far, been formally used in the National Accounts Statistics (NAS). Instead, the term used is the 'unorganised' sector. However, researchers often use the term 'informal' in place of the term 'unorganised'. For this study too, we have assumed the informal sector to be the same as the unorganised sector covered in the NAS. According to Kulshreshtha (1997), in the Indian NAS, the unorganised sector refers to a collection of those operating units whose activity is not regulated under any legal provision and/or which do not maintain any regular accounts. The unorganised segment broadly covers all of the agricultural sector except plantation crops, operations of the government irrigation system, minor minerals, unregistered manufacturing units and all units of non-manufacturing activities except those in the public, private corporate and cooperative sector.

SEGREGATING THE INFORMAL SECTOR

The income or value added by unorganised units is distributed among different households. For example, in general, in the agricultural sector, wages are given to agricultural labour households and the rest of the value added goes to the self-employed in the farming sector. Similarly, the value added in the unorganised parts of other activities are divided among different types of households. In the case of the organised sector, under different activities, in addition to the distribution of income among households there is a component of retained profits of the corporate sector and corporate taxes. The households receive all the incomes except retained profits by the corporate sector, and corporate taxes. Based on the MIMAP–India survey, the households have been classified into the following six occupational categories;

(i) self-employment in farm activities
(ii) self-employment in non-farm activities
(iii) agricultural labour
(iv) non-agricultural labour
(v) salaried
(vi) others

A household has been put into an occupational category on the basis of its principal source of income. The total value added, from unorganised segments of different sectors of the economy, has been divided among the above categories of households. Households belonging to the salaried category will, however, receive their income from both the unorganised and the organised segments of different sectors. On the basis of the data available from the survey these households are further divided into two parts: (i) those receiving income from the organised segments and (ii) those receiving income from the unorganised segments. Thus for the first four categories of households, the major share of the income came from the unorganised sector. The total income or value added of the unorganised segments have been distributed mainly among the first four and second part of the fifth category. Some parts of the incomes from organised segments of different sectors will be received by the above categories of the households in the form of secondary income. Also, some part of the income of this segment will go to households of the category 'others' which consists of households that could not be separated into those receiving their incomes from the organised and those from the unorganised segments. These households are included in the informal/unorganised sector.

In spite of some of the incomes of the formal sector being received by the different categories of households (as a secondary source of income), the broad structure of income and other variables of these categories will represent the informal sector. Hence, the total income of the unorganised (informal) sector will be covered by the above categories of households.

EMPIRICAL FINDINGS

The informal sector coverage under this study has been identified as a subset of the household sector. Except for those households whose major source of income originates from salary received from the organised sector, all other households have been defined as working in the informal sector.

The estimated size of the informal sector in terms of population was 91.5 per cent in rural and 56.5 per cent in urban areas. The size of this sector contributed 82.6 per cent of total population at the all-India level. Table 6.1 gives the percentage distribution of households and population by occupational categories in rural and urban areas in the informal and formal sectors. From this table it can be shown that the main source of income for 72 per cent of the population in the informal sector is either self-employed farming or wage-work, at the all-India level. In rural areas this proportion is higher at 81 per cent and in urban areas it is 28 per cent. In the urban informal sector 42 per cent of the population is engaged in self-employed non-farming activities. The family size in the informal sector of the households was comparatively higher at 5.51 compared to 5.41 in the formal. Table 6.2 provides the participation rates defined as the percentage of earners to total population in the informal and formal sectors in rural and urban areas by sex.

In rural areas, the participation rate of members of households in the informal sector is found to be higher than in the formal sector. However, the female participation rate, in urban areas, in the formal sector, is higher than the informal sector. This finding is revealing as it indicates that a majority of female earners prefer to work in the

Table 6.1
Percentage Distribution of Households and Population
by Occupational Category

	Rural		Urban		All-India	
Occupation	House-holds	Population	House-holds	Population	House-holds	Population
S.E. farm	30.59	32.98	1.22	1.68	22.55	25.02
S.E. non-farm	8.62	8.49	22.06	23.70	12.30	12.36
Agr. wage	32.64	31.18	2.21	2.59	24.31	23.91
Non-agr. wage	10.55	9.94	11.27	11.57	10.75	10.35
Others	3.81	3.08	7.83	5.53	4.91	3.70
Salary—Informal	6.04	5.81	11.42	11.47	7.52	7.25
All Informal	92.26	91.47	56.01	56.54	82.34	82.58
Salary—Formal	7.74	8.53	43.99	43.46	17.66	17.42
Total	100.00	100.00	100.00	100.00	100.00	100.00

Table 6.2
Participation Rates by Sex

(per cent)

	Informal			Formal			Total		
	Rural	Urban	All	Rural	Urban	All	Rural	Urban	All
Male	51.2	50.4	51.0	44.4	50.2	48.3	50.7	50.4	50.5
Female	17.0	6.5	15.3	8.7	9.6	9.0	16.2	7.8	14.2
Total	35.1	29.3	34.1	27.9	30.9	29.7	34.4	30.0	33.3

formal sector in urban areas. Work in this sector is organised and thus more secure. In the MIMAP survey, an earner is defined as the member participating in any economic activity. However, economic activities such as making dung cakes, and other home-based activities, may not have been netted in. The proportion of male earners engaged in the informal sector to total male earners is found to be

92.4 per cent in rural and 56.4 per cent in urban areas, while that of female earners was even higher, 96 per cent in rural but less, at 47 per cent, in urban areas.

The percentage of workers at the all-India level in the 1991 Census was reported at 37.5 per cent as against 33.3 per cent based on the MIMAP survey. The participation rate of females is reported to be much lower (14.2 per cent) compared to the 1991 Census figure of 22.3 per cent. However, the participation rate of males was found to be closer at 50.5 per cent, against 51.6 per cent in the 1991 Census. This difference could arise because of the fact that there is a tendency, especially by the male head of the household, not to report their female and child members as earners, unless these members take part regularly in economic activities. Given the invisibility of home-based workers, the underestimation of women's work participation is possibly greatest in the case of urban informal employment. Marginal workers who have taken part in economic activity for a very short duration may also have been left out. The distribution of these earners by their primary economic activity, reveals that more than 95 per cent of earners in rural and 62 per cent in urban areas worked in the informal sector for their livelihood. The distribution of these earners by type of economic activity is given in Table 6.3.

Table 6.3
Percentage Distribution of Earners by Type of
Economic Activity and by Sex

Type of Economic Activity	Rural			Urban			All-India		
	Male	Female	Total	Male	Female	Total	Male	Female	Total
S.E. farm	37.48	23.76	34.41	1.68	4.14	1.99	28.51	20.99	27.00
S.E. non-farm	10.35	3.18	9.75	28.08	9.12	25.72	14.80	4.02	12.65
Agr. wage	28.09	57.12	34.61	1.58	7.39	2.30	21.45	50.19	27.22
Non-agr. wage	11.19	8.44	10.57	11.08	14.12	11.45	11.16	9.24	10.77
Others	1.93	3.32	2.24	8.12	14.84	8.96	3.48	4.94	3.76
Salary—Informal	5.66	2.59	4.98	12.54	6.85	11.84	7.58	3.20	6.55
Salary—Formal	5.30	1.50	4.44	36.92	43.54	37.74	13.02	7.42	12.05
Total	100.00	100.00	100.00	100.00	100.00	100.00	100.00	100.00	100.00

As per the 1991 Census, the distribution of the working population indicates 26.4 per cent as agricultural labour at the all-India level. The census also indicated 21.1 per cent of total male workers and 44.9 per cent of female workers as agricultural labourers. The survey showed that the proportion of female workers had gone up during this period. The MIMAP survey indicates a drop in the proportion of cultivators to total working population, compared to that of the 1991 Census. The survey also revealed that 18.9 per cent of the total earners have a secondary occupation.

SAVINGS IN THE INFORMAL SECTOR

It is common knowledge that in survey research, despite intensive scrutiny at the investigation level itself, information on income and thereby saving is under reported. The saving of the household, in this study is derived by computing the difference between the total income earned by the household from all sources minus the consumption expenditure during the reference period net of tax. Consumption expenditure includes the amount spent by the household on food and non-food items and ceremonies, which includes gifts given in the form of gold and jewellery and consumer durables. Thus the savings in the MIMAP survey includes a part of gold and jewellery and consumer durables purchased for self consumption. The gross income as estimated from the MIMAP survey is found to be around 74 per cent of the personal income provided by the NAS. The differences between these two estimates may possibly be attributed to the following factors:

(i) Certain population groups (belonging to the non-household category and the inaccessible regions) are not covered in the survey. The survey covered around 98 per cent of the total population.

(ii) During surveys income generally tends to be under reported.

(iii) The survey estimates of income do not cover accrued but unrealised income from interest, reimbursements for medical and travel expenses, etc. There are practical difficulties in getting information on the contribution towards provident fund, etc.

(iv) The CSO estimates of domestic product and hence personal income are themselves not based on firm data, specially in the unorganised sectors of the economy. This fact is admitted to by the CSO itself (CSO 1989).

Table 6.4
Share of Expenditure on some of the Major Items
Obtained from MIMAP and NSSO (1994–95)

Items of Expenditure	Rural		Urban	
	MIMAP	NSSO	MIMAP	NSSO
Cereals	22.7	24.3	11.5	14.4
Pulses	5.5	3.7	3.3	3.2
Other food items	31.6	33.0	27.8	35.8
Total food items	59.8	61.0	42.6	53.4
Fuel and light	4.0	7.0	6.7	6.7
Clothing, footwear	11.1	8.0	10.5	6.5
Health	2.8	5.0	2.6	3.4
Education	2.7	1.6	5.6	4.0
Consumer durables	3.1*	5.2	5.3*	4.5
Gold and jewellery	3.6*	Neg.	4.9*	–
Other non-food items	12.9	12.2	21.8	21.5
Total	100.0	100.0	100.0	100.0
Average per capita per month expenditure	350.83	309.43	673.41	508.07

* These items of expenditure are part of savings in the MIMAP survey, but, for the sake of comparability with NSSO, these items are included in consumption expenditure.

The estimated consumption expenditure according to our survey is 80.4 per cent of the corresponding estimate of the NAS. The survey estimates, however, were found to be more than the projected NSS survey estimate of 1994–95. An attempt is made to compare the MIMAP ratio estimates of consumption expenditure and NSSO estimates. Table 6.4 provides the ratio estimates of comparable items of expenditure obtained from the NSSO and MIMAP survey. It is observed that these estimates are closer in rural areas except for health and education. In urban areas the share of other food to total consumption in MIMAP is much lower, although in absolute terms it is Rs 185 per capita per month according to MIMAP against Rs 188 in NSSO.

NCAER had earlier conducted a similar survey of *Household Income and its Disposition* in 1975–76, where estimates of savings included consumer durables, gold and jewellery (which were taken as a part of physical investment and savings). Savings was obtained as:

$$S = (\Delta PA + \Delta FA) - (\Delta L + CT)$$

where,

ΔPA = change in physical assets (acquisition minus liquidation)
ΔFA = change in financial assets (increases minus decreases)
ΔL   = change in liabilities (increase in borrowings minus increase in lendings)
CT   = net inflow of capital transfers (inflow minus outflow)

In the MIMAP survey, due to practical difficulties in collecting data on net inflow of capital transfers, the estimates of saving as the difference of income minus expenditure and the estimate of saving as calculated by the residual method did not match exactly. There was a difference of about 5 per cent in these two estimates. Saving was found to be higher by 5 per cent at an all-India level when it was computed by deducting expenditure from income. Thus, while calculating savings by computing the difference between the change in the value of physical and financial assets adjusted for liabilities, and net inflow of capital transfers, the net inflow of capital transfers, in fact, was derived as residuals.

Of the total gross savings, 50.6 per cent originated in rural households, the contribution by the informal and formal sectors being 41.24 and 9.39 per cent respectively. Thus the rural informal sector contributed 81.4 per cent of rural savings. In urban areas, the informal sector contributed 37.4 per cent of the total urban savings. Rural and urban regions in the informal sector, together contributed 59.7 per cent of the total savings at the all-India level (see Table 6.5).

The average savings of the rural households in the informal sector was Rs 4,464 and that of urban, Rs 8,720, while at the all-India level it was Rs 5,256 (see Table 6.6).

The overall estimated rate of savings in the household sector based on the MIMAP survey is 20.3 per cent. The rates of savings in the informal sector were 17.37 per cent and 19.25 per cent for rural and urban regions respectively. It can be seen from Tables 6.5 and 6.6 that the rate of savings in the informal sector is much lower that that of the households working in the formal sector. This is not surprising as the average income of households (Rs 29,347) in the informal sector is only 45 per cent of the average income of households engaged in the formal sector (Rs 65,276).

As per the CSO, the estimate of household sector savings as a percentage of personal income for the financial year 1994–95 is around 24 per cent which excludes gold, jewellery and consumer durables. The estimate of the savings rate (which partly includes gold,

Table 6.5
Contribution of the Informal and Formal Sectors in Population,
Income and Savings

(in per cent)

	Informal			Formal			All		
	Population	Income	Savings	Population	Income	Savings	Population	Income	Savings
Rural	68.20	48.20	41.24	6.40	7.50	9.39	74.60	55.80	50.64
Urban	14.40	19.50	18.45	11.00	24.80	30.93	25.40	44.20	49.36
All	82.60	67.70	59.69	17.40	32.30	40.32	100.00	100.00	100.00

Table 6.6
Annual Savings per Household and the Rate of
Savings in the Informal and Formal Sectors

	Average Savings (Rs)			Saving Rate (%)		
	Informal	Formal	All	Informal	Formal	All
Rural	4,464	12,114	5,056	17.37	26.34	18.45
Urban	8,720	18,632	13,080	19.25	25.37	22.68
All	5,256	16,557	7,252	17.90	25.36	20.32

Table 6.7
Comparison of the Distribution of Physical and
Financial Savings—CSO and MIMAP

		Physical Savings	Financial Savings
CSO (April 1994–March 1995)		44.30	55.70
MIMAP (July 1994–June 1995)	All-India	39.22	60.78
Excluding gold, jewellery	Rural	54.57	45.43
and consumer durables	Urban	20.93	79.07
MIMAP (July 1994–June 1995)	All-India	49.66	50.34
Excluding consumer	Rural	61.82	38.18
durables	Urban	35.61	64.39
MIMAP (July 1994–June 1995)	All-India	56.92	43.08
including gold, jewellery	Rural	66.50	33.50
and consumer durables	Urban	46.42	53.58

jewellery and consumer durables) is thus much less compared to the CSO. The household savings estimates by the NAS are obtained as residuals for most of the instruments of savings, and, according to the CSO itself, are not satisfactory at all (CSO 1989).

A comparison of the proportion of physical and financial savings based on the MIMAP Survey and CSO estimates revealed that the CSO estimate of the financial savings for the financial year 1994–95 was 55.7 per cent of the total, corresponding to 43.08 based on the MIMAP study. A similar exercise after deducting consumer durables, gold and jewellery from the physical savings in MIMAP increased this percentage to 60.7 per cent at an all-India level (see Table 6.7). The details of the comparison are given in the table.

The proportion of financial savings seemed to be more in urban areas (79 per cent) than in rural areas (45 per cent) excluding investment in gold, jewellery and consumer durables. However, when only consumer durables are excluded, the physical savings in urban areas improves to 35.6 per cent and in rural areas to 61.8 per cent. In all the cases, physical savings was found to be higher in rural areas and financial savings higher in urban areas.

PATTERN OF SAVINGS

The pattern of savings in the informal and the formal sectors differ widely. The households in the informal sector save more in the form of physical assets, while savings in financial assets dominate in the formal sector. This trend is more pronounced in rural than in urban areas. Thus there seem to be diverse patterns in utilisation of savings between the informal and formal sectors, with the informal sector dominantly acquiring physical assets for self use and formal sector savings generally being transferred to other sectors. Physical investment by the informal sector in the rural areas was 71.7 per cent, and in the urban areas it was 57.9 per cent (see Table 6.8).

Table 6.8
Components of Savings by Informal and Formal Sectors

	Change in Investment		Total Investment	Change in Liabilities	Net Inflow of Capital Transfers	Gross Savings
	Physical	Financial				
Informal						
Rural	3,494	1,376	4,870	334	72	4,464
Urban	5,931	4,316	10,247	44	1,483	8,720
All-India	3,947	1,924	5,871	280	335	5,256
Formal						
Rural	4,638	6,900	11,538	−554	−22	12,114
Urban	6,227	10,404	16,626	−205	−1,801	18,632
All-India	5,717	9,288	15,005	−316	−1,236	16,557
Total						
Rural	3,582	1,804	5,386	266	64	5,056
Urban	6,059	6,994	13,053	−65	38	13,080
All-India	4,260	3,225	7,485	175	58	7,252

It can be pointed out that a net increase in borrowing is more prominent in the households working in the informal sector than those in the formal sector, where the lending is more. The net inflow of the capital transfers is found to be higher in the informal households. The estimates show that the change in liability of informal sector households in rural and urban India is positive. This is a liability of the rural household sector compared with other sectors such as urban households, cooperatives, banks etc. It also shows that the net inflow of capital transfers is negative in the formal sector, indicating a net outflow of capital items from formal to informal sector households. The investment in physical and financial assets taken together is found to be 21 per cent of the total income in 1994–95. More than two-thirds of the investment in the informal sector came from physical investment while it was the reverse in the formal sector. It should be pointed out that the physical investment in MIMAP includes gold, jewellery and consumer durables.

A comparison of the results of the MIMAP survey with that of the 1975–76 survey with similar concepts and definitions is in Table 6.9.

The comparison revealed that not much change in the share of physical and financial investment to total investment, is observed at the all-India level during the last two decades, but there has been a significant increase in the preference for financial investment in rural areas in the MIMAP study compared to the 1975–76 study, and a preference for physical investment which, in urban areas, was only 21 per cent in 1975–76 compared with 46 per cent observed in 1994–95.

Table 6.10 provides the distribution of physical and financial investment in the informal and formal sectors, in rural and urban areas, after excluding only consumer durables and after excluding both consumer durables and gold and jewellery from physical investment.

Table 6.9
Comparison of Physical and Financial Investment
(1975–76) and MIMAP Surveys

	MIMAP (1994–95)			1975–76 Survey		
	Physical	Financial	Total	Physical	Financial	Total
Rural	66.50	33.50	100.0	76.2	23.8	100.0
Urban	46.42	53.58	100.0	20.9	79.1	100.0
All	56.92	43.08	100.0	56.8	43.2	100.0

Table 6.10
Percentage Distribution of Physical and Financial Investment
in Informal and Formal Sectors

Physical Investment Excluding Consumer Durables	Informal		Formal	
	Physical	Financial	Physical	Financial
Rural	68.15	31.85	27.69	72.31
Urban	48.18	51.82	26.15	73.85
All-India	62.04	37.96	26.52	73.48

Physical Investment Excluding Both Consumer Durables, Gold and Jewellery	Informal		Formal	
	Physical	Financial	Physical	Financial
Rural	62.81	37.99	4.10	95.90
Urban	37.50	62.50	8.04	91.96
All-India	55.24	44.76	7.14	92.86

The pattern of savings by occupational categories, and the rate of saving, is given in Annexure Table 6.1. It can be pointed out that the 'others' category of households whose major sources of income are rent, interest and dividend etc., and the salaried households report more inflows of capital transfer, thereby reducing their savings. The households in the agricultural wages category have the least investments, both of physical and financial, with a tilt towards financial savings. The saving rate is highest in the self-employed non-farm households, in the informal sector, working in business, arts and crafts, and professionals. Their income is also found to be higher than the other groups of households in the informal sector. The highest average income is reported in the households working in the formal sector, both in the rural and urban sectors.

COMPOSITION OF INCOME

The household sector, both informal and formal, derives its income from several types of activities, which are given below

- Farming, i.e., agriculture and allied pursuits
- Non-farming such as business, crafts and professions
- Agricultural wages

- Non-agricultural wages
- Salaried work
- Other sources

As expected, the importance of the sources differ between households working in the informal and the formal sector. While 86 per cent of total household income in rural areas originated from the informal sector, in urban areas this was found to be only 44 per cent. At the all-India level, 67.7 per cent of the total income, originated in the 82.3 per cent of the households working in the informal sector.

An attempt is made to estimate the income accruing from the formal sector of these households in the informal sector. Some members of the households in the informal sector deriving the major part of its income from the unorganised sector, also work in the organised sector. Their contribution is found to be 1.3 per cent of the total income in rural and 2.8 per cent in urban areas. Thus an overall 1.73 per cent of the total income in informal sector households came through organised salaried work. An income of around 16 per cent is reported to have come from informal sector activities in the households in the formal sector, whose major income came from the salary (organised) work, at an all-India level. The percentage distribution of income by sources of income in the informal and formal sector in rural and urban areas is given in Table 6.11.

PATTERN OF PHYSICAL INVESTMENT IN INFORMAL AND FORMAL SECTOR

Informal sector households accounted for 76 per cent of physical investment in the household sector. The share of physical investment in the informal sector in rural areas was found to be 90 per cent while that in urban areas was 55 per cent (see Table 6.12).

Of the rural physical investments in the informal sector, 53.2 per cent went to farm assets, which include land improvement, machinery and equipment, livestock assets, inventories etc. The corresponding share in urban physical investment was 9.5 per cent. The major component of urban physical investment in the informal sector was consumer durables (32 per cent), house property (25 per cent) and gold and jewellery (24 per cent) whereas the rural households invested more in gold and jewellery (17.8 per cent) followed by consumer durables (15.7 per cent) and house property (12.8 per cent) (see Table 6.13). It may be noted that according to National

Table 6.11
Source of Income by Informal and Formal Sectors

	Farm	Nom-farm	Salary—Formal	Salary—Informal	Agr. Wage	Non-agr. Wage	Others	Total
Rural								
Informal	39.73	12.62	1.30	5.90	23.24	8.70	8.51	100.0
Formal	7.48	1.80	82.89	–	1.37	0.24	6.21	100.0
Total	35.37	11.16	12.31	5.11	20.29	7.56	8.20	100.0
Urban								
Informal	2.88	45.33	2.82	12.45	1.65	10.80	24.12	100.0
Formal	0.81	1.51	84.55	–	0.03	0.29	12.81	100.0
Total	1.72	20.74	48.70	5.47	0.74	4.94	17.78	100.0
All-India								
Informal	29.14	29.99	1.73	7.79	17.04	9.32	13.00	100.0
Formal	2.36	1.58	84.16	–	0.34	0.28	11.27	100.0
Total	20.48	15.40	28.36	5.27	11.65	6.40	12.44	100.0

Table 6.12
Share of Physical Investment in Informal and Formal Sectors

	Informal	Formal	All
Rural	90.00	10.00	100.00
Urban	54.83	45.17	100.00
All-India	76.29	23.71	100.00

Table 6.13
Percentage Distribution of Physical Investment in
Informal and Formal Sectors

Components of Physical Investment	Informal			Formal		
	Rural	Urban	All-India	Rural	Urban	All-India
Farm assets	53.24	9.45	40.98	-8.75	-0.25	-2.44
Business	0.47	9.57	3.02	-	7.83	5.81
House property	12.83	24.65	16.14	15.51	7.05	9.13
Gold and jewellery	17.77	23.99	19.51	50.57	44.58	46.12
Consumer durables	15.69	32.34	20.35	43.00	40.79	41.38
Total	100.00	100.00	100.00	100.00	100.00	100.00

Sample Survey Organisation (NSSO) and CSO both consumer durables and gold and jewellery are part of consumption expenditure and not saving. At the all-India level for the households engaged in the informal sector the other important items of physical investment seem to be consumer durables and gold and jewellery followed by house property.

The details of the components of investment by type of economic activities are given in Table 6.1 in Appendix 6.

PATTERN OF FINANCIAL INVESTMENTS IN INFORMAL AND FORMAL SECTORS

The share of financial investment in the informal sector accounted for 49 per cent at the all-India level. The share of rural areas was

Table 6.14
Share of Financial Investment in Informal and Formal Sectors

	Informal	Formal	All
Rural	70.39	29.61	100.00
Urban	34.56	65.46	100.00
All-India	49.12	50.88	100.00

Table 6.15
Percentage Distribution of Composition of Financial Investment

Components of Financial Investment	Informal			Formal		
	Rural	Urban	All-India	Rural	Urban	All-India
Provident fund/PPF	1.26	1.46	1.36	27.22	36.32	34.17
Deposits	69.43	60.92	65.88	52.27	47.00	48.25
Shares and units	4.89	9.75	6.92	0.49	1.21	1.04
Chit fund	5.13	11.91	7.96	2.15	1.24	1.46
LIC	3.74	9.52	6.15	10.53	8.56	9.03
Others	15.54	6.41	11.73	7.34	5.67	6.06
Total	100.00	100.00	100.00	100.00	100.00	100.00

70.4 per cent compared to the contribution of 34.6 per cent by urban areas (see Table 6.14). Both rural and urban households in the informal and formal sectors favoured deposits and small savings with commercial banks and post offices as the major component. At the all-India level the investment was 65.9 per cent, while the rural and urban areas showed an investment of 69.4 and 60.9 per cent respectively. Financial investment in 'other' forms of saving was the second best at the all-India level and in rural areas, while in urban areas the chit fund at 11.9 per cent was the second best. Provident fund/public provident fund seem to be the second major form of financial savings in the formal sector (see Table 6.15).

DISTRIBUTION OF HOUSEHOLDS BY SEX OF THE HEAD OF THE HOUSEHOLD

Households were classified by the sex of the head of the household. Female-headed households constitute 7.3 per cent of total households in the informal sector at the all-India level while in the formal sector it was lower at 5.9 per cent. The saving-income ratio of the female-headed households in the informal sector was found to be lower (10.8 per cent) than that of the male-headed households (17.8 per cent) at an all-India level. The savings rate in female-headed households in the urban informal and formal sectors is found to be much higher than that of the male-headed households (see Table 6.16).

In the informal sector the male-headed households preferred to invest in farm assets as physical investment to the extent of 41.88 per cent followed by gold and jewellery (19.50 per cent), while the female preference was for consumer durables (41.37 per cent) at the all-India level. However, in the formal sector, both male and female-headed households preferred investing in gold and jewellery (45.58 per cent), closely followed by consumer durables. About 50 per cent of the total physical investment in the rural informal sector by both male and female-headed households was dominated by farm assets. In urban areas both male and female-headed households preferred consumer durables. While male-headed households invested 29.6 per cent, the female counterpart investment was as high as 50.98 per cent in the urban informal sector (see Table 6.17).

In the case of financial investment both the male and female-headed households distinctly showed a preference for deposits in commercial banks and post offices etc. in the informal as well as formal sectors. However, while the male-headed households had a second preference for 'others' which includes cash at the all-India level (12 per cent), the female-headed households preferred units, shares and securities (22.56 per cent) in the informal sector. In the formal sector provident fund was the second best investment for both (see Table 6.2 in Appendix 6).

DISSAVERS/SAVERS IN INFORMAL SECTOR

The dissavers in this study are defined as those households whose total consumption expenditure exceed or equals the total income from all sources during 1994–95. Nearly one-fifth (20.18 per cent) of the total households at an all-India level are found to be dissavers (see Table 6.18). The informal sector covered 93 per cent of the total dissavers while only 7 per cent of the dissavers are found in the formal sector. The rural informal sector accounted for 79.1 per cent of the total dissavers in the country. In the rural areas 23.82 per cent

Table 6.16
Distribution of Households by Average Income, Saving Rate and Sex of the
Head in the Informal and Formal Sectors

Sex of Head	Informal				Formal			
	Per cent of Household	Avg. Income	Avg. Saving	Saving Rate	Per cent of Household	Avg. Income	Avg. Saving	Saving Rate
Rural								
Male	92.76	26,207	4,652	17.75	95.38	47,114	11,794	25.03
Female	7.24	19,186	2,062	10.75	4.62	62,295	18,732	30.07
All	100.00	25,695	4,464	17.37	100.00	47,815	12,114	25.34
Urban								
Male	92.56	44,840	8,332	18.58	93.46	73,823	18,383	24.90
Female	7.44	50,988	13,536	26.55	6.54	67,862	22,194	32.70
All	100.00	45,298	8,720	19.25	100.00	73,473	18,632	25.36
All-India								
Male	92.72	29,670	5,336	17.98	94.08	65,201	16,256	24.93
Female	7.28	25,240	4,246	16.82	5.92	66,481	21,335	32.09
All	100.00	29,348	5,256	17.91	100.00	65,276	16,557	25.34

Table 6.17
Percentage Distribution of Physical Investment by
Sex of the Head of the Household

Rural

Components of Physical Investment	Informal		Formal		All	
	Male	Female	Male	Female	Male	Female
Farm assets	53.50	55.31	-12.13	56.34	46.77	55.53
Business	0.46	0.99	–	–	0.42	0.77
House property	12.82	13.31	15.89	–	13.12	10.38
Gold and jewellery	17.58	6.95	51.32	35.96	21.23	13.34
Consumer durables	15.60	23.46	44.92	7.69	18.46	19.98
All	100.00	100.00	100.00	100.00	100.00	100.00

Urban

Components of Physical Investment	Informal		Formal		All	
	Male	Female	Male	Female	Male	Female
Farm assets	10.60	6.18	-0.46	3.42	5.59	4.98
Business	10.55	–	8.57	–	9.65	–
House property	24.90	22.27	6.43	13.66	16.52	18.55
Gold and jewellery	24.34	20.57	43.50	56.00	33.04	35.88
Consumer durables	29.61	50.98	41.96	26.92	35.20	40.59
All	100.00	100.00	100.00	100.00	100.00	100.00

All-India

Components of Physical Investment	Informal		Formal		All	
	Male	Female	Male	Female	Male	Female
Farm assets	41.88	23.35	-3.66	12.23	31.43	19.16
Business	3.13	0.35	6.29	–	3.86	0.22
House property	16.01	19.14	8.95	11.39	14.39	16.25
Gold and jewellery	19.50	15.81	45.58	52.68	25.48	29.54
Consumer durables	19.47	41.37	42.84	23.72	24.85	34.82
All	100.00	100.00	100.00	100.00	100.00	100.00

Table 6.18
Percentage Distribution of Dissaver and Saver Households
in the Informal Sector

	Rural		Urban		All-India	
	Dissavers	Savers	Dissavers	Savers	Dissavers	Savers
Informal	23.82	76.18	18.29	71.71	22.80	77.20
Formal	8.05	91.95	7.97	91.03	8.00	92.00
All	22.60	77.40	13.75	86.25	20.18	79.82

Table 6.19
Average Saving per Household

(in rupees)

Average Saving	Rural		Urban		All-India	
	Dissavers	Savers	Dissavers	Savers	Dissavers	Savers
Informal	−3,987	4,666	−7,774	8,996	−4,556	5,519
Formal	−5,646	12,680	−11,594	19,241	−9,687	17,154
All	−4,035	5,404	−8,776	13,805	−4,929	7,888

were reported as dissaver households in the informal sector against 8.05 per cent in the formal sector. The proportion of dissavers in the urban informal sector was much lower, at 18.3 per cent, than in the rural informal sector. The survey reveals that every fourth household dissaves in the rural informal sector.

The annual per household dissaving was Rs −3,987 in the informal sector in rural areas, while the formal sector had a higher dissaving of Rs −5,646 (see Table 6.19).

Investment in the physical and financial components by dissavers and savers in the informal and formal sectors is presented in the following tables. In the area of physical investment, while the dissavers disinvested in gold and jewellery and house property in the informal sector, the formal sector dissaved in all the asset areas except consumer durables (see Table 6.20).

On the financial investment front, the household dissaved both in deposits in commercial banks, post offices and in units, shares and securities, in the informal as well as the formal sector. The average dissaving in financial investment in the informal and formal sector

Table 6.20
Average Physical Investment by Dissaver and Saver Households, all-India

Components of Physical Investment	Informal		Formal		All	
	Dissavers	Savers	Dissavers	Savers	Dissavers	Savers
Farm assets	344	2,002	–958	–63	253	1,582
Business assets	15	150	–	361	14	193
House property	–169	875	–394	602	–185	819
Gold and jewellery	–270	1,077	–3,107	3,136	–469	1,497
Consumer durables	294	954	625	2,517	317	1,272
All components	221	5,048	–3,834	6,548	–63	5,353

Table 6.21
Average Financial Investment by Dissaver and Saver Households, all-India

Components of Financial Investment	Informal		Formal		All	
	Dissavers	Savers	Dissavers	Savers	Dissavers	Savers
Provident fund	6	32	1,121	3,352	84	708
Deposits	–610	1,822	–2,802	5,114	–763	2,492
Shares and securities	–111	205	–2,231	299	–260	224
Chit fund	195	141	70	141	186	141
LIC	82	129	293	886	97	283
Others	58	275	–6	612	53	344
All components	–381	2,604	–3,555	10,405	–603	4,192

was Rs –381 and Rs –3,555 respectively at the all-India level (see Table 6.21).

An analysis of dissavers by occupational categories revealed a higher concentration of dissavers in agriculture wage earning households, followed by self-employed farm and non-agriculture wage earning households. About 50 per cent of dissavers are reported from wage earning (both agricultural and non-agricultural) households alone (see Table 6.22).

Table 6.22
Percentage Distribution of Households by Dissavers/Savers
and Occupation Group

(percentage)

Occupational Group	Rural		Urban		All-India	
	Dissavers	Savers	Dissavers	Savers	Dissavers	Savers
Farming	32.10	33.48	1.37	2.36	27.51	27.35
Non-farming	5.16	10.35	28.84	41.74	8.70	16.78
Agr. wage	41.32	33.59	11.16	2.33	36.65	27.43
Non-agr. wage	13.32	10.85	17.85	20.63	13.99	12.78
Others	3.69	4.27	21.03	12.40	6.28	5.87
Salary—Informal	4.61	7.16	19.75	20.54	6.87	9.79
Total informal	100.00	100.00	100.00	100.00	100.00	100.00
Informal sector	97.24	90.80	74.49	53.06	93.00	79.64
Formal Sector	2.76	9.20	25.51	46.94	7.00	20.36

SAVINGS BY PER CAPITA INCOME IN THE INFORMAL SECTOR

The distribution of households in the informal sector by per capita income indicated a steady increase in the per capita savings and the saving rate. On an average, a dissaving is reported by 28 per cent of the households with a per capita monthly income below Rs 250 in the informal sector. Households with a threshold per capita monthly income of more than Rs 250 to Rs 300 a year, reported a marginal saving rate of 5 per cent at the all-India level. This level of income in the urban areas was not sufficient for the household to save, and it had in fact, shown a marginal dissaving, but in rural areas a marginal positive saving of 6.5 per cent was reported. The rate of saving at the higher level of income in rural areas was higher compared to urban areas, although the proportion of households in the higher income bracket was much greater in urban areas. The household's saving per capita seemed to depend largely on the per capita income of the household (see Appendix Table 6.3).

APPENDIX 6

SAMPLE DESIGN

Over the years NCAER has conducted a number of household surveys to estimate household income, savings and consumption, both in rural and urban parts of the country, through a three-stage stratified design, with the district, village and household as first, second and final stage units in rural areas and towns, blocks and households in urban areas. On the basis of the earlier studies and the cost factor, it was decided to select a sample of around 5,000 households for the MIMAP survey, which would be adequate to yield an estimate of average household income with a reasonable margin of error. These studies suggested that the major component of sample error was contributed by variations between the first stage units of selection, of districts in rural areas and towns in urban areas. The contribution due to variations between households within a village or a block was quite small, suggesting the possibility of a significant improvement in precision through an increase in the number of first and second stage units of selection without increasing the overall sample size. Keeping this in view, it was decided to select a larger number of first and second stage units for the MIMAP survey, relative to the earlier surveys.

ALLOCATION OF RURAL AND URBAN SAMPLE

According to the 1991 population census, 25.7 per cent of the population was found to live in urban areas in India. A proportional allocation on this basis would suggest a sample size of 1,285 urban and 3,725 rural households. A more efficient way of allocation would, however, be on the basis of the relative variance of income in two regions rather than a proportional one. Taking a cue from the earlier study, the optimal allocation of the samples for rural and urban areas were worked out as 3,400 and 1,600 households respectively. Since the most important characteristics of the present study is to estimate income distribution at rural/urban/all-India level, it was decided to select a sample of 3,400 rural households and 1,600 urban households.

In any large scale survey, where data are to be collected from a number households, a few non-responses are inevitable, due either to absence, non-cooperation or unwillingness of respondents to give information. There are two possible ways of tackling non-responses, viz.,

- by substituting households with similar households in the sample,
- by increasing the initial sample size to provide for possible non-response, so that the effective sample size would be around the required level.

The latter approach is adopted in this study.

Based on the experience of earlier surveys where the non-responses ranged between 8 to 10 per cent, a sample of 3,666 households from rural and 1,757 households from urban areas were selected for the study to cover an effective sample of 5,000 households.

The study covered more than 98 per cent of the population covering all the States and Union territories of India excluding Jammu and Kashmir, Mizoram, Andaman and Nicobar Islands, Lakshadweep and Dadra and Nagar Haveli.

RURAL AREAS

A three-stage sample design was adopted to select the households with the first and second stage units as districts and villages respectively. In each state, 50 per cent of the districts covered by the Human Development Indicators (HDI) Survey, 1993, were selected for this study by adopting a systematic random sampling technique. For each selected district, a random sample of four villages was selected from among the villages selected for the HDI survey. From each selected village, roughly 50 per cent of the households of the HDI Survey were selected from each category (as defined by HDI Survey) of households, with the condition that at least one household of each existing category is selected. A total of 392 villages were selected for this study.

URBAN AREAS

In all, 53 towns were selected for this survey. These towns formed a sub-sample of the towns selected for the Market Information Survey of Households (MISH), 1993 study. The towns were selected in such a manner that, as far as feasible, in each state one town is selected from each town-size category. All the four metropolitan cities were selected for the survey. The total number of blocks were allocated to towns by giving higher samples to towns in a higher size category. The blocks from each town were selected randomly from the MISH blocks. For each selected block the list of households was available in the listing for the MISH study according to income classes. Households were selected from each income category in such a way as to give a higher relative sampling fraction to higher income households (because of larger variation in higher income households). Nine households were selected from each block so as to achieve the required sample.

The effective number of households selected for the analysis were 3,364 in rural and 1,492 in urban areas; the non-response was found to be 8.2 per cent in rural and 15.1 per cent in urban areas. The rate of non-response in an earlier survey of income and its disposition in 1976, was 6.6 per cent and was 11.1 per cent in rural and urban areas respectively. The percentage margins of error, for the estimate of per household and per capita income, were worked out for both rural and urban areas. The margin of error per household and per capita income, worked out from the MIMAP Survey in rural households, was 3.2 per cent and 3.1 per cent respectively, while for urban households it was 5.8 per cent and 6.2 per cent respectively.

CONCEPTS AND DEFINITIONS

Sampling Unit: The household unit of the study is defined as a composition of persons living in the same dwelling unit, sharing food from a common kitchen. The number of members in the household thus defined above, constituted the household size.

Head of the Household: The person, male or female, who takes all major decisions related to the household activities is recognised as the Head of the Household.

Reference Period: In view of the predominance of rural households in the country, and agriculture being the dominant activity, Agriculture year, July 1994 to June 1995, was adopted as the accounting period for the study.

Household Income: Household income is defined as the sum of earnings of all members of the household, from all sources of income during the reference period.

The various sources of income of the household are categorised as:

Self-employment in farming
Self-employment in Non-farming
Salary
Agriculture wages

Non-agriculture wages
Others

Farming activity for the study covered cultivation, plantations, and other allied agricultural activities, such as orchards, sericulture, forestry, bee-keeping, fishery, piggery, poultry and livestock.

Income from self-employment in farming, i.e., agriculture and allied pursuits, is obtained by deducting from the total gross receipts or value of output (including by-products) from agriculture, animal husbandry, poultry, bee-keeping etc., all the paid out operating expenses incurred by the household to obtain the gross receipts during the reference period. The value of the output from a crop is derived as follows:

If a farmer has not sold any part of his output, the entire output is valued at the farm harvest prices. If a farmer has sold a part of his output and retained the other, then the actual value of the part sold plus the value of the output retained by him at farm harvest prices, is taken as the total value of his agricultural produce. In the case of by-products, their value as indicated by the farmer, has been adopted. From the gross receipts from agriculture, thus obtained, operating expenses for the production of crops (e.g., cost of seeds, fertiliser, manure, hired labour, irrigation charges, marketing charges, land revenue etc.) have been deducted. It may be relevant to note that imputed value of family labour employed in the production crops is neither treated as imputed income nor as part of the current operating expenses incurred by the farmer. Gross income from self-employment in farming is derived by adding the income from crops and other agricultural activities.

Non-farm activity comprised business/trade, crafts like blacksmithy, goldsmithy, weaving and professions such as doctors, lawyers, etc. Gross income under this category is accounted for separately for the purpose of analysis, by deducting from the gross receipts any operating expenses incurred by them during the reference year.

Income from salaries received by the members of a household is shown separately for analysis if they are employed on a regular salary payment basis during the reference period. It may be noted that the salary income includes the basic pay plus allowances, bonus, commission, other receipts and also employer's contribution to the provident fund, if any.

Income from wages earned by members of a household working as agricultural and non-agricultural labourers include both the cash receipts as well as the imputed value of the payments in kind (such as meals, crop produce, etc.) received during the period they worked as labourers.

All other sources of income like house property, current transfers etc. are put under 'Others' category. Gross income from house property is derived by deducting the current expenses incurred for maintenance of the residential building including house tax paid, if any, during the reference period from the income from the house property which includes actual rent received by the household, if any, as well as the imputed value of the rental income of the house property owned and occupied by the household. Income received by the members of the household from other sources such as interest, dividends, pensions and regular receipts is also included.

The algebraic sum of income from self-employment in farming (SEF), self-employment in non-farming (SENF), salaries, agricultural wages, non-agricultural wages and other sources received by all the members in a household is defined as the gross income of the household during the reference year.

Household Investment: For an individual economic unit, acquisition of all income-generating assets, physical and financial assets, were covered under household investment.

Physical Investment comprised both fixed assets and inventories. The various items of fixed assets covered in the study were:

- Farm assets like land improvement, irrigation assets, farm machinery and equipment, other farm assets like bullock cart, livestock assets.
- Business assets like building, plant and machinery and other assets like transport equipment.
- House property, both residential and non-residential.
- Gold and jewellery.
- Consumer durables.

Investment in each fixed asset was estimated for the household as Purchase/Construction – Sales + Additions/Improvements + Net inflow of transfers.

Inventories were covered for farm, business and livestock. The value of change in the volume of inventories for both farm and non-farm activities was estimated by taking into account the opening stock and all receipts and outgoing stock during the reference period. In livestock, births and deaths were taken into account in computing the change in inventory.

Financial Investment: The change in the value of financial assets held by the household during the reference period was regarded as its financial investment. The various components of financial investment considered for the study were:

- Deposits with commercial banks, cooperatives, companies and post offices including small saving instruments.
- Shares and Securities in companies including Unit Trust of India.

- Contributions to provident fund.
- Contributions to chit funds.
- Premium paid to Life Insurance Corporation.
- Others include currency holdings.

In provident fund, both the employee's and employer's contributions were regarded as household savings. In estimating financial investment of the household, only gross contributions were considered. Liabilities were estimated by taking the net change in borrowings and lendings of the household as well as outstanding payments to be made for purchases and advances received for sale of assets. Savings of the household were obtained by computing the difference between the total income earned by the household from all sources minus consumption expenditure net of tax.

Consumption: Expenditure on consumption is an essential part of the household. Items of consumption covered for the study were:

- Cereals
- Pulses
- Other food items
- Clothing and foot wear
- Fuel and light
- Ceremonies
- Health
- Education
- Other non-food items
- Imputed rental value of owner occupied houses

Consumption of food items comprises cereals, pulses and other food items. Apart from regular items of cereals and pulses, 'other food items' category include such items as edible oils, vegetables, meat products, milk and milk products, sugar, confectionery, beverages, etc. Clothing consists of cloth for garments, readymade garments, hosiery items, tailoring charges, bedding, footwear and others. Consumption of fuel includes both commercial fuels like kerosene, soft-coke, charcoal, gas, electricity and non-commercial fuels like firewood, twigs, crop waste etc. Non-commercial fuels are purchased as well as collected by a household. Where a household reported collection of such fuels, the imputed value of the quantity collected was considered.

Ceremonies are of regular and irregular expenditure in nature. However, every household spends some part of its income on ceremonies such as performing marriages, celebrating festivals and other functions. The gifts given by the household in the form of cash, gold and jewellery, consumer durables etc. are also covered under expenditure on ceremonies for this study. Expenditure on health covers the amount spent on doctor's fees, purchase of medicines, hospital/nursing home charges, transport expenses for visiting a hospital/doctor etc. Education expenditure on the children incurred by the household, includes school/college fees, books and stationery, uniform, hostel and mess charges, transport expenses etc. Apart from the above items of consumption expenditure, a household spends some proportion of its income regularly on non-food items.

Non-food items covered for the study includes expenditure on toiletry/cosmetics, furnishings, intoxicants, entertainment, hotels/restaurants, house rent, payment to domestic servants, barber, dhobi, travel expenses and other non-food items such as repairs of durables.

Table 6.1
Components of Investment per Household by Activities

	Change in Physical Assets	Change in Financial Assets	Change in Liabilities	Net Inflow of Capital Transfers	Total	Rate of Savings
Rural						
S.E. farm	7,146	1,827	656	1,227	7,090	21.91
S.E. non-farm	6,489	5,011	307	–1,363	12,556	31.86
Agr. wage	402	405	85	–496	1,218	6.76
Non-agr. wage	657	463	52	–27	1,095	6.08
Others	2,584	152	1,164	–904	2,476	9.29
Salary—Informal	2,959	1,519	61	125	4,292	16.05
Total informal	3,494	1,376	334	72	4,464	17.37
Formal	4,638	6,900	–554	–22	12,114	25.34
All	3,582	1,804	266	64	5,056	18.45
Urban						
S.E. farm	4,044	3,497	–109	–7,880	15,530	27.37
S.E. non-farm	11,695	5,508	596	1,989	14,618	24.05
Agr. wage	295	644	–174	1,144	–31	–0.15
Non-agr. wage	1,188	1,112	31	–442	2,711	10.20
Others	2,484	10,493	449	3,020	9,508	17.67
Salary—Informal	3,134	1,737	–1,227	2,420	3,678	11.65
Total informal	5,931	4,316	44	1,483	8,720	19.25
Formal	6,227	10,404	–205	–1,801	18,632	25.37
All	6,059	6,994	–65	38	13,080	22.68
All-India						
S.E. farm	7,100	1,853	645	1,092	7,216	22.05
S.E. non-farm	9,045	5,255	449	283	13,568	27.19
Agr. wage	399	411	79	–456	1,187	6.56
Non-agr. wage	809	649	46	–147	1,559	7.62
Others	2,540	4,667	852	809	5,546	14.40

	Change in Physical Assets	Change in Financial Assets	Change in Liabilities	Net Inflow of Capital Transfers	Total	Rate of Savings
Salary— Informal	3,032	1,610	−475	1,080	4,037	14.04
Total informal	3,947	1,924	280	335	5,256	17.91
Formal	5,717	9,288	−316	−1,236	16,557	25.36
All	4,260	3,225	175	58	7,252	20.32

Table 6.2
Percentage Distribution of Financial Investment by
Sex of the Head of the Household

Financial Investment Components	Informal		Formal		All	
	Male	Female	Male	Female	Male	Female
Rural						
Provident fund	1.33	0.23	29.73	8.32	9.40	3.76
Deposits	70.55	53.08	47.58	87.50	64.03	68.10
Shares and securities	4.72	7.40	0.44	0.91	3.50	4.57
Chit fund	4.56	13.53	2.30	1.33	3.92	8.07
LIC	3.44	8.19	11.81	0.91	5.81	5.01
Others	15.40	17.57	8.14	1.33	13.34	10.48
Total	100.00	100.00	100.00	100.00	100.00	100.00
Urban						
Provident fund	1.32	3.01	36.58	33.25	24.65	20.49
Deposits	62.42	48.22	46.67	50.93	52.00	49.78
Shares and securities	6.72	35.31	1.13	2.20	3.02	16.17
Chit fund	12.43	7.49	1.25	1.13	5.03	3.81
LIC	10.02	5.25	8.61	7.92	9.09	6.79
Others	7.09	0.72	5.76	4.59	6.21	2.96
Total	100.00	100.00	100.00	100.00	100.00	100.00
All-India						
Provident fund	1.33	1.74	35.01	25.21	18.42	14.03
Deposits	67.25	50.44	46.88	62.71	56.91	56.86
Shares and securities	5.53	22.56	0.97	1.78	3.22	11.68
Chit fund	7.76	10.25	1.49	1.10	4.58	5.46
LIC	6.11	6.59	9.35	5.66	7.75	6.10
Others	12.02	8.42	6.30	3.54	9.12	5.86
Total	100.00	100.00	100.00	100.00	100.00	100.00

Table 6.3
Distribution of Households in the Informal Sector by Monthly
Per capital Income and their Income and Savings

(in percent)

Per capita Income	HH	Income	Savings	Saving Rate
Rural				
Upto Rs 150	7.45	3.00	-3.12	-18.06
151–200	12.10	6.57	-0.94	-2.50
201–250	12.82	8.11	-0.45	-0.96
251–300	11.80	8.82	3.35	5.60
301–400	21.35	18.72	10.81	10.03
401–600	19.76	22.00	17.37	13.72
601–800	6.63	9.22	11.87	22.36
801–1,200	4.66	9.99	19.32	33.61
1,201–1,800	1.83	5.31	15.71	51.44
>1,800	1.59	8.27	26.07	54.80
All	100.00	100.00	100.00	17.37
Urban				
Upto Rs 150	2.50	0.55	-0.57	-19.73
151–200	2.98	1.09	0.29	5.12
201–250	3.57	1.39	-0.31	-4.29
251–300	12.10	5.16	-0.03	-0.11
301–400	10.52	5.74	0.69	2.33
401–600	22.91	15.86	11.89	14.44
601–800	13.82	11.66	6.87	11.34
801–1,200	15.51	19.09	18.06	18.21
1,201–1,800	8.01	12.46	11.18	17.27
>1,800	8.07	27.00	51.91	37.02
All	100.00	100.00	100.00	19.25
All-India				
Upto Rs 150	6.53	2.30	-2.33	-18.17
151–200	10.40	5.00	-0.56	-2.02
201–250	11.09	6.18	-0.41	-1.18
251–300	11.85	7.77	2.31	5.32
301–400	19.34	14.99	7.69	9.19

(Continued)

(Continued)

Per capita Income	HH	Income	Savings	Saving Rate
401–600	20.35	20.24	15.68	13.88
601–800	7.97	9.92	10.32	18.64
801–1,200	6.68	12.60	18.93	26.91
1,201–1,800	2.98	7.36	14.31	34.82
>1,800	2.80	13.65	34.05	44.69
All	100.00	100.00	100.00	17.91

REFERENCES

Central Statistical Organisation (1989), *National Accounts Statistics: Sources and Methods*, Central Statistical Organisation, Government of India, New Delhi.

———— (1994), *National Accounts Statistics: Factor Incomes, 1980–81 to 1989–90*, New Delhi.

———— (1997), 'A concept paper on Informal Sector', Paper presented at the First Meeting of the Expert Group on Informal Sector Statistics, 20–22 May, New Delhi.

———— (1998), *National Accounts Statistics 1998*, Government of India, New Delhi.

Kulshreshtha, A.C. (1997), 'Informal sector in the Indian National Accounts Statistics', Paper presented at the First Meeting of the Expert Group on Informal Sector Statistics, 20–22 May, New Delhi.

National Council of Applied Economic Research (1980), *Household Income and its Disposition*, New Delhi.

National Sample Survey Organisation (1998), 'Household Consumption Expenditure and Employment Situation in India 1994–95', *Report No. 436*, July 1998.

Planning Commission (1993), *Report of the Expert Group on Estimation of Proportion and Number of Poor, July 1993*, Government of India, New Delhi.

7

Health Insurance for Workers in the Informal Sector: A Case Study of Gujarat

ANIL GUMBER AND VEENA KULKARNI

INTRODUCTION

It is estimated that about two-fifths of India's GDP originates from the informal sector and almost 90 per cent of families depend on this sector for their livelihood. Despite this fact, a large number of workers engaged in the informal sector in both rural and urban areas are illiterate, poor and vulnerable. They live and work in unhygienic conditions and are susceptible to many infectious and chronic diseases. These workers neither have fixed employer–employee relationships nor do they obtain statutory social security benefits (Ahmad et al. 1991). They do not have the bargaining power to fight against discrimination and victimisation or for protecting their rights to lead a minimal standard of living.

Persistent poverty and disease syndromes have pushed families in the unorganised sector into the process of decapitalisation and indebtedness to meet their day-to-day contingencies, which certainly includes healthcare. The latter is the subject of this paper. The studies on the use of healthcare services show that the poor and other disadvantaged sections, such as scheduled castes and tribes, are

218 ◈ Anil Gumber and Veena Kulkarni

forced to spend a higher proportion of their income on healthcare than the better off. The burden of treatment is unduly large on them when seeking inpatient care (Visaria and Gumber 1994; Gumber 1997). The high incidence of morbidity cuts their household budget both ways, i.e., not only do they have to spend a large amount of money and resources on medical care but they are also unable to earn during the period of illness. Very often they have to borrow funds at very high interest rates to meet both medical expenditure and other household consumption needs. One possible consequence of this could be the pushing of these families into a zone of permanent poverty.

On the other hand, there are issues related to accessibility and use of subsidised public health facilities. A majority of the poor households, especially the rural ones, reside in backward, hilly and remote regions where neither government facilities nor private medical practitioners are available. They have to depend heavily on poor quality services provided by local, often unqualified practitioners and faith-healers. Further, wherever accessibility is not a problem, the primary health centres are either dysfunctional or provide low quality services.

Overall about 6 per cent of the household income is spent on curative care which amounts to Rs 250 per capita per annum (Shariff et al. 1999). The burden of expenditure on healthcare is however unduly heavy for households belonging to the informal sector indicating a potential for voluntary comprehensive health insurance schemes for such sections of the society. It is estimated that only a small fraction (less than 9 per cent) of the Indian work force is covered by some form of health insurance through the Central Government Health Scheme, Employees' State Insurance Scheme and *Mediclaim*; a majority of the covered population belongs to the organised sector (Gumber 1998). Further, the low level of health insurance coverage is due to the fact that the government policies have been designed to provide free health services through the public sector. The reality however, is that the public sector health agencies charge for their services on the one hand and have a poor outreach both in terms of quantity and quality on the other. Also, the public insurance companies so far have paid very little attention to voluntary medical insurance because of low profitability and high risk, coupled with deficient marketing and management strategies.

Hence a majority of the rural and urban slum population in India remains outside the health insurance system. This could be due to a lack of information regarding available health insurance schemes or because the mechanisms used by the health insurance providers are not suitable to them. There is also a gender bias with men having better access to healthcare when compared to women due to various socio-economic and cultural reasons. More specifically, the poor women are most vulnerable to diseases and ill-health due to unhygienic living conditions, heavy burden of child bearing, low emphasis on their own healthcare needs and severe constraints in seeking healthcare for themselves. Institutional arrangements have so far been lacking in correcting these gender differentials. This study undertaken on a pilot basis attempts to explore some critical issues relating to the availability and needs of health insurance coverage for the poor and especially women, and the likely constraints in extending current health insurance benefits to workers in the informal sector.

The objectives of the study were:

- to estimate the burden of healthcare expenditure on households, protected under varied health insurance environments,
- to assess the extent to which health insurance has helped in mitigating the burden,
- to estimate the demand for health insurance and willingness to pay for services, and
- to suggest an affordable health insurance plan for workers in the informal sector.

METHODS AND MATERIALS

To achieve the objectives of the study, a primary survey of 1,200 households was undertaken in Ahmedabad district of Gujarat. The survey included households from four types of health insurance enrolment status in rural and urban areas. About 360 households belonged to a contributory plan known as Employees' State Insurance Scheme (ESIS) for industrial workers. Another 120 households subscribed to a voluntary plan (*Mediclaim*) and 360 households were members of the community and self-financing scheme, which was run by a trade union, the Self-Employed Women's Association (SEWA). The remaining 360 households were non-insured and purchased healthcare services directly from the market. This last sub-sample, namely the non-insured households, was taken to serve as a control group. The idea of selecting such stratification was to understand the healthcare needs, use pattern and the types of benefits received by sample households protected under different health insurance environments. Also, the survey was designed to estimate the demand for health insurance and the willingness and capacity to pay for services across socio-economic categories of households.

The survey was conducted in eight localities dominated by slum populations in the city of Ahmedabad and six villages in the neighbourhood. On an average 60 households per village and 90 households per urban locality were selected. The selection criterion of a village or an urban locality was that the settlement should have a cluster of households benefiting from SEWA and ESIS plans. The sample canvassed from each of the settlements was such that it covered approximately an equal number of households from the ESIS, SEWA and the non-insured categories (20 each from a village and 30 each from an urban locality). The sample was purposive and no house listing prior to the survey was carried out. On the other hand, the sample of *Mediclaim/Jan Arogya* beneficiaries belonging to Ahmedabad city was selected from the list of subscribers obtained from the offices of the United India Insurance and New India Assurance companies.

SEWA HEALTH INSURANCE SCHEME

SEWA has been providing health insurance to its members as part of the integrated social security scheme. SEWA's members typify workers who are poor women and are engaged in occupations of the unorganised sector. The SEWA Bank introduced the scheme in March 1992 with initial enrolment of 7,000 women from Ahmedabad city (Chatterjee and Vyas 1997; Srinivas 1997). Later on it was extended to cover rural woman members from nine districts of Gujarat. Now its enrolment is 30,000, of which 50 per cent is from rural areas.

Health insurance is an integral part of the insurance programme of SEWA. The main motivation behind the initiation of a health insurance scheme for women is that the maintenance of an active health-seeking behaviour is a vital component for ensuring a good quality of life, and women tend to place a low priority to their health-care needs. The poor women's health is most vulnerable, both because of their unhygienic living conditions as well as the burden of bearing children. Persistent poor health of such workers costs them a loss of working days and the corresponding income.

Statement I
Type of Coverage under SEWA Scheme

Provider	Description of Coverage	Coverage Amount (Rs)	Premium (Rs)
National Insurance Company Ltd.	Accidental death of the woman member	15,000	3.00
	Loss of assets		
	Accidental death of a member's husband	15,000	3.00
SEWA	Loss during riots, fire, floods, theft, etc.:		9.00
	(a) of work equipment	2,000	
	(b) of the housing unit	3,000	
	Health Insurance (including coverage for:	1,300	32.50
	[a] gynaecological ailments		(10)
	[b] occupational health related diseases)		(5)
	Maternity benefits	300	
Life Insurance Corporation of India	Natural death	3,000	22.50
	Accidental death	25,000	

Note: Total premium for the entire package is Rs 70 plus Rs 5 as service charge.

The coverage of the SEWA health insurance programme includes hospitalisation coverage for a wide range of diseases, and insurance for occupational health related illnesses and other diseases specific to women (see Statement I). More specifically its main features are:

- Occupational health coverage.
- Coverage for women-specific diseases.
- Maternity benefit.
- Coverage for a broader range of diseases (not covered by the GIC's *Mediclaim* plan).
- Simplified administrative procedures.
- Life and asset insurance coverage of the woman member.
- Life coverage for members' husband.

SEWA health insurance scheme, functions in coordination with Life Insurance Corporation of India (LIC) and National Insurance Corporation (NIC). SEWA has integrated the schemes of LIC and NIC into a comprehensive health insurance package to address women's basic needs. The claimants are the needy health-benefit seekers; as the insurance is an additional benefit, the beneficiaries willingly pay the premium. Most of the insurers opt for a fixed deposit of Rs 700 with the SEWA Bank, and the interest accrual goes towards the annual payment of the premium. It is the large membership and assets of the SEWA Bank that has made possible the provision of the insurance coverage at low premiums.

Box 7.1: Evolution of SEWA Insurance Plan

SEWA is a trade union of 270,000 women workers of the unorganised sector in Gujarat. It organises them towards the goals of full employment and self-reliance at the household level. Full employment includes social security, which in turn incorporates insurance.

SEWA's experience repeatedly revealed that despite women's efforts to come out of poverty through enhanced employment opportunities and increased income, they were still vulnerable to various crises in their lives. These prevented them from leading a life free of poverty. The crises they continue to face are death of a breadwinner, accidental damage to, and destruction of, their homes and work equipment, and sickness. Maternity too often becomes a crisis for a woman, especially if she's poor, malnourished and lives in a remote area. One of the SEWA studies observed that women identified sickness in themselves or a family member as the major stress event in their lives. It was also a major cause of indebtedness among women.

It was with the goal of increasing women's ability to cope with risks like illness that SEWA began its integrated insurance programme in 1992. Through health insurance, it was hoped that:

- Women's vulnerability to sickness would be reduced and the claims received would be a 'buffer' during times of illness.
- Women would no longer become indebted during illness, i.e., their illness-related economic losses would be reduced.
- Women's healthcare needs would be taken care of to some extent and healthcare seeking behaviour for their own health and well-being would be enhanced.

The health insurance programme was, from the start, linked to SEWA's primary health care programme, which includes occupational health services. Thus insured members also have access to preventive and curative healthcare with health education. Health insurance accounts for the majority of claims and for 50 per cent of the premium paid out to the insurance programme by SEWA members. This is operational in the city of Ahmedabad and the nine districts where SEWA members live and work.

Mirai Chatterjee
SEWA, Ahmedabad

MORBIDITY AND UTILISATION OF HEALTHCARE SERVICES

Before going into details of accessibility and use of healthcare services, let us discuss the broad socio-economic characteristics, including health insurance coverage among the sampled households.

The households subscribing to *Mediclaim* generally belong to the higher income strata and their average annual income was twice that of the households enrolled with SEWA and ESIS as well as that in the non-insured category. In the remaining categories the average household income of the ESIS households is marginally higher than the SEWA and non-insured households, in both rural and urban areas. Similar differentials are revealed in the average household monthly expenditure (see Table 7.1).

In terms of major source of income, a considerable proportion of both non-insured and SEWA households in rural as well as urban areas has earnings from self-employment and casual labour. As expected ESIS households are dependent on salaried income primarily from the organised sector in both rural and urban areas. However, for *Mediclaim* households, besides salaried income from the organised sector, self-employment and salaried jobs in the unorganised sector are equally important sources of income.

The literacy rate among the surveyed population is high in both rural and urban areas. The gender disparity in the literacy rates is much lower, as compared to the 1991 census figures for the state as a whole, for urban and rural areas. Interestingly, the literacy rate is very close to 100 per cent for both males and females among the

Table 7.1
Select Characteristics of the Surveyed Population by
Health Insurance Status

	Rural			Urban			
Characteristics	Non-insured	SEWA	ESIS	Non-insured	SEWA	ESIS	Mediclaim
Number of households	127	121	113	240	236	239	116
Main source of household income							
Self-employed	37.0	43.9	2.7	26.2	22.9	0.4	29.3
Casual labour	36.2	35.6	1.8	28.8	18.7	–	0.9
Salaried-Organised	5.5	11.6	93.8	15.4	23.3	88.3	46.6
Salaried-Unorganised	19.7	8.3	1.8	27.5	34.7	11.3	20.7
Others	1.6	0.8	–	2.1	0.4	–	2.6
Mean household annual income	31,164	31,182	36,711	33,537	37,715	38,197	79,086
Mean household monthly exp.	2,319	2,299	2,793	2,484	2,869	2,887	5,123
Mean household size	5.13	5.50	5.47	5.42	5.88	5.64	4.63
Literacy rate (Aged 7+) (%)							
Males	89.3	86.3	94.0	·87.7	87.1	90.0	99.6
Females	63.5	68.2	75.7	68.6	75.6	73.4	96.8
Both sexes	76.6	77.0	85.1	77.9	81.4	81.8	98.2
Worker-population ratio (%)							
Males	54.0	53.7	48.8	49.5	50.5	50.8	56.1
Females	31.0	33.9	22.5	22.9	28.3	16.9	11.7
Both sexes	42.8	43.9	36.7	36.2	39.4	33.8	34.1

Source: NCAER–SEWA Survey, 1999.

Mediclaim households. In terms of economic activity, the female participation is higher among the SEWA households in both rural and urban areas. As expected, the overall work participation rate is higher in rural than in urban areas.

The health insurance coverage is not mandatory for all the SEWA households. Only 47 per cent of rural and 66 per cent of urban SEWA households opted for the health insurance scheme. As the SEWA scheme is limited to woman members, the percentage of beneficiary population is just 11 per cent in rural and 18 per cent in urban areas. The proportion of sample population insured is between 82 and 86 per cent in the ESIS and 68 per cent in the *Mediclaim* categories (see Table 7.2). Only a couple of households in the non-insured category receive medical reimbursement from their employers. On average, the insured persons among the SEWA households pay an annual premium between Rs 70 and Rs 80; the figure for ESIS households is between Rs 126 and Rs 130 and for *Mediclaim* households it is Rs 221.

To understand the health seeking behaviour of the surveyed population, information was collected on three types of morbidity:

Table 7.2
Extent of Health Insurance Coverage among the Surveyed Households

| Characteristics | Rural | | | Urban | | | |
	Non-insured	SEWA	ESIS	Non-insured	SEWA	ESIS	Mediclaim
Health insurance coverage							
Households (%)	3.1	47.1	100.0	4.6	66.1	100.0	100.0
Population (%)	2.5	10.8	82.5	3.3	17.7	86.1	67.6
Males	1.8	3.6	81.5	2.9	6.1	85.3	71.2
Females	3.2	18.1	83.7	3.7	29.6	86.8	63.9
Annual premium (Rs)							
Per household	4	44	525	5	77	540	648
Per capita	1	8	96	1	13	96	140
Per insured	41	70	130	25	80	126	221

Source: NCAER–SEWA Survey, 1999.

acute morbidity (using 30 days recall period), chronic morbidity and hospitalisation (using 365 days recall period).[1] The incidence of acute morbidity is the highest for SEWA households among the three categories of SEWA, ESIS and Non-insured for both males and females in rural and urban areas. The incidence of acute morbidity is the lowest among the *Mediclaim* households. All the three types of morbidity rates are higher for females as compared to males in almost all the population groups. For a meaningful comparison we have converted three types of morbidity into annual illness rate. On an average, the population experiences about two episodes of illness per year; the rate however is higher for SEWA households and lower for *Mediclaim* households. We have also asked the surveyed population how they rate their 'overall health status' on a scale ranging from very poor to excellent. As compared to rural, a higher percentage of the urban population (very close to 90 per cent) perceived their health status to be good or excellent. The rural–urban differentials are sharper for perceived health status than emerged from the empirical morbidity rate (see Table 7.3).

As expected, both in rural and urban areas the private sector has played a dominant role in providing services for ambulatory care (acute and chronic morbidity). Surprisingly, even the households covered under the ESIS facility, particularly in rural areas, relied heavily on the private facility for treatment of acute illnesses. The results clearly highlight the poor outreach of ESIS panel doctors, dispensaries and hospital facilities, for the rural insured households. In urban areas too, only a little over 50 per cent of both acute and chronic cases of the insured population are handled by the ESIS facilities. For the rest of the population groups, there is some reliance on government hospitals for inpatient care (see Table 7.4).

To estimate the total burden of treatment, three types of cost are computed—medical cost, other direct cost and indirect cost. The medical cost includes expenses towards fees and consultations, medicines, diagnostic charges and other hospital payments. There are other kinds of out-of-pocket expenditure, which relate to accessing health care, such as transportation, special diet, etc. While undergoing treatment there is a loss of income of the patient (if working) and/or of the caring person (if working). Sometimes the household has to borrow money at a very high interest rate to meet treatment-related exigencies. All these account for the indirect cost of treatment.

As nearly 90 per cent of rural households have used private facilities for the treatment of acute morbidity, the direct medical cost does not vary much by insurance status of households. However, the total

Table 7.3
Morbidity Profile of the Population, by Health Insurance Status
of the Household, in Rural and Urban Ahmedabad

Type of Morbidity	Rural			Urban			
	Non-insured	SEWA	ESIS	Non-insured	SEWA	ESIS	Mediclaim
Acute morbidity (last 30 days)							
Male	131	170	146	130	149	140	55
Female	152	209	145	165	181	167	94
Both sexes	141	189	146	147	165	154	75
Chronic morbidity							
Male	45	33	37	38	53	53	37
Female	57	70	76	64	63	72	45
Both sexes	51	51	55	50	58	62	41
Hospitalisation (last 365 days)							
Male	42	72	58	52	43	62	19
Female	57	48	87	67	74	54	19
Both sexes	49	60	71	59	59	58	19
Annual morbidity rate*							
Male	1,663	2,146	1,845	1,652	1,888	1,799	720
Female	1,937	2,619	1,907	2,106	2,305	2,129	1,192
Both sexes	1,796	2,381	1,874	1,877	2,095	1,965	953
Percent reporting their overall health status as good/ excellent	77.3	78.1	82.4	90.5	88.2	86.2	90.9

Source: NCAER–SEWA Survey, 1999.

Notes: Various morbidity rates are per 1,000 population.
Annual morbidity rate = Acute morbidity rate* 12 + Chronic rate + Hospitalisation rate.

cost of treatment varies within a narrow range of Rs 295 and Rs 401, primarily due to differences in indirect costs of treatment (see Table 7.5). Spending by the non-insured and SEWA households in urban areas is similar however, the urban ESIS households spend much less on treatment, because they avail the ESIS facility to a greater extent than their rural counterparts. On the contrary, the

Table 7.4
Source of Treatment, by Health Insurance Status of
the Household, in Rural and Urban Ahmedabad

Type of Morbidity	Rural			Urban			
	Non-insured	SEWA	ESIS	Non-insured	SEWA	ESIS	Mediclaim
Acute morbidity							
Government	10.3	6.1	3.5	9.2	15.2	3.1	–
ESI facility	–	–	15.1	1.1	1.3	54.1	–
Private	89.7	93.9	81.4	89.7	83.5	42.9	100.0
Chronic morbidity							
Government	21.9	20.0	9.1	40.3	31.6	7.7	9.5
ESI facility	–	–	30.3	1.6	–	53.8	–
Private	78.1	80.0	60.6	58.1.	68.4	38.5	90.5
Hospitalisation							
Government	40.6	27.5	29.5	51.9	50.6	14.5	10.0
ESI facility	–	–	20.5	1.3	2.4	64.5	–
Private	59.4	72.5	50.0	46.8	47.1	21.1	90.0

Source: NCAER–SEWA Survey, 1999.

Mediclaim beneficiaries spend three times more than the non-insured or SEWA households.

In the case of treatment of chronic illnesses, the expenditure per episode is higher than that of acute illnesses in both rural and urban households. Surprisingly, rural households spent about 50 per cent more on treatment whereas for urban households it was just 10 per cent higher than the expenditure on treatment of acute illnesses. The reason for such a difference could be a delay in seeking treatment by rural households, thus raising the indirect cost of treatment. This fact is also reflected in the case of hospitalisation. Further, the indirect cost of treatment for both chronic and hospitalisation episodes is higher among rural patients, as a relatively higher percentage of them have reported loss of income as well as amount borrowed in the course of treatment, than their urban counterparts. Thus, in several population groups, indirect cost of treatment turns out to be substantial (between one-fifths to one-third of the total cost) for seeking ambulatory and/or inpatient care. Another observation worth noting is that the average cost of treatment is lower among urban than rural patients irrespective of health insurance status.

Table 7.5
Cost of Treament, by Health Insurance Status
of the Household, in Rural and Urban Ahmedabad

Type of Morbidity	Rural			Urban			
	Non-insured	SEWA	ESIS	Non-insured	SEWA	ESIS	Mediclaim
Acute morbidity							
Medical cost	233	200	224	234	228	97	686
Other direct exp.	77	62	69	48	54	49	152
Indirect cost	90	33	93	50	54	55	85
Net total cost	401	295	380	331	336	202	923
Chronic morbidity							
Medical cost	347	284	214	210	261	135	216
Other direct exp.	115	81	215	56	51	74	43
Indirect cost	236	86	225	98	60	25	5
Net total cost	697	451	644	364	371	234	263
Hospitalisation							
Medical cost	2,427	3,072	2,200	3,246	2,099	621	4,045
Other direct exp.	444	557	589	431	780	318	935
Indirect cost	631	694	305	439	413	206	464
Net total cost	3,502	4,323	3,076	2,954	3,280	1,146	4,034

Source: NCAER–SEWA Survey, 1999.

Notes: Medical Cost includes expenses towards fees, medicine, diagnostic and other hospital charges.
Other Direct Expenditure includes expenses on transport, special diet, etc.
Indirect Cost includes loss of income of the ailing person as well as of the caring person and one year interest payment (@ 24 per cent) on the amount borrowed during the course of treatment.
Net total cost = Direct cost + Indirect cost – Reimbursement.

UTILISATION OF MATERNAL AND CHILD HEALTH SERVICES

In the survey the details of use of maternal and child health services (antenatal care, delivery, postnatal care and child immunisation) were recorded from married women who had reported delivery.

during the two years prior to the date of the survey. About 98 per cent of urban women and 93 per cent of rural women used antenatal services. Here once again the private sector has played a significant role in providing such services. More than 50 per cent of women had incurred expenditure while seeking antenatal care. On an average the expenditure per reporting case was Rs 679 for a rural woman and Rs 691 for an urban woman (see Table 7.6).

The share of institutional delivery was only about 47 per cent among rural women as compared to 77 per cent among urban women. In the latter case, it is the government hospital where the highest proportion of deliveries took place. For rural women, however the percentage of deliveries taking place in government hospitals was 20.8 per cent, lower than the private hospital where the corresponding figure was 26.4 per cent. Also, 54 per cent of the deliveries in the rural sample were assisted by a trained mid-wife or a nurse. The average expenditure on delivery was higher for urban than rural women. The difference in expenditure is larger in the 'other expenses' category than in the 'institutional payments' category.

A majority of women did not avail of the postnatal care services and surprisingly the number was higher among urban women. In the sample villages, the government dispensary/clinic seemed to be most sought after followed by the Primary Health Centre/Community Health Centre. In urban areas, it was the private hospital where a higher number of women used the facility. As far as immunisation status is concerned, most children were immunised against six diseases and almost all against five diseases (excluding measles) in both rural and urban areas. Here the government clearly dominated in providing such services free of cost.

The average total expenditure on using various MCH services during the last two years turned out to be Rs 2,128 per rural woman and Rs 2,653 per urban woman. The higher total expenditure for the urban woman was mainly due to other out-of-pocket expenditure (Rs 1,066 per urban woman as opposed to only Rs 668 per rural woman).

BURDEN OF HEALTHCARE
EXPENDITURE ON HOUSEHOLDS

The total burden of out-of-pocket expenditure on households is estimated while taking into account three types of expenditure—namely, per capita annual expenditure on treatment of illnesses, use of MCH services and health insurance premium. The per capita expenditure

Health Insurance for Workers in the Informal Sector ◈ 231

Table 7.6
Use Pattern of Maternal and Child Healthcare Services,
in Rural and Urban Ahmedabad

Type of Service	Rural	Urban
Number of women reported delivery during last two years	87	213
I. Antenatal services		
Source: Public	43.7	51.7
Private	49.4	46.0
Did not use	6.9	2.3
Expenditure on antenatal services		
% reported institutional payment	57.5	61.5
% reported other expenses	50.6	62.9
Average institutional payments per reporting case	608	640
Average other expenses per reporting case	266	323
Average total expenses per reporting case	679	691
II. Delivery		
Place: Home	40.2	17.4
Govt. institution	20.8	42.7
Private institution	26.4	34.7
Other places	12.6	5.2
Expenditure on delivery		
% reported institutional payment	71.3	69.5
% reported other expenses	75.9	81.2
Average institutional payments per reporting case	1,366	1,628
Average other expenses per reporting case	595	1,017
Average total expenses per reporting case	1,494	2,004
III. Postnatal services		
Source: Public	26.5	9.4
Private	11.4	10.8
Did not use	62.1	79.8
Expenditure on postnatal care		
% reported institutional payment	24.1	10.3
% reported other expenses	21.8	12.7
Average institutional payments per reporting case	533	492
Average other expenses per reporting case	371	290
Average total expenses per reporting case	730	518
IV. Immunisation of children		
Number of surviving children	82	210
% immunised for: DPT	92.6	94.8
Polio	100.0	97.6
BCG	96.4	96.1
Measles	74.4	85.7

(Continued)

Table 7.6 *(Continued)*

Type of Service	Rural	Urban
% used private facility for: DPT	3.6	14.7
Polio	3.6	14.2
BCG	3.6	14.7
Measles	2.4	13.3
% reported expenditure	2.4	7.1
Average expenses per reporting case	360	154
Average expenditure on MCH		
Institutional payments	1,460	1,587
Other expenses	668	1,066
Total expenses	2,128	2,653

Source: NCAER–SEWA Survey, 1999.

on treatment was higher for rural households irrespective of health insurance status. In urban areas the per capita out-of-pocket expenditure among both ESIS and *Mediclaim* beneficiaries was lower than that among the non-insured and SEWA households (see Table 7.7). Among three categories of households common in rural and urban areas, the average expenditure on treatment of morbidity for rural households in the non-insured, SEWA and ESIS categories was higher by 27, 7 and 102 per cent respectively, than their urban counterparts. When one converts the average expenditure on treatment as proportion of income (burden of treatment), the rural–urban differences increase further (because of lower levels of income in the rural areas).

The burden of treatment as a percentage of per capita income ranged between 16 and 19.1 per cent for rural households and between 4.7 and 17.0 per cent for urban households. Overall, the burden of treatment turned out to be the lowest for *Mediclaim* and the highest for rural SEWA households. If we include the expenditure on MCH and insurance premium then the burden increases further. The increase was higher among ESIS households mainly due to their regular contribution towards health insurance. The burden of total healthcare costs varied between 18 and 21 per cent in three categories of rural households and the corresponding range for urban households was 10 and 18 per cent. Although the *Mediclaim* households spent the highest amount per illness episode, having reported the lowest incidence of illness the annual per capita expenditure turned out to be small; and as a result the burden was just 6 per cent of their income. On the contrary, the SEWA households

Table 7.7

Out-of-pocket Expenditure on Healthcare, by Health Insurance
Status of the Household, in Rural and Urban Ahmedabad

Indicator	Rural			Urban			
	Non-insured	SEWA	ESIS	Non-insured	SEWA	ESIS	Mediclaim
Annual per capita health exp.							
Direct	968	1,036	868	888	966	438	855
Indirect	280	196	286	167	191	131	87
Total (net)	1,247	1,232	1,149	981	1,156	569	905
As % of per capita income	19.1	20.4	16.0	14.6	17.0	7.9	4.7
Av. annual health insurance premium by the household	9	44	523	7	74	538	648
Av. expenditure on MCH	492	577	466	722	659	709	576
Burden of total healthcare costs on households (%)	19.9	21.4	17.9	15.6	18.0	10.1	5.7

Source: NCAER–SEWA Survey, 1999.

Notes: Expenditure on MCH has been incurred during the last two years.
Burden is estimated as the sum of per capita expenditures on
(a) treatment of morbidity, (b) maternal and child health care, and
(c) health insurance premium and divided by per capita income.

bore the highest burden of all the categories of households in both
rural and urban areas.

UTILISATION OF
HEALTH INSURANCE SERVICES

This section discusses in detail the use pattern of SEWA, ESIS and
Mediclaim health insurance services by the respective beneficiary
households. Beside enrolment status, amount of premium paid and

the nature of service used, the problems encountered while availing of the services are investigated. The opinions and suggestions for improvement in service delivery of the respective health insurance schemes are also highlighted.

SEWA HEALTH INSURANCE SCHEME

The percentage of SEWA member households where at least one woman has been enrolled in the SEWA health insurance scheme is 46.3 in rural and 161.9 in urban areas. It is surprising that 25.2 and 15.3 per cent of the SEWA households in rural and urban areas, respectively, have no knowledge of the existence of such a scheme. The major reasons which emerge for non-enrolment both in rural and urban SEWA households are 'low income/can't afford' and 'no knowledge of insurance'. The former (reason) has been reported by 38.5 percent of rural and 30.3 per cent of urban respondents. The second reason has been cited by 44.6 percent of rural and 55.3 per cent of urban respondents. About 6 and 3 per cent of rural and urban households did not enrol because of 'not being interested' in the scheme.

Although the plan was introduced in March 1992, it took some time for the coverage to extend to rural SEWA households. As a result, the bulk of enrolment in rural areas took place in 1996 whereas for the urban areas it was before 1995. In 1998 however, there was a higher enrolment figure of rural than urban households. The type of coverage subscribed by the SEWA households does not vary much for the urban and the rural areas. The majority takes life insurance coverage—about 90 per cent in both rural and urban areas. The subscription to maternity insurance is stronger in the urban (87.4 per cent) as compared to the rural sample (73.7 per cent). Depending upon the type of coverage of benefits, the annual premium is charged. The premium varies between Rs 60 and Rs 90. Also, three types of methods are used to collect the premium: one time payment annually, fixed deposit and monthly recurring deposit with SEWA Bank.[2] A majority of households have gone for fixed deposit of either Rs 500 or Rs 700. The average premium paid is Rs 65.3 by the rural and 68.3 by the urban household. In the rural areas 5.3 per cent of the beneficiaries have reported a claim whereas the percentage is 11.3 for the urban areas.

The beneficiaries of SEWA health insurance seem to be satisfied on the whole with the various aspects of the functioning of the system, since the frequency of the responses in the 'fully satisfied' category is the highest. There is a lot of similarity between the responses in the urban and the rural sample. In the rural as well as urban sample, the SEWA health insurance beneficiaries seem to be most satisfied with the mode of premium payment—80.7 per cent in rural and 78 per cent in urban Ahmedabad (see Table 7.8).

The aspects, for which a lot of dissatisfaction is expressed, are 'claim settlement time' and 'documents required for claim', and the degree of dissatisfaction is higher among the rural than the urban subscribers. The next factor against which there is dissatisfaction is 'amount of reimbursement' even though from mid-1998 the coverage of a maximum of Rs 1,000 hospitalisation expenses in a year for the insured women has been raised to Rs 1,200. There is also a high degree of non-response, more among the rural than urban beneficiaries, particularly when asked about the working of the system vis-à-vis 'claim settlement time', 'documents required for claim' and 'amount of reimbursement'. It needs to be noted that these are the same factors against which there is dissatisfaction too.

The opinion regarding the SEWA scheme, when asked to the rural subscribers (despite having a higher level of dissatisfaction as compared to their urban counterparts), is that 98.2 per cent of them find the SEWA scheme better than the schemes that have been the subject of the study. The corresponding figure for the urban subscribers is 92.5. Among the reasons cited for calling the scheme better, the important ones are 'low premium', 'maternity benefits' and coverage of woman-specific diseases.

There are suggestions for the improvement of the specific aspects of the scheme like 'coverage of services', 'coverage of family members', etc. There are more suggestions put forward by the urban than the rural respondents. In the urban sample, 81.1, 84.9 and 76.1 per cent of the responses suggest improvements in 'coverage of services', 'coverage of family members' and 'additional benefits', respectively. In the rural sample, while 68.4 per cent, which is incidentally the highest frequency recorded, want improvement in the aspect of 'coverage of family members', 63.2 per cent desire improvement in the provision of 'additional benefits'.

Various benefit options were put forward to the members of SEWA, irrespective of whether or not they are the beneficiaries of the health insurance schemes. This was followed by their preference of the scheme and the premium that they are willing to pay. There were six options in all and they are as follows:

Table 7.8

Extent of Satisfaction with the SEWA Health Insurance Scheme in Rural and Urban Ahmedabad

Items	Rural				Urban			
	Fully Satisfied	Some-what	Not Satisfied	NR	Fully Satisfied	Some-what	Not Satisfied	NR
Coverage of diseases	63.2	12.3	7.0	17.5	56.6	17.0	11.3	15.1
Coverage of family members	45.6	15.8	31.6	7.0	50.3	20.1	25.2	4.4
Sum assured	52.6	5.3	10.5	31.6	56.0	6.9	16.4	20.8
Mode of premium payment	80.7	5.3	1.8	12.3	78.0	6.9	6.9	8.2
Claim settlement time	33.3	7.0	12.3	47.4	42.8	10.7	13.8	32.7
Documents required for claim	36.8	8.8	5.3	49.1	42.1	10.7	14.5	32.7
Amount of reimbursement	40.4	5.3	5.3	49.1	42.8	12.6	10.7	34.0

Source: NCAER–SEWA Survey, 1999.

(a) Raising hospitalisation coverage to Rs 2,000 for the woman.
(b) Extending current hospitalisation coverage to the spouse also (Rs 1,200 per head).
(c) Extending current hospitalisation coverage to all family members (Rs 1,200 per head).
(d) Hospitalisation coverage up to Rs 1,200 plus OPD up to Rs 300 to the woman only.
(e) Coverage up to Rs 1,200 plus OPD up to Rs 300 to all family members.
(f) Coverage up to Rs 1,000 (hospitalisation plus OPD) to all family members.

There is a higher degree of willingness to accept these various options among the urban as compared to the rural respondents. However, the responses in both the locations are similar in the sense that at both places there is a majority which is ready to accept the plans at a higher premium (see Table 7.9). In rural areas, the most popular option appears top be Option (a) where there are only 19.5 who are not interested and 73.2 are willing to accept the option at a higher premium. In the urban sample, Option (b) is the most acceptable with 89.4 per cent of the respondents willing to opt for the same at higher premium. The least acceptable in rural areas is Option (d) (30.1 per cent) and in urban it is Option (f) (8.9 per cent). There is, however, not a very wide range of variation in the responses across the various options. Another feature worth noting is that though the degree of willingness for the various options is higher in urban than in rural areas, the percentage of respondents who are willing to buy the various options at existing or lower premiums is higher in the urban sample. However, such percentage varies only between 3 and 10 per cent among various options.

Overall, the average premium willingness-to-pay tends to increase with the amount of benefits in both rural and urban samples. However, in the rural sample it increases from Rs 86.3 to Rs 100.5 as opposed to Rs 86.6 to Rs 92.5 in the urban sample. As compared to the average premium they are currently paying (Rs 65.3 by the rural and Rs 68.3 by the urban women), the increase is of the order of 33 to 54 per cent for rural and 27 to 35 per cent for urban households. There is a threshold limit to pay the premium for various benefits. The median value suggests that at least 50 per cent of the households in rural areas are willing-to-pay between Rs 84 to 100 in the increasing order of benefits whereas the range for urban households is Rs 84 to Rs 96. The modal value comes out to

Table 7.9

Percentage of SEWA Households willing to opt for a Better Plan, within the SEWA Health Insurance Scheme, in Rural and Urban Ahmedabad

Plans	Rural				Urban			
	Not Interested	Willing at Existing Premium	Willing at Higher Premium	Willing at Lower Premium	Not Interested	Willing at Existing Premium	Willing at Higher Premium	Willing at Lower Premium
(a) Raising hospitalisation coverage to Rs 2,000 for women	19.5	3.3	73.2	4.1	2.1	4.7	88.1	5.1
(b) Extending hospitalisation coverage to the spouse (Rs 1,200 per head)	22.8	2.4	70.7	4.1	2.9	4.7	89.4	3.0
(c) Extending hospitalisation coverage to all family members (Rs 1,200 per head)	22.0	2.4	72.4	3.3	3.7	4.7	88.6	3.0
(d) Hospitalisation coverage up to Rs 1,200 + OPD up to Rs 300 to the woman only	30.1	2.4	65.0	2.4	5.5	4.2	87.7	2.5
(e) Hospitalisation coverage up to Rs 1,200 + OPD up to Rs 300 to all family members	28.5	1.6	68.3	1.6	6.8	4.2	86.0	3.0
(f) Rs 1,000 coverage (hospitalisation + OPD) to all family members	22.0	2.4	74.0	1.6	8.9	3.8	83.9	3.4

Source: NCAER–SEWA Survey, 1999.

be Rs 100 for both rural and urban households, irrespective of benefits.

ESI SCHEME

There is a much higher proportion of ESIS households who are currently using the facility in urban (96.3 per cent) as compared to rural areas (70.8 per cent). The figure for those who have used the facility in the past is higher in rural (7.1 per cent) than in the urban locations (1.7 per cent). Among the facilities that are being used by the beneficiaries, the ones, which are used the most are clinical examination, prescription, medication/topical application. The facilities for which ESIS is least used are 'advice/education', 'cash compensation'. One of the most often used facilities of the ESIS is to avail of 'leave sanctions'. The use of this particular facility is as high as 90 per cent in the rural and 91.1 per cent in the urban sample. The degree of usage of all the listed facilities is higher among urban than among rural households.

The majority of the urban beneficiaries are affiliated to a dispensary (96.6 per cent) whereas considerable proportions of rural beneficiaries (30 per cent) are attached to only a 'panel doctor'. The average premium paid by the beneficiary is between Rs 45 and Rs 46 per month. The bulk of the beneficiaries (nearly 52 per cent) in urban and rural samples fall in the premium payment category of Rs 30–50. When asked about the types of benefits available in the plan, the least reported benefit is the 'funeral expenses' both by urban and rural respondents. The knowledge about the availability of maternity (77.8 per cent) and dependent benefit (76.7 per cent) is not so high among rural as compared to urban households (93.2 and 83.1 per cent, respectively).

The average distance, to be commuted, to access the services of the panel doctor and dispensary from the workplace, for the rural ESIS subscribers, is nearly half of that for the urban ones. Also, from home, the corresponding distance to be traversed for the rural beneficiaries is three times that required for their urban counterparts. The cost of travel to be incurred to access the services of a dispensary by the rural beneficiaries is higher than that required to access the services of a panel doctor. For the urban beneficiaries, this cost pattern is the reverse. It is more expensive (in terms of travel cost) to avail of the facility of a panel doctor than of the dispensary. Nearly 88 to 89 per cent of the rural beneficiaries report the working hours of the panel doctor and dispensary as convenient. In the urban sample too, 87.5 per cent of the beneficiaries find the working hours of the dispensary convenient but only 62.5 per cent of them have reported the same for the panel doctor. As far as the percentage reporting the availability of the doctor during working hours is concerned, exactly the same pattern is observed.

The level of satisfaction as far as the various services are concerned is higher in urban than in rural areas (see Table 7.10). The percentage of responses falling in the 'fully satisfied' category is 49.6 among rural and 67.6 per cent among urban households. Among the specific items for which this kind of satisfaction is expressed are 'coverage of illness' and 'facilities available', irrespective of the area of residence. The factor against which the highest level of dissatisfaction reported by the rural households that fall in the category of 'not satisfied' is 'distance to dispensary' (45.1 per cent of the responses). The urban respondents are most dissatisfied with 'time spent for seeking treatment' (15.8 per cent of the responses).

When asked, the bulk of the rural ESIS beneficiaries (48.7 per cent) do not wish to opt out of ESIS facility whereas for urban beneficiaries the respective figure is 33.6. Surprisingly, even 36.7 per cent of the rural and 15.4 per cent of the urban beneficiaries in the 'not satisfied' category do not want to opt out of the plan. There are 42.3 per cent of the urban respondents who wish to subscribe to SEWA as an alternative. The proportion wanting to choose *Mediclaim* is surprisingly higher in rural (8 per cent) than in urban areas (6.3 per cent). There are a substantial number of responses in 'can't say' category—16.7 per cent in rural and 17.8 per cent in urban areas.

The percentages of beneficiaries not satisfied accordingly are 50.4 in the rural and 32.4 in the urban sample. The reason which scores the most in this respect among the rural households, is 'large distances and inconvenient locations' (73.7 per cent) followed by 'inadequate facilities' (49.4 per cent). Among the urban beneficiaries, the factor 'inadequate facilities' is the one that has been reported as very dissatisfactory by most (48.7 per cent) which is followed by 'poor quality of services' (35.9 per cent).

MEDICLAIM AND JAN AROGYA SCHEME

The percentage of enrolment in the *Mediclaim*-individual scheme is 64.7 in the sample whereas that for *Jan Arogya* and *Mediclaim*-group are 26.7 and 8.6, respectively (see Table 7.11).

Table 7.10
Extent of Satisfaction from the ESIS Facility in Rural and Urban Ahmedabad

Items	Rural				Urban			
	Fully Satisfied	Some-what	Not Satisfied	NR	Fully Satisfied	Some-what	Not Satisfied	NR
1. Coverage of illnesses	66.4	8.8	15.9	8.8	81.7	9.1	9.1	–
2. Facilities available	60.2	15.0	20.4	4.4	77.6	10.4	12.0	–
3. Cost, i.e., monetary expenses and wage loss	52.2	18.6	20.4	8.8	74.7	10.8	14.1	0.4
4. Time spent for seeking treatment	52.2	16.8	23.9	7.1	74.7	9.5	15.8	–
5. Quality of services—medical and paramedical staff	46.0	19.5	18.6	15.9	73.0	13.7	13.3	–
6. Quality of infrastructure available	43.4	24.8	15.0	16.8	75.5	11.2	12.9	0.4
7. Distance to dispensary	30.1	23.0	45.1	1.8	78.8	12.4	7.9	0.8
8. Administrative procedure to process papers	44.2	13.3	20.4	22.1	66.4	10.4	13.7	9.5
Overall system	49.6	22.1	26.5	1.8	67.6	15.8	16.2	0.4
Percentage do not want to shift to any other scheme	60.7	36.0	36.7	50.0	38.0	34.2	15.4	–

Source: NCAER–SEWA Survey, 1999.

Table 7.11
Profile of Households Enrolled with
the *Mediclaim* Plan in Urban Ahmedabad

Type of Plan	Characteristics		
	% Enrolled	Av. Months Back Enrolled	Av. Annual Premium (Rs)
Jan Arogya	26.7	19.3	197
Mediclaim-individual	64.7	30.8	844
Mediclaim-group	8.6	16.2	578
All	100.0	26.4	648

Reasons for enrolment (multiple response)

1. Agent persuaded	41.3
2. Group insurance	9.5
3. Employer's recommendation	19.8
4. Neighbour/friends motivated	12.1
5. Expected to incur major medical expenses	32.7
6. Prolonged sickness	3.4
7. Income tax benefits	5.2

Type of knowledge about the purpose of *Mediclaim* plan

1. Reimbursement of all medical expenditure	30.2
2. Only hospitalisation expenses	56.0
3. Only expenses for major illnesses	15.5
4. Reimbursement of medical expenses in the 2nd year of the policy	24.1
5. Other	0.9

Knowledge about period for which *Mediclaim* policy is issued

1. One year	88.8
2. Six months	0.9
3. No specific period	3.4
4. Don't Know	5.2
5. Other	1.7
Percentage reported any claim	13.8

Extent of satisfaction

1. Fully satisfied	56.0
2. Partially satisfied	13.8
3. Not satisfied	0.9
4. No response	29.3

Source: NCAER–SEWA Survey, 1999.

The subscribers, on average, got themselves enrolled about 26.4 months prior to the survey. The bulk of the beneficiaries fall in the category of having bought the scheme in the previous 12–23 months. On average, they pay Rs 648 as an annual premium. Obviously, the premium is much lower for *Jan Arogya* than other *Mediclaim* policies. The major reasons for enrolment are 'persuasion by agent' and 'expected major medical expenses'. About one-fifth of them enrolled as per a suggestion made by their employers. The majority of the beneficiaries (56 per cent) feel the main purpose of the *Mediclaim* policy is to take care of the hospitalisation expenses. A substantial percentage of subscribers (30.2 per cent) say that attainment of reimbursement of all medical expenditure is the objective of *Mediclaim*. Also, 24.1 per cent of the respondents feel that reimbursement of hospitalisation expenditure in the second year of the policy is obtained by buying *Mediclaim* policy. The remaining 15.5 per cent cite the coverage of expenses for major illnesses as the purpose achieved by subscribing to *Mediclaim*. The knowledge about the period for which *Mediclaim* is issued is known as one year by 88.8 per cent of the beneficiaries, 5.2 per cent of them have no knowledge about the period and 3.9 per cent feel that there is no specific period for that. Only 13.8 per cent of the beneficiaries have reported a claim in the past.

When asked about the level of satisfaction, 56 per cent of subscribers reported the response as 'fully satisfied', 13.8 'partially satisfied' while 29.3 per cent chose not to respond. The proportion of those 'not satisfied at all' is minimal at 0.9 per cent. We took the opinions of subscribers on three broad issues, namely, service improvement, popularity and expectation from medical insurance. A lot of suggestions were floated which are grouped into four categories related to better service delivery, waiver of existing exclusions/ conditions, extended benefits and other suggestions. Between 17.2 and 27.6 per cent of respondents did not give any suggestions, whereas the opinions those who responded, by giving a maximum of two suggestions on the three questions, were recorded (see Table 7.12).

Nearly 26 per cent of the beneficiaries agreed that one of the areas where improvement in service can take place is the quick settlement of claims, and another 4.3 per cent said that the process of filing the claims should be made easier. There are 9.5 per cent of them who feel that overall service delivery should be improved. Other aspects where improvement can be made, according to the beneficiaries are developing the faith of the *Mediclaim* authorities in a doctor's certificate and an improvement in the behaviour of the staff (4.3 per cent each). Quick settlement of the claim and overall improvement

Table 7.12
Households' Opinion about their Expectations and Steps to be Taken for Improving Health Insurance Services and the Popularity of the Company

Steps	Service Improvement	Popularity	Expectation
1. Better service	56.9	25.9	40.5
Quick settlement of the claim	25.9	3.4	13.7
Easy process for filing claim	4.3	–	0.9
Faith on doctor's certificate	4.3	–	3.4
Full payment of the claim/expenses	3.4	–	7.9
Improve customer service/better information	2.6	6.9	0.9
Improve behaviour of the staff	4.3	0.9	1.7
Prompt issue of the policy/ timely delivery	2.6	0.9	2.6
Renewal notice at least two months in advance	0.9	–	–
Premium payment on monthly basis	0.9	0.9	0.9
Improve overall service delivery	9.5	12.9	9.5
2. Waiving off exclusions/conditions	7.7	0.9	2.6
No condition for a minimum of 24 hours hospitalisation	0.9	0.9	–
Coverage of multiple hospitalisation	2.6	–	–
No condition of registered hospital	–	–	0.9
Inclusion of pre-existing diseases	1.7	–	–
No such condition that benefits would accrue from 2nd year	–	–	1.7
Inclusion of pre-/post-hospitalisation expenses	2.6	–	–
3. Extended benefits	31.9	12.9	62.9
Coverage of all diseases	1.7	1.7	2.6
Coverage of chronic diseases	8.6	0.9	18.9
Coverage of dental care/eye care	–	0.9	0.9
Coverage for emergency/ accident care	1.7	–	1.7
Coverage for clinic and diagnostic services	1.7	–	1.7
Coverage for OPD expenses/ domicilary hospitalisation	13.8	4.3	25.9
Extend coverage to all wage workers and their families	–	0.9	0.9
Coverage of chronic and OPD	–	0.9	3.4
More benefits	4.3	3.4	7.8

Steps	Service Improvement	Popularity	Expectation
4. Other Suggestions	6.9	71.6	9.5
Advertisement through electronic and print media	–	37.0	–
Door to door canvassing	–	11.2	–
Extend more benefits to the agent	–	17.3	0.9
Enhanced accidents would generate more demand	0.9	3.4	–
Direct payment to hospital by the company	0.9	–	0.9
Part payment of expenses while undergoing treatment	1.7	–	0.9
Provision for no-claim bonus	–	0.9	0.9
Reduce premium	2.6	2.6	5.2
Make it a long-term policy	–	3.4	–
No discrimination while paying through 'Unique Card'	–	–	0.9
No dual pricing system by the hospital	–	0.9	–
Privatisation of insurance co. to increase efficiency	0.9	–	–
Raise sum assured/initiate group insurance in *Jan Arogya*	–	1.7	–
Non response	27.6	17.2	21.6

Source: NCAER–SEWA Survey, 1999.

in service delivery (in the opinion of 3.4 and 12.9 per cent of the respondents, respectively) will enhance the popularity of the scheme; and 6.9 per cent feel that improving customer service/better information will add to the popularity of the scheme. As far as expectations are concerned, 13.7 per cent expect quick settlement of claim and easy process for filing the claim. There are 7.9 per cent of the respondents who expect full payment of the claim/expenses.

There are not many responses worth discussing in the category of waiving of exclusions/conditions. Only 2.6 per cent of the respondents are of the opinion that the coverage of multiple hospitalisation will improve the services. The extended benefits, which the respondents believe will help in improving the services, are coverage for OPD expenses/domicilary hospitalisation. There are 25.9 per cent of the respondents who expect the coverage of OPD expenses/domicilary hospitalisation and another 18.9 per cent of them expect coverage of chronic diseases.

As far as other suggestions are concerned, 37 per cent of the respondents say that advertisements in the electronic and print media will make the scheme popular. There are 17.3 per cent who believe that more benefits should be extended to the agent. The overall response for these three broad categories of steps, which can be taken to make possible better delivery of services, exclusions, benefits and others, is: A majority feels that 'better services' among all the four steps will lead to service improvement and that is also the expectation of many. On the other hand, 71.6 per cent say that 'the other suggestions' when carried out will enhance the popularity of the scheme.

EXPECTATIONS FROM THE NEW HEALTH INSURANCE SCHEME

Over 92 per cent of the non-insured households in both rural and urban areas have no awareness about the existing health insurance schemes (see Table 7.13). This is a very critical issue despite living in the neighbourhood of ESIS and SEWA households. Further only a miniscule number of insured households were aware of the other insurance plans available in the market. When we told them about the various plans, almost all of them became interested in joining them. The SEWA plan turns out to be very appealing not only among the non-insured but also among the insured households. Further, the *Jan Arogya* plan was preferred over the *Mediclaim* plan mainly because of its lower premium.

We asked the respondents about their expectation from a new health insurance scheme in terms of influencing factors to subscribe, types of benefits coverage, type of management preferred, types of costs coverage, types of additional benefits, amount of premium willing to pay for each additional benefit, and mode of premium payment.

As far as broad expectations from a new health insurance scheme are concerned, among rural households the coverage of all illnesses and timely attention seem to be paramount (see Table 7.14). Among urban households, however it is the price of the insurance scheme that seems to be the most important factor considered for determining enrolment. Among the specific medical care benefits, coverage of hospitalisation expenditure is desired by more than 90 per cent of the

Table 7.13

Health Insurance Awareness by Health Insurance Status
of the Household in Ahmedabad

	Rural			Urban			
Indicator	Non-insured	SEWA	ESIS	Non-insured	SEWA	ESIS	Mediclaim
% reporting awareness							
None	93.0	43.0	0	91.7	26.7	0	0
Mediclaim	2.3	2.5	1.8	0	0	0.8	98.3
ESIS	1.6	4.1	100.0	1.7	3.8	97.9	1.7
SEWA	1.6	54.6	1.8	2.9	71.2	2.1	0
Other plan	1.6	2.5	0.9	5.0	2.5	0	0.9
% willing to join							
None	8.1	13.9	–	6.1	5.3	–	–
SEWA	79.8	80.0	53.1	82.6	80.0	66.5	37.1
Mediclaim	24.2	10.8	25.7	26.5	26.7	37.7	58.6
Jan Arogya	30.7	18.5	30.1	43.5	46.7	43.1	31.0

Source: NCAER–SEWA Survey, 1999.

Note: Percentages do not add to 100 because of multiple response.

respondents in both rural and urban areas. Hospitalisation being expensive, there is a strong demand for the coverage of its costs among respondents. The coverage includes that of fees, medicines, diagnostic services and hospital charges in rural areas. The urban respondents expect specialist consultation (as part of the coverage of hospital expenses). Also about 50 per cent of households expressed the coverage of expenses for transport in the plan. The expectation of coverage of Out Patient Department (OPD) and MCH services follows next to that. The availability of OPD facilities at government hospitals rather than at dispensaries and clinics is a better way of providing coverage towards expenses incurred for OPD health care. Among the coverage of additional benefits, life insurance coverage was desired most, by households in both rural and urban locations. Personal accident, permanent disability compensation, provision of cash benefits, and reimbursement of wage/income loss follows this. It is worth noting that all three household types and Mediclaim subscribers follow this preference pattern, the figures pertaining to the latter vary significantly. There are 73.3 per cent of the responses, which elicit inclusion of the life insurance coverage as additional benefits whereas

Table 7.14
Expectation from a New Health Insurance Scheme, by Health
Insurance Status of the Household, in Rural and Urban Ahmedabad

Types of Expectations/ Preferences	Rural			Urban			
	Non-insured	SEWA	ESIS	Non-insured	SEWA	ESIS	Mediclaim
% of households reported	91.3	96.7	96.5	100.0	100.0	99.6	87.1
Influencing factors to subscribe							
Cheaper	48.8	49.6	41.6	75.8	74.2	79.5	57.8
Quality	35.4	37.2	41.6	64.6	63.1	57.7	37.9
Nearby/ Accessibility	40.9	37.2	37.2	60.4	59.7	64.0	59.5
Timely attention	51.2	49.6	52.2	49.6	57.2	50.6	41.4
Coverage of all illnesses	67.7	61.2	58.4	60.0	64.0	64.9	62.1
Coverage of all services	27.6	24.0	33.6	25.0	30.5	25.9	22.4
Community managed services	1.6	0.8	–	1.7	2.1	1.3	–
Coverage of benefits							
Hospitalisation	90.6	93.4	91.2	100.0	100.0	99.6	85.3
Chronic ailment	82.7	88.4	83.2	99.6	98.7	99.2	82.8
General OPD	76.4	78.5	79.6	99.2	99.2	99.2	84.5
Specialist consultation	75.6	74.4	70.8	99.6	98.7	99.2	83.6
Reproductive and maternity care	68.5	79.3	62.8	95.8	97.5	97.1	81.0
% reporting mode of premium payment on an annual basis	77.6	65.8	73.6	67.1	64.3	69.7	78.8
Type of management preferred							
Public hospital based	29.9	29.8	25.7	14.2	11.4	17.6	25.0
Private hospital based	2.4	9.9	8.0	0.8	–	–	15.5

Types of Expectations/ Preferences	Rural			Urban			
	Non-insured	SEWA	ESIS	Non-insured	SEWA	ESIS	Mediclaim
Public insurance company	12.6	12.4	21.2	25.0	17.4	26.8	13.8
Private insurance company	2.4	2.5	3.5	8.3	–	0.8	11.2
Through bank/ financial inst.	20.5	25.6	23.9	18.3	19.5	24.7	23.3
Village level/ panchayat	9.5	6.6	8.0	–	–	–	–
NGOs	33.1	38.8	27.4	45.4	54.2	40.2	5.2
Factors for success of the plan							
Coverage of all benefits	23.6	28.9	22.1	25.4	21.6	32.6	22.4
Coverage of additional benefits	6.3	20.7	15.0	7.1	8.9	5.9	0.9
Better delivery and management	15.0	17.4	21.2	9.6	10.6	13.0	0.9
Premium related	15.8	18.2	18.6	13.8	12.3	13.4	13.8
Quick settlement of claims	3.9	2.5	7.1	3.3	2.1	1.3	4.3
Better benefits	10.2	8.3	8.0	29.6	24.6	21.8	22.4
Others	15.8	14.9	13.3	15.8	19.9	20.9	16.4

Source: NCAER–SEWA Survey, 1999.

for the rest of the urban households the corresponding figure hovers around 87.

It is not that the respondents expect the above mentioned health insurance services free of charge. The rural respondents are willing to pay an annual per capita premium between Rs 80 and Rs 95 for the coverage of services of hospitalisation, chronic ailment, specialist consultation and the like (see Table 7.15). Further, with the coverage of the costs (such as fees, medicine, diagnostic charges, transportation, etc.) the respondents are willing to pay an amount that is higher by 16 per cent. For additional benefits (such as life coverage, personal accident, etc.) however the respondents are willing

Table 7.15

Average per Capita Premium Willingness-to-pay for a New Health
Insurance Scheme, by Health Insurance Status of the
Household, in Rural and Urban Ahmedabad

	Rural			Urban			
	Non-insured	SEWA	ESIS	Non-insured	SEWA	ESIS	Mediclaim
Stage 1: After asking type of service to be covered	80.4	82.6	95.3	82.1	83.3	84.1	206.5
Stage 2: After enlisting types of costs to be covered	93.5	98.2	111.0	93.1	95.8	105.1	255.1
Stage 3: After enlisting types of additional benefits to be covered	100.4	99.8	118.9	103.9	102.9	120.2	304.2
Percentage change from							
Stage 1 to 2	16.3	18.9	16.5	13.4	15.0	25.0	23.5
Stage 2 to 3	7.4	1.6	7.1	11.6	7.4	14.4	19.2
Stage 1 to 3	24.9	20.8	24.8	26.6	23.5	42.9	47.3

Source: NCAER–SEWA Survey, 1999.

Notes: **Types of services** include coverage of hospitalisation, chronic disease,
general OPD, specialist consultation and maternity care.
Types of costs include coverage of expenses towards fees, medicine,
diagnostic service, hospital charges, specialist consultation and transportation.
Types of additional benefits include coverage of life insurance, personal
accident, permanent disability benefits, reimbursement of wage/income
loss, etc.

to pay an additional amount that is higher by around 7 per cent when
compared to the amount that they are willing to pay for coverage of
costs. The urban respondents (barring *Mediclaim* beneficiaries) are
willing to pay an amount ranging from Rs 82 to Rs 84 by type of
coverage of services. In addition to the above services, the respondents are willing to pay an amount extra by 13 to 25 per cent for the
coverage of costs and further 11 to 14 per cent more for the coverage of additional benefits. The corresponding percentages for the
Mediclaim beneficiaries are 23.5 and 19.5.

The preference for the type of management for a new health insurance scheme varied according to the place of residence. A substantial proportion of the rural respondents preferred management by non-governmental organisations (NGOs); the next to follow was public hospital based management. Also, a section of the rural respondents are of the opinion that village level institutions such as the Panchayat should be delegated the responsibility of running the new heath insurance scheme. In urban locations too, with the exception of *Mediclaim* beneficiaries, management by NGOs is most preferred. Public insurance company management follows it. Thus, it is quite indicative that most of the low-income households have faith in the public system for delivering of services.

Among the factors, which determine the success of the scheme, the 'coverage of additional benefits' scores the most both in the rural and urban samples. The SEWA beneficiaries in particular are interested in coverage of additional household members. The others are 'better delivery and management' and 'premium related' factors. In urban areas, more than the 'premium related' factors, it is the provision of 'better benefits' which determines the success of a health insurance scheme.

POLICY IMPLICATIONS

This study addresses some critical issues with regard to extending health insurance coverage to poor households in general and those working in the informal sector in particular. These issues have become extremely important in the current context of liberalisation of the insurance sector in India. There is no doubt that health insurance will be one of the high priority areas as far as consumers, providers, and insurance companies are concerned. However, developing and marketing of unique and affordable health insurance packages for low-income people would be a great challenge.

First of all, there is a strongly expressed need for health insurance among low-income households in both rural and urban areas. This need has arisen primarily because of the heavy burden of out-of-pocket expenditure on them while seeking healthcare. Despite a significant reliance on public health facilities, the poor households tend to spend nearly one-fifth of their income on treatment. Even among the fully insured households under the ESIS, the burden is unduly large, particularly among rural households. This clearly reflects upon the large-scale inefficiency prevalent in the delivery of healthcare services by both government and ESIS sectors.

The ESIS, with its large infrastructure set-up, however has substantial scope for improvement, especially through the introduction of private initiatives. The latter can be of such nature as the opening of underutilised facilities to the general public for the payment of nominal charges, allowing the private practitioners to use labs, radio-diagnostic services, operation theatres, evening OPDs, etc. The panel doctors can be replaced with mobile facilities. This will specially benefit the rural beneficiaries since most of them are affiliated to the panel doctors who are very irregular in delivering the services. There are in fact, instances of such initiatives being undertaken in some of the ESIS hospitals. A recent World Bank study suggests some more drastic options too, like the separation of the health service delivery function (of ESIS) from the cash benefits component. Over time, the health service delivery elements of ESIS can be transferred to a separate state-owned entity, which may be privatised fully at a later point in time. These steps could both improve the quality of health care services, as well as reduce the corruption that is substantial in the area of issuing cash compensation (Naylor et al. 1999).

Mediclaim, which is presently the only public sector managed health insurance scheme, too will have to gear up if it wishes to remain in the race. There is lot of ignorance regarding the scheme. *Jan Arogya Bima* policy, which is one of the schemes (of the General Insurance Corporation) specially designed for people in the low-income group, is not known by the majority. The other areas where there is scope for improvement is the coverage of problems such as those related to ophthalmic and dental care, making the process of filing claims easy and quick settlement of claims.

While, measures for improvement in the ESIS and the *Mediclaim* programmes are a necessity, nevertheless these will continue to cover a small proportion of the population. There are hence many other emerging issues as far as future health insurance schemes are concerned. The expectations of low-income households from a new scheme indicate that coverage of illnesses, coverage of services, amount of the premium to be paid as well as the procedural aspects such as filing claims are critical in the decision to buy insurance. A strong preference for SEWA type of health insurance schemes reinforces the notion that the beneficiaries desire a system, which is not only affordable but also accessible in terms of easy settlement of claims and other related administrative procedures. The range of services expected to be covered include hospitalisation, maternal and outpatient facilities.

As far as the management of a health insurance scheme is concerned, the responses indicate a preference for some version of community financing. It appears that a scheme where the disbursement of services will take place from a public sector hospital with monetary contribution from the beneficiaries will be in demand. A pure privately managed health. insurance scheme was among the least preferred ones. In rural areas, a preference for the management of health insurance schemes by the *panchayats* was also cited.

Finally, the need for education about the insurance concept and information on health insurance for rural and urban folk alike is a crucial aspect in extending health insurance coverage on a large scale. This study demonstrates that while there is great interest, the concept of health insurance and paying for a service, which may or not be availed of, is new to low-income people. This calls for effective Information Education and Communication (IEC) activities which will generate an understanding of insurance by the public and hence help in developing a market for health insurance.

Box 7.2: Implications for Future Action

This study brings out a number of issues with regard to developing health insurance for urban and rural working people. These issues are extremely relevant in the current context of deregulation of the insurance sector in India, and consequently the expected development of competitive insurance packages. There is no doubt that health insurance will be one of the high priority areas as far as both clients and insurance companies are concerned. It is also an area that is fraught with unanswered questions, given our large, poor and hence more disease-prone, population.

A host of questions arise when health insurance is considered, especially in the context of the poor who are primarily engaged in work in the unorganised sector. This study has implications for future action and also further study.

(Continued)

Box 7.2 (Continued)

1. There is a strongly expressed need for health insurance among families of the working poor, both urban and rural. Once the knowledge and understanding of health insurance increases and spreads, an even stronger demand can be expected from these workers of both the unorganised and organised sectors.

2. There is both a willingness and ability to pay among urban and rural families alike, the range of ability to pay, being between Rs 90 to Rs 111. Given this, as well as existing experience, one may surmise that substantial health insurance coverage—i.e., of major expenses—can be achieved.

3. Hospitalisation is the main need to be considered in developing health insurance. However, some OPD services and reproductive health care are also expressed needs. Women expressed maternity benefits as a need which will have to be considered seriously, given the continuing high maternal mortality ratios in India, and the fact that increasing numbers of women are entering the workforce.

4. The nature, range and extent of coverage are important factors determining people's willingness to pay for health insurance. The cost of the premium and timely disbursement of benefits are also critical factors. This implies that apart from the economics of health insurance, the mechanisms and procedures adopted and developed by the insurer merit close attention.

Strong preference for the SEWA-type of health insurance among the general population—those SEWA members insured in existing government schemes who are as yet not enrolled in the insurance programme—also suggests that a health insurance system which is both affordable and accessible is in high demand. The paying capacity has already been mentioned, but the accessibility issues will have to be examined in more depth.

One possibility is that of developing client-owned and client-run health insurance with decentralised systems for timely disbursement of benefits. This would imply the setting up of a worker/client-owned form of organisation like a cooperative. The worker-clients would put up the share capital, develop their own bye-laws and systems, and would have a democratically elected executive committee to function and manage the health insurance scheme according to the set bye-laws.

In addition, decentralised branches of the organisation could be developed at the district level for increased accessibility and speedy disbursement of benefits. Intensive extension work is an essential part of this approach. Having a large number of client shareholders would keep administrative costs low and also offer more possibilities for coverage. Further studies analysing costs of such an approach would be useful to determine the viability of this.

5. With regard to payment of premium, one interesting finding is that rural people prefer post-harvest lump sum payments, as at this time they are in a position to pay out the required sums. This has implications for the development of schemes to cover rural families. Perhaps the client-oriented, decentralised approach would be able to incorporate this preference of rural people.

6. The need for education on the insurance concept and information on health insurance is an important need of both urban and rural people. While there is great interest, the concept of health insurance, and planning for the future by setting aside a premium is new to most people. This implies that educational activities aimed at both generating understanding of insurance and marketing of this insurance product are essential elements in developing a health insurance programme.

7. One interesting finding of this study is that both urban and rural people prefer a package of insurance products. For example, along with health, accident and life insurance are expressed as needs. These additional products may be considered to both enhance the marketability and competitiveness of the package offered and also provide additional essential risk coverage to poor families.

8. There are a number of emerging issues vis-à-vis future coverage. People clearly want more coverage in health insurance—both in terms of the total amounts covered and the range of coverage (OPD, reproductive health, maternity benefits, specialist services, etc.). But they also want total

(Continued)

Box 7.2 (Continued)

family coverage. Of course all of these involve balancing out costs with the ability to pay. But the fact that these are expressed needs means that additional coverage may be considered and even developed in a phased manner in the future.

Mirai Chatterjee
SEWA, Ahmedabad

NOTES

1. For details regarding conceptual problems in measurement of perceived morbidity see Gumber and Berman (1997).
2. On fixed deposit, the annual accrual interest @ 12 per cent is considered as premium. Those who have opted for a recurring deposit of Rs 20 per month will become entitled for benefits after two years.

REFERENCES AND SELECT BIBLIOGRAPHY

Ahmad, Ehtisham, Jean Dreze, John Hills and Amartya Sen (eds) (1991), *Social Security in Developing Countries*, Oxford: Clarendon Press.

Chatterjee, Mirai and Jayshree Vyas (1997), *Organising Insurance for Women Workers: The SEWA Experience* (Mimeo), Self-Employed Women's Association, Ahmedabad.

Gumber, Anil (1997), 'Burden of Disease and Cost of Ill Health in India: Setting Priorities for Health Interventions During the Ninth Plan', *Margin*, vol. 29, no. 2: 132–72.

——— (1998), 'Facets of Indian Healthcare Market—Some Issues', *Saket Industrial Digest*, vol. 4, no. 12.

Gumber, Anil and Peter Berman (1997), 'Measurement and Pattern of Morbidity and the Utilization of Health Services: Some Emerging Issues from Recent Health Interview Surveys in India', *Journal of Health & Population in Developing Countries*, vol. 1, no. 1: 16–43.

Naylor, David C., Prabhat Jha, John Woods and Abusaleh Shariff (1999), *A Fine Balance: Some Options for Private and Public Health Care in Urban India*, World Bank, Washington, D.C.

Shariff, Abusaleh, Anil Gumber, Ravi Duggal and Moneer Alam (1999), 'Health Care Financing and Insurance Perspective for the Ninth Plan (1997–2002)', *Margin*, vol. 32, no. 2: 38–68.

Srinivas, Smita (1997), *Providing Health Insurance and Social Security for Over 15000 Poor Women workers: A profile of the SEWA Health Insurance Scheme and the Women Who Use it* (Mimeo), SEWA, Ahmedabad.

Visaria, Pravin and Anil Gumber (1994), *Utilization of and Expenditure on Health Care in India, 1986–87*, Gujarat Institute of Development Research, Ahmedabad.

❽

Bringing Informal
Workers Centrestage

RENANA JHABVALA

Today, the unorganised sector is taken far more seriously than it was two decades ago. It has been a long journey for these workers from the margins towards the centre, which has happened not because of any changes in the conditions of the workers and but far more due to the changes in perception that have come about with the historical shifts due to globalisation. In Self-Employed Women's Association (SEWA) we have been experiencing these changes firsthand. When SEWA first started it was considered, by all who we talked to, that these were marginal workers and that their issues are really not very important. Over the years, women workers in the unorganised sector are being taken more seriously at the local and national levels. We have experienced these changes in very concrete ways at the ground level during the last 15 years. At the same time at the national level we experienced that our work was being taken more seriously, and that policies began changing to first recognise, then accommodate unorganised workers. At the international level too we experienced that these workers began moving out of the margins. We experienced real changes in the economy which reflected in our work deepening and expanding.

However, a change in real conditions needs to be accompanied by changes in perceptions, thinking, interpretation and theory. At the international level, there was a growing dominance of neo-liberal thought, which began to be reflected in India. The new thinking affected budgets and policies in drastic ways, but it also opened up space for new ways of looking at the unorganised sector, and over the last decade there has been a change in thinking and writing, to which the joint studies of SEWA, National Council of Applied Economic Research (NCAER) and Gujarat Institute of Development Research (GIDR) have contributed.

The process of bringing the unorganised workers centrestage is still going on. In alliance with other actors, SEWA has contributed to this process, and continues to do so. Because we are in the midst of it, we have been able to see the ongoing changes reflected at the ground level and in changes in SEWA's own role and structure, at the national level and at the international level. Being in the midst of events we see the changes in many layers—in income and employment opportunities, in policies, in attitudes. We also see the changes reflected at many levels—among the workers themselves, among the general public, in trade unions, nationally and internationally. These many layers of change work and interact on each other, leading to widening ripples which eventually engulf society as a whole.

Here I would like to describe the changes in the economy and in the thinking as we experienced it at SEWA, and will try to link our own experiences with the larger changes occurring both nationally and internationally.

THE INITIAL YEARS: THE INDUSTRIAL MAN

Initially, in the early 1970s, SEWA found a great deal of resistance even to the idea of organising women in this sector. Most people believed that to qualify as a worker a person had to be an employee, the problem being compounded by the belief that women were not workers but only wives and mothers. The initial resistance to SEWA came from the Labour Commissioner who refused to register SEWA as a trade union. First, he said, these workers had no definite employer, so they did not fit the traditional definition of worker. Who would they bargain with? Second, these workers had no fixed occupation. They went from one kind of work to another, they did a number of different types of work together. A proper worker had only one permanent occupation, and trade unions were formed by occupation. And finally, these workers often had no fixed place of work, such as a factory, so how would it be possible to organise them. Interestingly, the Trade Union Act, does not in fact specify all these conditions, but the officials had a certain type of worker in mind and the women we brought to them did not fit into their idea of a worker.

In fact, women did not fit into anyone's idea of a worker. In India there is a very large category of home-based workers making a variety of goods in their own homes either for direct sale or for a contractor or employer. When we first started organising the women garment stitchers, we were told by the employers that these women were not workers but just housewives who were stitching in their 'leisure time'; whereas we found that they were working anywhere between eight to 10 hours a day. We were also told by the labour commissioner's office that since there was no direct employer–employee relationship between the employer and the women, they were not covered by any labour laws, although we found that there was complete control of production by the employers. Even the husbands of the workers said 'my wife does not work' but only does this as a 'hobby'. Statistical agencies too ignored these women and their work did not appear in population censuses.

These attitudes reflected a larger perspective, which defined a worker as one who conformed to the image of the 'labouring or industrial man'. This was a full time, generally male, worker, with one skill and one occupation, working for a well-defined employer in a factory or office, a workplace under the control of the employer. This worker, or employee, sold his labour to the employer and received a wage or salary in return. It was the security of this 'industrial worker' around which the systems of security or social protection were based. This prototype of the worker was imported from the industrialised countries into India:

The twentieth century has been the century of the labouring man. From the earliest years, his needs and contribution to economic expansion became the primary impetus to social and labour market policy... Subordinated to the dictates of mass production and large scale organisations, worker stability was regarded as the desirable norm for industrial society... the two models in competition were welfare state capitalism and state socialism. Although there were crucial differences these had much in common... there were common developmental goals that were in one form or other exported to developing countries.

These two models of desirable society were based on the interests of the labouring man, and the pursuit of his basic needs and aspirations. Everywhere people were to be made more like the norm of the labouring man (Standing 1999: 51).

Within this prototype of the industrial or labouring man, is subsumed the housewife woman. The industrial man through his earnings supports a family, and the woman's role is nurturing the worker and his children. These norms were reflected even in the labour laws—for example, the recommended guidelines for fixing the minimum wage, is that one wage earner should support three consumption units, which would include the man himself, his wife and two children. (Man is one consumption unit, woman is 0.8 consumption unit and children are 0.6 consumption units each.)

SEWA, in the initial years, was part of a larger trade union called the Textile Labour Association, and to us, the contrast between the security of the organised or formal sector worker and the insecurity of the unorganised sector was very obvious. The textile workers, like workers in other big factories and in public sector offices were protected by a variety of labour laws and machineries. These laws guaranteed them economic security and social security. Their work was protected, in that they could not be easily dismissed. Their income was enough to meet their needs and was protected through dearness allowances. Their old age needs were met by the Employees Provident Fund system and their health needs by the Employees Social Insurance Corporation. They had voice representation through the statutory bargaining mechanisms and through the Industrial Disputes Act and through being represented on boards and committees which decided and administered these acts. In contrast, the unorganised workers had no security of work, no access to social security and no voice.

Once it was recognised that the unorganised were workers too, the major question was what were the methods and mechanisms, which would help them to move towards greater security. The only available instruments were the statutory regulations and SEWA began to try and use these regulations, as well as modify and adapt them. The experiences were mixed. Where the laws and schemes were open to flexibility, a certain measure of security could be achieved. However, in general, we found that the laws were actually designed for the industrial worker and could not be adapted. Two examples will illustrate this point. Unorganised workers often have accidents in the course of their work. SEWA went to court on behalf of a cart-puller, with a hired cart, who was involved in a street accident and broke both legs, in the process of delivering cloth from a wholesaler to a retailer. Although the cart-puller had been delivering goods for the wholesaler for more than 20 years, the court ruled that there was no employer–employee relationship, and so no one could be held liable under the Workmen's Compensation Act. On the other hand we were more succesful with the Bidi Workers Welfare Fund Act, where there is no intrinsic need to prove an employer–employee relationship. The employer is not directly liable for particular employees, but pays contributions, through a cess into a fund, which provides social protection to bidi workers. This law was more easily adapted to unorganised workers since social protection is not linked to the employer–employee relationship, and we were able to get a large number of bidi workers covered.

However, these were lonely struggles, in an almost hostile environment. The unorganised sector was 89 per cent of the workforce, and policy-makers were definitely concerned about the poverty and vulnerability of these workers. But there were few attempts to either extend the existing social protection regulatory framework or to think about alternative methods of social protection for them.

The *Report of the National Commission on Labour, 1969* reflected the prevalent mind-set. The bulk of the report was concerned with industrial labour, with less than 10 per cent of the report, 45 pages out of over 500, explicitly referring to non-industrial workers. The objectives of the report are stated as: To 'review the existing legislative and other provisions intended to protect the interests of labour and to advise how far these provisions serve ... the national objective of establishing a socialist society and achieving planned economic development' and second 'our approach throughout has to be inspired by a quest for industrial harmony' (*Report of the National Commission on Labour* 1969: 45, 55).

The bulk of the report is concerned with the working of the protective legislative framework—i.e., the various labour laws, the concern with employment security through training, employment agencies, income security through wages, bonuses etc., social security through the ESIS, Labour Welfare and Housing Boards, representation security through organisations, wage councils, tripartite machinery, etc.

THE BEGINNING OF CHANGE

In India the first challenge to the model of the 'industrial man' came from the women's movement, which began gathering momentum in the 1970s. The leaders of this movement recognised that in addition to being wives and mothers, women were also active workers and that it was important to recognise their worker role. Furthermore, they saw that most of these women workers were in the unorganised sector.

94% of the women workers are engaged in the unorganised sector of the economy, 81.4% in agriculture and the rest in non-agricultural occupations. The major problems that affect them spring from the unorganised nature of all industry in this sector. They are outside the reach of most laws that seek to protect the security and working conditions of labour. Labour organisations are mostly absent. Where they do exist they are still in the formative stages and have had little impact on women (*Towards Equality:* 157).

The 1970s also saw a number of protests and workers movements, which carried on into the 1980s. The large numbers of workers who were left out of the security provided by the statutory legal protections, began to organise and demand a share. There was the rise of the fisherman's movement, the contract workers especially in the mines, forest workers, construction workers and agricultural labourers too had begun to organise. There were also large-scale farmer's movements. However, in most cases the existing laws proved to be irrelevant. Some new laws such as the Contract Labour Act and the Inter State Migrant Act, were enacted during this time. However, even these acts were based on the 'Industrial man' and so could never really be applied to workers who did not fit that mode.

Internationally, too the informal sector was discovered in the early 1970s, perhaps the first international acknowledgement of the existence of alternative forms of work. The International Labour Organisation adopted and popularised the term informal sector in a series of studies that focussed on the problems of employment in the urban areas of developing countries. The growth of the urban labour force in the developing countries brought home the fact that the jobs as envisaged in the European models of development, just did not exist for the majority of workers, and were unlikely to do so in the near future.

Although there were the beginnings of recognition that the unorganised, or informal, sector did indeed exist and was unlikely to disappear in the near future, there seemed to be a great deal of reluctance to actually extend the facilities of social protection to this sector. Most policy-makers were reluctant to even begin the task as they were afraid that once they began to think about this huge unorganised sector, it would open a 'Pandora's Box' (Personal conversation with senior trade unionist). The following attitude was typical:

The main obstacle in the extension of social security coverage to the wage earners in small and tiny establishments is the formidable task of identifying the potential insured persons, their registration and the formulation of a working plan for their coverage. More than this, the high operational costs of extension to the unorganised workforce, fishermen, small artisans and other unprotected groups impel the government and other social security planners to shrink from the administrative and financial consequences that might arise out of extended coverage (Singh 1994).

RAPID WINDS OF CHANGE

But in the 1980s and 1990s there were rapid changes taking place internationally with the ascendancy of the forces of globalisation and trade liberalisation. The macroeconomic changes in industrialised countries were supported by the rise of neo-liberalism which shifted the emphasis from security to growth. Regulations which promoted security were seen as inimical to economic growth, and 'deregulation' was to be promoted in order to facilitate the working of the market.

According to the Chicago school of law and economics, statutory or institutional regulations can be justified only if they promote, or do not impede growth. If they do not do that, they are impediments to efficiency, and therefore, because efficiency and growth are equated with improvements in social welfare, most regulations are suspect. This perspective was to become pervasively influential (Standing 1999: 75).

In India, this school of thought gradually began to gain ascendancy in the mid to late 1980s, and became the dominant school of thought with the debt crisis in 1991. The main targets of this new school of thought were the public sector undertakings, the visible face of the socialist economy. In addition, there were persistent demands for the 'deregulation' of markets, which included delicensing of industry, lowering import and excise taxes and removal of reservations and quotas for categories such as small-scale industries. The popular image of the 'License-Permit Raj' caught the imagination not only of the industrialists, but of the middle classes as well as the poor, all of whom continually suffered under the high-handed treatment and corruption of the entrenched bureaucracy.

The statutory regulatory system for labour too came under attack with demands for an 'exit' policy to increase the 'flexibility' of firms and allow them to compete internationally. More and more came to be written about the privileged position of formal sector labour. The focus began to shift towards workers who were not part of the formal sector.

We were able to see some of the effects of the 'informalisation', very early in the process. Ahmedabad, where SEWA is based, was a prosperous city, with its wealth based on the production of more than 60 textile mills with a labour force of 150,000 workers employed in them. These workers had, over the course of the century, acquired a certain degree of security. They had secure jobs with a living wage, they were covered by social security schemes protecting their health and old age. They had a strong union, which not only represented them in disputes but also ran activities for the welfare of the workers and their families. The textile workers of Ahmedabad had begun to enter the ranks of the middle classes.

In the early 1908s, textile mills all over the country began to close down. In some places, such as Mumbai, the mills closed rapidly. In Ahmedabad, the process of closure was long drawn out, and spread over 10 years. Over this period approximately over 80,000 permanent workers and over 50,000 non-permanent workers lost their jobs and were driven into the informal sector. The city experienced an economic recession and public disturbances, especially communal riots. A whole class of workers were thrown back from the middle class into the informal sector, into poverty. There was widespread alcoholism and suicides, children were withdrawn from school and sent to work.

We witnessed the rapid decline of the formal sector in Ahmedabad and the insecurity and misery it brings. In one of the studies in this volume Jeemol Unni has shown how the formal sector reduced from over 70 per cent to under 30 per cent of the workforce. The process of informalisation of the workforce made workers and trade unions begin to realise the importance of organising the informal workers. Once the mill-workers lost their jobs, they were no longer members of the trade union and no longer had a collective voice.

SEWA was one of the leading voices demanding recognition for the workers of the unorganised sector. In 1984 the SEWA Annual Conference passed a resolution, which stated

We are part of the vast majority of the working population who earn their meagre living through self-employment. We are agricultural labourers working in fields all over the country. We are construction workers building roads, dams, monuments. We fetch and carry, load and unload. We provide a variety of services such as washing, cleaning, cooking, transport. We are piece-rate workers making *bidis*, garments, paper products *aggarbattis*. We are artisans and small producers doing brassware, block printing, patchwork, paintings, milk production. We are vendors selling fruits, fish, cooked eatables ...

We feel that a first step to amelioration of our extreme poverty is a proper study of the conditions under which we live and work ... We therefore ask for a Commission for the Self-employed (in the broader sense of Self-employed) to study our situation and our problems and to propose solutions.

SEWA took a delegation to the Labour Minister in 1985 and subsequently to the Prime Minister in 1986 to press for this resolution. It is a measure of the changing times that the National Commission on Self-employed Women and Women in the Informal Sector was set up in 1986 with Smt Ela Bhatt, General Secretary of SEWA as its Chairperson. The National Commission on Self-employed Women and Women in the Informal Sector was set up to with the explicit purpose of recognising these as yet unrecognised workers and recommending steps for their social protection:

Despite the existence of various constitutional legal provisions safeguarding women's employment a large number of women workers particularly in the unorganised sector suffer from various disadvantages relating to their working lives as well as in their homes. The coverage of labour laws has not benefited these women workers in many crucial areas especially health, maternity and social security. With the changing social and economic conditions, women's productive roles have assumed new significance but without back-up support and services a healthy combination of women's productive and reproductive roles cannot be sustained ... (*Shram Shakti* 1987: 1).

The Commission decided that it will cover and study the entire gambit of unprotected labouring women to include self-employed and wage labour, paid and unpaid labour and contract labour. The Commission decided to cover the following categories of workers:

(a) Women doing manual work like agriculture, construction labour and other sectors.
(b) Home-based producers (including artisans and piece-rate workers).
(c) Women engaged in processing work in traditional and non-traditional areas.

(d) Providers of services like washerwomen, scavengers and domestic help.

(e) Petty vendors and hawkers who do not hire labour except for taking the assistance of family members.

(f) And all other poor labouring women, in the unprotected sector not covered in the preceding sections.

In view of the wide scope of the concept of worker the Commission has used the terms 'self-employed', 'informal' and 'unorganised' interchangeably.

The Commission also decided that all the terms of reference should be addressed to the following three objectives:

1. To bring into visibility poor unprotected labouring women to which the large majority belong.

2. To bring out the contribution of the target group of women as mentioned at (1) above to the family economy and the national economy.

3. To identify and examine the succesful methodologies in organising the unorganised women labour (*Shram Shakti* 1987: 2–3).

However, once these larger groups of workers began to be considered the solutions began to take on a different character. Although, the statutory regulation route was still recommended, non-statutory schemes became the norm.

In India, during the 1980s, a plethora of schemes were instituted for the social protection of unorganised workers. Most of these were social assistance schemes administered by the state or central governments. These included pensions for widows, welfare funds for fishermen, maternity benefits for agricultural workers and many more. However, given the inherently inefficient nature of bureaucracy-administered schemes, these measures, although expensive to the public exchequer, tended to remain marginal, except in areas where there were effective organisations of the workers.

During this period some innovative regulatory schemes too were developed. The Bidi and Cigar Welfare Fund Act, and the Bidi and Cigar Cess Act though passed in 1976, were implemented in the 1980s. This act, which provided social security schemes like health-care, childcare and housing could be extended to the unorganised sector because it did not require an employer–employee relationship. The Government of Kerala, passed a large number of laws providing social security to various sectors of unorganised workers—coir workers, toddy tappers, agricultural workers, etc. Various state governments'— Tamil Nadu, Maharashtra, Gujarat—laws called the 'Manual Workers' Acts got around the lack of an employer–employee relationship in setting up tripartite boards.

Another major change that SEWA began to notice was the acceptance of the unorganised sector worker as a worker, by the trade unions who, in the earlier years were almost hostile to the existence of these workers. When SEWA first took up the issue of recognition and protection of homebased workers, it was ridiculed.

> When I first raised the issue of homebased workers in the National Convention of our own federation the National Labour Organisation in 1981, I was ridiculed. The speakers responding to me said that these were not workers, only housewives. They said 'What can we demand? They have their own bathrooms and canteens right in the house.' They just laughed away the issue (author's interview with Ela Bhatt, Founder, SEWA).

However, by 1991, the National Trade Union Centres in India, had begun supporting the demand for a Law for Home-based workers.

The international trade unions too changed their views on unorganised workers. In its world congress in Dublin, March 1976, the International Textile, Garment and Leather Workers Federation (ITGLWF) resolved: 'It is essential that we reaffirm our determination to fight against the evil of industrial home work as a threat to the well-being of workers throughout the world' (ITGLWF Resolution 1976).

However, by 1988, the International Confederation of Free Trade Unions (ICFTU) had recognised the existence of large and growing numbers of home-based workers worldwide, and in its World Congress in 1988 it passed a resolution calling for recognition of and protection for home-based workers.

> ... Calls on its affiliated organisations to develop special organising programmes directed at homebased worker ... to press for legislation for protecting homebased workers and to resist economic policy decisions that destroy the livelihood of homebased workers and to give them access to collective bargaining ... (ICFTU Resolution 1988).

Perhaps the most relevant development during this period was the rise of 'market-based solutions' to the question of social protection. This is in keeping with the worldwide swing from statutory to market regulation of the labour market.

In the mid-1970s began what can be called the era of market regulation. An important part of the agenda amounted to a strategy for changing the boundaries of control over labour relations ... What supply-siders have promoted is pro-individualistic regulations (or anti-collective regulations) and greater use of fiscal and promotional regulations (Standing 1999: 75).

In India too we saw a growth of 'market-based' organisations which grew with the opening up of the economy. Private initiative of course grew at a tremendous rate. Government social services were replaced, often undermined, by private services. Private medical practitioners, for example, replaced government clinics in most states. These private practioners ranged from highly skilled surgeons and specialists, offering services in expensive 'five-star' hospitals, to village level 'compounders'. However, along with private practioners there was also a less obvious growth of more social market-based solutions. Many hospitals and clinics were set up by charitable trusts. Non-governmental organisations promoted community-based healthcare which was notably more succesful than the public sector clinics.

Perhaps the best known initiatives have been in the area of micro-finance—a system of extension of financial services, savings, credit and now insurance, to the poor, most of whom are in the unorganised sector. Mainstream financial institutions too became players in the field. In 1988, the Government of India deposited Rs 1 billion with the Life Insurance Corporation of India to provide insurance for this sector. The nationalised banks were instructed to provide loans at easy terms to the self-employed sector.

SEWA, during this period, experienced changes connected with the more liberal policy atmosphere. As unorganised workers were more generally recognised as workers, SEWA's membership grew during the last decade (see Table 8.1).

During this period, the cooperatives providing service health care—Lok Swasthya—and child care—Sangini—grew. SEWA bank benefited from a more permissive Reserve Bank and was able to expand to the rural areas. The figures in Table 8.2 show how growth in the bank has responded to the changes in policies. The 10 years from 1977 to 1987 showed a doubling of depositors and a tenfold growth in working capital. Whereas within the next 10 years depositors grew almost four times and capital 20 times.

In 1991 SEWA was also able to begin an insurance scheme for its members which grew to cover nearly 100,000 members in 10 years.

Table 8.1
Increase in SEWA Membership, 1975–95

Year	Membership
1975	3,850
1985	15,741
1995	218,797

Table 8.2
Increase in Depositors and Capital in SEWA Bank

Year	No. of Depositors	Working Capital	Profit
1977–78	11,656	Rs 1,448,600	Rs 13,700
1987–88	23,156	Rs 14,931,000	Rs 370,000
1997–98	8,410,000	Rs 209,578,000	Rs 1,758,000

PROMOTING THE PEOPLE'S SECTOR—AN ECONOMIC DECENTRALISATION APPROACH

Society can function well only if there are accepted rules that everyone is ready to obey and that can be enforced or implemented through sanctioned mechanisms. Three types of mechanisms have been identified which regulate work and labour markets. First are statutory regulations which include protective rules and laws to protect the weaker members of society; fiscal regulations that encourage certain forms of activity and discourage other forms; and promotional regulations, which are rules and mechanisms, other than fiscal; and facilitating regulations that permit activities to take place if there is a desire to do so.

Second, there are market regulations, where authorities seek to maximise reliance on market forces. Market regulation tends to increase market dependency, whereas statutory regulations decrease it.

Finally there is voice regulation, where practices and changes are managed through bargaining and negotiation between representatives of different interests. Voice regulation requires that the parties involved have reasonably sustainable strength and that there is a willingness to engage over a period of time (Standing 1999: 41–43).

Rapid changes are taking place in India today. The effects of globalisation are being felt in almost every sphere of life, with its resultant opportunities on the one hand and dislocations and insecurities on the other. There are few studies on the effects of globalisation on the unorganised sector, although anecdotal information confirms major dislocations of employment and growing costs of social protection. On the other hand, there is a fast rise in education, awareness and expectations and the workers in this sector are in search of a better life, if not for themselves, at least for their children.

At the policy level, too, there seems to be a search for policies which can deliver the benefits of globalisation to this section and at the same time reduce its negative effects. However, in today's world some policies are more acceptable than others. As we have explained earlier, statutory regulations, especially protective regulations have had their heyday, and not only is there considerable resistance to new laws, but also a process to dismantle many of the existing ones. Market regulations and market-based solutions are more acceptable, and in fact fit in better with the extensive 'marketisation' and 'privatisation' of all spheres of economic life that are occurring with globalisation. Voice regulation, is an area that has been thoroughly explored in the political sphere and hardly at all in the economic one.

However, proposed policies cannot just be an expediency to the current thinking but must reflect the current need and more importantly lead in a specific direction. In other words, policies and regulations are both a response to an existing situation and a step towards a different vision of society. In the unorganised sector, the need is fairly clear and has been spelled out by various National Commissions quoted earlier, in particular, the National Commission on Self-employed Women and the National Commission on Rural Labour. These needs centre around three aspects of economic life. First, is the need for work and income security; second, the need for social protection and finally, the need for organisation and voice.

The policies recommended to fulfil each of these needs would reflect the approach, or vision, if you will, of the proposer. The earlier policies of protective statutory regulations which reflected the ideal society of state socialism, has been replaced by a vision of a free and globalising market, which through rapid economic growth and expanding political democracy, would fulfil the needs of employment and income, social protection and voice. However, at this stage in the world's development, there is an acknowledgement that neither of these approaches has worked, at least for the weaker and poorer members of society. Here we would like to suggest an alternative approach which draws on both the market and different forms of voice regulation.

As we have seen, most workers in India are in what has been called the 'unorganised' sector. This is neither the public sector, controlled by the government, nor the private sector, controlled by large corporate interests. Most of these workers are in small enterprises, own-account workers, small farmers or linked through a series of contractors and chains to the large enterprises. Their method of work is through sale of their labour, such as construction labour or agricultural labour, or through self-employment as small producers, vendors or service providers. Most worker families, especially in rural areas, use a combination of methods for their livelihood.

Often, they organise themselves into larger work systems, which may or may not be officially registered. These may be cooperatives, which predominate in India in the milk sector, handloom sector and agricultural sector. Or they may be unregistered groups such as chit funds, farmer's irrigation groups and groups of producers supported by non-government organisations (NGOs). There are literally millions of such groups across the country, they are the basis of production systems, yet they remain undocumented and unrecognised. We call this vast system of small producers/vendors/service providers with its network of formal and informal organisations the 'people's sector'.

The private and public sector at present, dominate the economy in terms of control and visibility. Prices and markets are generally controlled by these sectors as are the laws and policies. However recent years have seen the public sector giving way to the private sector as more and more industries and enterprises earlier controlled by the public sector are being privatised.

All three sectors, the private, the public and the people's sector, have been interdependent on each other. Whereas much of the actual production is in the people's sector, it depends for its marketing on the private or sometimes the public sectors. In agriculture for example, although most produce is grown by small farmers, the markets are controlled by the large private traders or by the Food Corporation of India. More recently, a number of multinational companies have been buying produce from cooperative societies and marketing products under their brand names. The infrastructural support such as electricity, transport and water have generally been provided by the public sector, although the private sector is beginning to take over some infrastructural functions. The public sector banks and the private moneylenders have been, till recently, the main source of credit for the people's sector.

However, the interdependence has rarely been on equal terms. The people's sector have never had a level playing field but have been dominated and controlled by both the public and private sectors. The terms of trade have been heavily weighted against the people's sector. An artisan who makes products out of bamboo, for example, faces a raw materials (bamboo) market dominated by a monopolistic Forest Department, and a market for finished products dominated by a single trader or a cartel of traders, operating in the area. In both these markets the terms of trade are against him (or her). Furthermore, neither the public or the private sector has encouraged growth of people's sector organisations, but have tried either to suppress or supplant them, or to control them. For example, it has been our experience that if they are successful, they have been taken over by private companies. Similarly, the government has often tried to destroy the independence of cooperatives by putting government administrators in charge of them.

Perhaps the dominance of the private sector in recent policies can be seen most clearly in the terms and conditions which have brought in liberalisation. The 'License-Permit Raj' was certainly liberalised for large industry, but it remained in place for the street vendor, who needs and cannot get a license to sell her goods; for the forest producer who is illegal without a license and even when she gets one, can only sell to a monopoly public sector corporation; for the small farmer who is not allowed to sell his products freely across state borders. At the same time the market regulations for new opportunities have encouraged the bigger players and discouraged the people's sector. When the insurance sector was opened up, for example, it required a capital base for a new insurance company to be a minimum of Rs 1 billion which ruled out any market share for the thousands of small registered and unregistered mutuals which flourished all over the country.

The basis for people's organisations has been one of mutual trust and cooperation. Unlike the private sector, it is not pure self-interest, rather a mixture of self-interest and cooperation. The people's sector, which relies on and uses market forces, has also been called the 'Civil Economy'.

A too narrow interpretation of the notion of market economy has brought us to believe that 'the market leaves us with no way to appreciate disinterest'. I believe it is time to reexamine that very foundation of economic theory according to which rational economic man is conceived as a calculating self-interested maximiser. I argue for a more realistic and solid view that takes into account the possibility of visualizing a market society as composed of both a private economy and a civil economy (Zamagini 1999: 1).

If we can identify the public economy with the set of activities organized and legitimized by coercive powers, and the private economy with the set of profit-oriented activities organized according to the principle of exchange of equivalents, the civil economy is represented by all those activities in which neither coercion nor profit are the *primum movens* or the ultimate target. In other words, while in public and private spheres the principle of legitimization of economic decisions is represented, in the one case by the right of citizenship, in the other case by purchasing-power, in the civil economy it is represented by the *reciprocity principle...* reciprocity cannot be explained in terms of *self-interest* alone: motives and relations are basic elements of the concept of reciprocity ... One should recognize however that reciprocity owns a strategic dimension of its own (ibid.: 8–10).

The future for unorganised workers lies in the people's sector. However, in spite of the vibrancy of this sector, it will not happen on its own. Our experience in SEWA has been that in order to build sustainable organisations used, managed and owned by the workers a number of inputs and changes are required. First, is the need for policies which recognise and promote this sector. It has to be recognised that people's economic organisations are a viable alternative. There has to be serious thinking also on the legal forms of people's economic organisations; the existing legal forms of people's organisations tend to be outdated. For example, in the field of microfinance the only forms of organisation available are either those of private companies or of charitable societies. There is no legal recognition of the people's sector. We need flexible and simple legal structures which allow people to manage their economic organisations at the primary level and also at the federated and national levels.

Privatisation policies too need to take this sector into account. Privatisation of health care for example, has come to mean a focus on the corporate sector. In fact, especially in the rural areas there are health providers of the unorganised sector, like midwives. Promoting and encouraging these would mean a fast spread of inexpensive health care as well as a growth of employment. Similarly, privatisation of insurance services with promotive and regulatory policies could lead to the mushrooming of small mutuals throughout the country, thereby reaching a large number of unorganised workers.

Finance policies too need to be changed if this sector is to flourish. Budgetary allocations need to be made to the people's sector, directly rather than through the bureaucracy. Tax policies and monetary policies too need to promote rather than inhibit this sector. In particular, the policies need to be helpful and promotive, rather than controlling and suppressing people's own initiatives.

The second major initiative required is capacity building of the people's sector organisations. The workers of the unorganised sector have enthusiasm, energy and risk bearing capacities, but they lack the skills to run organisations and they lack the technical skills that would make these organisations succesful. Both the public sector and private sector organisations can contribute towards building up the skills of this sector, of bringing modern technologies and knowledge to them.

Finally, a belief in people's inherent capacities is required. We need to believe that people will indeed cooperate if provided with the right structures, that people will be able to learn and run organisations and that the people's sector is a viable alternative.

REFERENCES

Government of India (1987), *Shram Shakti*, Report of the National Commission on Self-Employed Women, New Delhi: 1–3.

International Confederation of Free Trade Unions Resolution (1988), Resolution passed at the World Congress of the International Conference of Free Trade Unions, Melbourne.

International Textile, Garment and Leather Workers Federation Resolution (1976), Resolution passed during the World Congress, of the International Textile, Garment and Leather Workers Federation, Dublin.

National Commission of Labour (1969), *Report of the National Commission on Labour, 1969*, Government of India, New Delhi: 45, 55.

SEWA Annual Conference Resolution (1984), SEWA, Ahmedabad.

Sankaran, Subrahmanya, Wadhan and Social Security Association of India (1994), *Development of Social Security Programmes in Developing Countries*. New Delhi: Har Anand.

Standing, Guy (1999), *Global Labour Flexibility: Seeking Distributive Justice*, London: Macmillan: 41–43, 51, 75.

Towards Equality (1974), Report of the Committe on the Status of Women in India, Ministry of Human Resource Development, Government of India: 157.

Zamagini, Stefano (1999), 'Social Paradoxes of Growth and Civil Economy', in G. Gandolfo and F. Marzano (eds), *Economic Theory and Social Justice*, London: Macmillan: 1, 8–10.

About the Editors
and Contributors

THE EDITORS

Renana Jhabvala is National Coordinator of the Self-Employed Women's Association (SEWA). Among other recognitions, she is the recipient of the Padmashri and the Outstanding Social Worker award of the Federation of Indian Chambers of Industries' Ladies Organisation. Ms Jhabvala has also served as Chairperson of the Group on Women Workers and Child Labour of the National Commission on Labour, and as Chairperson of the Task Force on Unorganised Labour for the state of Madhya Pradesh. Some of her recent publications include *The Unorganised Sector: Work Security and Social Protection* (2000) and *'Speaking Out': Women's Economic Empowerment in South Asia* (1997), both co-edited. Ms Jhabvala has also contributed several articles on issues of social security and women's economic empowerment to journals such as *Seminar* and the *Economic and Political Weekly*.

Ratna M. Sudarshan is Principal Economist, Human Development Programme Area, National Council of Applied Economic Research (NCAER), New Delhi. Prior to joining the NCAER, Ms Sudarshan worked as Research Officer at the South Asia Regional Office of the International Development Research Centre (1990–95) and as Project Leader at the Institute of Social Studies Trust, New Delhi (1987–90). At NCAER, her work primarily centres on initiating, managing and implementing research projects. Ms Sudarshan has contributed several articles on women's work and education to journals like the *Indian Journal of Gender Studies*, *Indian Journal of Labour Economics* and *Asian Journal of Women's Studies*. She has previously co-edited *Gender, Population and Development* (1998). E-mail: *ratnamangala@yahoo.com*

Jeemol Unni is Professor, Gujarat Institute of Development Research (GIDR), Ahmedabad. She has been a Visiting Post-Doctoral Fellow at the Economic Growth Center, Yale University, USA, and Senior Research Fellow at the Institute of Social Studies, The Hague. Dr Unni's research focuses on issues pertaining to rural and urban labour markets in developing countries, informalisation of labour and production systems, the gender implications of this process and issues of social protection and education. A prolific writer, Dr Unni has contributed numerous articles to edited volumes and journals and has previously published *Sustainable Development and Social Security: Role of the Non-Farm Sector* (2000), *Women's Participation in Indian Agriculture* (1992) and *Self-Employed Women, Population and Human Resource Development* (1992).
E-mail: *jeemol@icenet.net*

THE CONTRIBUTORS

Keshab Das holds M. Phil. and Ph.D. degrees in Economics from Jawaharlal Nehru University, New Delhi (through the Centre for Development Studies, Trivandrum). Dr Das is presently a faculty member at the Gujarat Institute of Development Research (GIDR), Ahmedabad and was a visiting fellow at the Institute of Development Studies, Sussex, the Maison des Sciences de l'Homme, Paris and a CNRS visiting faculty at REGARDS, Bordeaux, France. He has co-authored *The Growth and Transformation of Small Firms in India* and has also published on industrial clustering, the informal sector, labour and rural infrastructure.
E-mail: *dastara@hotmail.com*

Anil Gumber, Senior Research Fellow at the Centre for Health Services Studies, Warwick Business School, Coventry, UK, is currently engaged in evidence-based policy research in ethnicity and health in Europe. Dr Gumber, previously at the National Council of Applied Economic Research (NCAER), New Delhi, was responsible for several studies relating to health care utilisation, financing and insurance at NCAER. He was awarded his Ph.D. from Gujarat University, Ahmedabad and a Post-Doctoral Takemi Fellowship from the Harvard School of Public Health, Boston. Dr Gumber's research papers have focused on issues relating to human development including health, nutrition and poverty. He is the author of *Displaced by*

Development: Oustees of an Irrigation Project and co-author of *Inter-Village Difference in Social Overheads and Their Correlates in Matar Taluka.*
E-mail: *anilgumber@yahoo.co.in* or *anil.gumber@wbs.ac.uk*

Veena Kulkarni is currently a Ph.D. student at the University of Maryland, College Park. She has a Masters in Economics from the Delhi School of Economics, University of Delhi, and a Masters in Population Studies from the International Institute for Population Sciences. She has worked in the Human Resource Development Programme Area of NCAER before joining the University of Maryland.
E-mail: *vkulkarni@socy.umd.edu*

N. Lalitha is Assistant Professor at the GIDR, Ahmedabad. Her fields of interest include industrial policy, growth dynamics of small firms, commercialisation of infrastructure and intellectual property rights issues, relating to the developing countries.
E-mail: *lalitha_narayanan@hotmail.com* and *gidradl@sanchar-net.in*

Basanta K. Pradhan is Chief Economist at the NCAER. His responsibilities include directing the MIMAP–India (Micro Impact of Macro and Adjustment Policies in India) research programme.
E-mail: *bkpradhan@ncaer.org*

Uma Rani is Assistant Professor at the GIDR, Ahmedabad. She did her Ph.D. at the University of Hyderabad. Her areas of interest relate to understanding the dynamics in the labour market in developing countries, informal employment and social protection.
E-mail: *ums_r@hotmail.com*

P.K. Roy is currently Project Coordinator, NCAER, in the IDRC sponsored MIMAP–India Project. He has been the project leader of several NCAER pioneering studies viz., Market Information Survey of Households (MISH), Evaluation and Demand for Household Energy Studies, Mobilisation of Savings for Housing, Income-Expenditure and Poverty studies.
E-mail: *pkroy@ncaer.org*

M.R. Saluja is a Senior Consultant at NCAER. He was previously a Professor in the Planning Unit of the Indian Statistical Institute, New Delhi and specialises in problems connected with input-output analysis, the social accounting matrix, national accounts, official statistics, poverty and other related planning problems.
E-mail: *mrsaluja@ncaer.org*

N. Sangeeta is an M.Phil (Statistics) from the University of Delhi. Working in the capacity of Research Assistant at the Macroeconomic Monitoring and Forecasting Division at the NCAER, she had been involved in research on the informal sector and gender since 1998. She has co-authored many research articles and documents with Dr Anushree Sinha which have been presented at different national and international seminars.
E-mail: *nsangeeta@hub.nic.in*

K.A. Siddiqui is an Economist in the Macroeconomic Monitoring and Forecasting Division at NCAER. He joined the Council in 1980. Since 1990 he has been intensively involved in building Social Accounting Matrices (SAMs) with different sectoral classifications, as base data for Computable General Equilibrium Models for India for different years.
E-mail: *kasiddiqui@ncaer.org*

Anushree Sinha is a Principal Economist in the Macroeconomic Monitoring and Forecasting Division at the NCAER. She is a Ph.D. in Economics from Jadavpur University, Kolkata, India, and has conducted post-doctoral research at the University of Pennsylvania and the University of Oxford. Her specialisation is in Input-Output Techniques, Social Accounting Matrices and macro modelling on which she has written a number of papers. She has developed macro models with applications for socio-economic and development issues during the last few years. Presently she is extensively involved in research on macro analysis of the Indian informal sector and gender.
E-mail: *asinha@ncaer.org*

Index

enrolled with the, 242; households subscribing to, 223
Micro Impact of Macro and Adjustment Policies (MIMAP–India), 181
micro-enterprises, 26; positive features of, 26
micro-entrepreneurs, search for, 26
microfinance, 269
Minimum Wages Act, 90
moneylenders, private, 272
morbidity, and utilisation of health services, 223; high incidence of, 218; incidence of acute, 226
Morris, S., 75
Morrisson, Christian, 22
Mukherjee, M., 159

Nagaraj, 73, 172
National Account Statistics (NAS), 105, 113; series, 65, 111, 164, 166, 176
National Commission on Rural Labour, 271
National Commission on Self-employed Women, 266, 271
National Council of Applied Economic Research (NCAER), 75, 76, 181, 188
National Income Statistics of the League of National Committee of Statistical Experts, 28
National Industrial Classification, 67, 108
National Insurance Corporation, 221
National Labour Organisation, 268
national product, international recommendations on the measurement of, 28
National Sample Survey Organisation (NSSO), 31, 68, 118, 158
Naylor, David, 252
net domestic product (NDP), 67, 105
net inflow of capital transfers, 193
New India Assurance, 220
non-farming, self-employed activities, 184

non-agriculturists, rural informal, 134
non-directory manufacturing establishments (NDME), 163, 166
non-government organisations, 64, 269
non-profit institutions, 180
NSSO, 75; Report, 118

occupation, of the majority of the members in a household, 136; non-agricultural, 263
official database, inadequacies and complexities of the, 73
OPD, coverage for, expenses, 245
organised sector, trends in the, 172
Oughton, E., 107
output, informal, 132, 133
Own Account Enterprises (OAEs), 52, 53, 54, 68, 176, 182
Own Account Manufacturing Enterprises (OAME), 166, 169
own-account, 115; home-based, units, 54; self-employed, workers, 48; work, 125, 133

Parmar, R., 84
partnerships, 180
Paul, S., 64
payment, mode of, 83, 92; mode of, and earnings, 89; mode of, of wages, 91
pension, for widow, 267; gratuity, 83
piece rate, job work in the manufacturing sector, 52; system, 91
Piore, M.J., 25, 41
poor, urban informal, 134
population, belonging to informal households, 126; India's urban, 34; measurement of economically active, 28; overall high rural, 124; total working, 187
Portes, A., 26, 63
pottery, growth of small-scale, units, 78
annual payment of the premium, 222
private sector, dominance of the, 273